Nixon and His Men

The Road Through Watergate

By Timothy D. Holder

PublishAmerica
Baltimore

ISBN: 1-4241-8424-X
PUBLISHED BY PUBLISHAMERICA, LLLP
www.publishamerica.com
Baltimore

Printed in the United States of America

Acknowledgments

The author is grateful for the contributions and encouragement of many individuals. Thanks to Bud Krogh, Rev. Jeb Stuart Magruder, and John Dean for answering questions and giving their unique perspectives on things. Thank you also to Chuck Colson's colleague, Linda McGraw, for helpfully providing a copy of some of Mr. Colson's reflections on the Watergate era.

Thanks also to Drs. W. Brian Shelton and Mark A. Smith and to Erin Schneider for graciously reading portions of this manuscript and offering helpful suggestions.

I have appreciated the encouragement of many individuals as I have worked on this project, including my parents, Judy and Charles Holder; close friends Darrin Thomas and the aforementioned Brian Shelton; and especially from my wonderful wife, Dr. Angela E. Holder.

Finally, I would like to express my thanks to the Author of life for every good thing.

Table of Contents

Eleven Key Men
to Nixon and/or Watergate

The Men Nixon Most Admired
1. Henry Kissinger, National Security Advisor/Secretary of State
2. John Mitchell, Attorney General/Head of Committee to Re-Elect the President
3. John Connally, Secretary of Treasury/Democrat

Other key staffers
1. Bob Haldeman, Chief of Staff
2. John Ehrlichman, Chief Domestic Policy Advisor
3. Chuck Colson, Legal Counsel/"Hatchet Man"
4. John Dean, Legal Counsel/Part of Watergate Cover up

Other staff members who had major roles in Watergate
1. Jeb Stuart Magruder, Mitchell's Chief Assistant at CRP (a.k.a. CREEP)
2. G. Gordon Liddy, Member of the Plumbers Unit
3. Bud Krogh, Assistant to Ehrlichman/Promoter of Liddy

* Bebe Rebozo was not a Nixon staffer, but he was a loyal and very influential friend.

INTRODUCTION

Interest in Richard Nixon and Watergate has led to numerous books over the years. The purpose of this book is to provide a look at Nixon, the men who were closest to him, and the other men most responsible for the Watergate break-ins and coverup. Why did Nixon let these men get out of control, and why did they let him? Where did they-Nixon and his men-come from, and how did they rise to such influential positions? What happened in those Watergate offices, and how did these men handle it?

One of the difficulties with approaching this topic was determining its scope. Numerous men were involved in the break-ins and went to prison, but since they were not initiators, less time, if any, is spent on them. Others were highly visible in the Nixon administration, but since they were not as central to the President and White House affairs as they might seem, little attention is paid to them either.

Conversely, some Nixon men who did not go to jail were nevertheless relevant to this study. For example, despite the fact that Henry Kissinger was not implicated in the Watergate scandal, he fell within the scope of this book because he consistently urged the President to take a hardline approach with political enemies. Kissinger simply reinforced the President's own thinking, but such a mentality did help produce Watergate. Also, Kissinger is central to this book because he was Nixon's foreign policy expert, and foreign policy concerns drove the Nixon administration. John Connally was picked for inclusion in this work because Nixon was so interested in this Democrat and his political future that it helped alienate Republicans who might otherwise have gone to bat for the President, giving liberal Democrats another reason to want to undermine Nixon. He had made himself a threat to their party's cohesion. Additionally, Connally's conduct in the White House is noteworthy. Nixon insiders never bullied John Connally; he stands out as proof that one did not have to give in to the corporate culture. His behavior undermines the excuse used by some of the men around Nixon that the culture drove their actions.

This book is not entirely laid out in chronological fashion because it made more sense to start at the beginning of the White House years, introducing the main figures, before going back to their roots in the middle chapters. People who have never heard of Bud Krogh, for example, might not be interested in where he came from, but after understanding his role in the Nixon administration, his origins might seem more relevant.

Those who have a passing familiarity with Watergate know that the unique nature of Richard Nixon helped create the atmosphere that produced the break-ins, so a good deal of attention will be given to Nixon's personality. Two key facets of that personality were that he was an introvert who was too reliant on a small group of men to communicate his will down the chain of command, and he was a battler who sometimes seemed to relish a hard fight more than a victory.

Nixon's personality has generated much analysis. Carl Luna described Nixon as "a man flawed to tragic Greek proportions."[1] One of Nixon's speech writers, journalist William Safire, described Nixon's personality as a layer cake. According to Safire, in the first layer under the icing (presumably the icing, the exterior, is that of a conservative), one finds a politician open to liberal ideas. But "underneath that is an unnecessarily pugnacious man who had to scrape for everything…who gets furious with…bums who expect the world on a platter." Under that "the next layer is the poker player with the long record of winning…not quitting until he absolutely had to quit." There was Nixon the mean spirited, the realist, the loner "who identifies with 'the people' but hates to deal with more than a very few persons." As Safire points out, the problem is "one layer or another is chosen as 'real' and the perceiver roots for that one layer's success. But the whole cake is the real Nixon."[2]

Other Nixon associates expressed basically the same view as Safire, though without the depth of detail. Another speech writer, Ray Price, described Nixon as having light and dark sides at war with each other. Chief of Staff and future Watergate defendant H.R. "Bob" Haldeman saw Nixon's personality "as a multifaceted quartz crystal. Some facets bright and shining, others dark and mysterious. And all of them constantly changing as the external light rays strike the crystal." Haldeman chose to build up the light side rather than confront the dark side. He observed that friends and employees of Nixon, like Bob Finch and Herb Klein, sometimes tried to confront the dark side, but then their influence in the White House waned. Nixon did not like to be challenged by subordinates, so Haldeman decided not to make that mistake.[3]

Haldeman saw Nixon as a man plagued by an insecurity that he tried desperately to overcome. This led to Nixon's iron-willed self-discipline. He was obsessive about dressing and acting appropriately, which made him quite charming on some occasions yet extremely awkward at other times. Once, he insisted on wearing his dress shoes during a photo op on the beach; then he could not understand why people laughed about it. His great need to appear to be in control and proper was both a cause and effect of his obsession with the Kennedys, who seemed to exude effortless charisma.[4]

National Security Advisor and Secretary of State Henry Kissinger saw Nixon as a man so divided that both the liberals and the conservatives on his staff thought they stood for the real Nixon. A manifestation of Nixon's dual nature was, in Kissinger's opinion, that Nixon "lived out a Walter Mitty dream[5] of toughness that did not come naturally and who resisted his very real streak of gentleness." Kissinger argued, "The fact was that there was no true Nixon; several warring personalities struggled for preeminence in the same individual. One was idealistic, thoughtful, generous; another was vindictive, petty, emotional." Kissinger believed that "it was the failure of some more literal-minded White House advisers to understand the requirements of his complex personality that gave such momentum to Watergate."[6]

The way Nixon handled adversity provoked comment from several men. As William Safire put it, "Whenever Nixon was challenged he usually responded well; when he won, he responded badly."[7] Author Kenneth Franklin Kurz believed the same thing, writing that Nixon could handle losing better than winning. Likewise, Counsel to the President Chuck Colson, one of the subjects of this book, described his boss as "noble in defeat, but…without grace in victory."[8] Kissinger noted, "Strangely enough, the thoughtful analytical side of Nixon was most in evidence during crises, while periods of calm seemed to unleash the darker passions of his nature."[9]

Some would argue that it is impossible to understand Nixon's personality without considering the influence of alcohol. Close aides like Kissinger and Chief Domestic Advisor John Ehrlichman, both central figures in this work, thought Nixon had a drinking problem. Kissinger was convinced, or at least acted convinced,[10] that Nixon was a drunk. Ehrlichman once said, "There were times when he got drunk-no question about it. But it wasn't that frequent, and he had a sense of when he was on and when he was off duty." Other, equally close if not closer, aides disagreed. Haldeman, for one, said he had never seen the President intoxicated. After both he and Nixon resigned, Haldeman had felt betrayed by Nixon, so Haldeman's reason to lie would be hard to discern. Haldeman contended that sometimes when Nixon seemed to be drunk, he was simply very fatigued, even to the point of slurring his words.[11] Ray Price said the same thing, adding that a sleeping pill with one drink would also cause the President to suffer from slurred speech.[12] It would seem that if Nixon did have a drinking problem it did not have such a hold on him that it caused him to lose control of White House operations for great periods or time, or Haldeman and Price would have viewed the President differently. It is worth noting that neither his aides nor his critics ever tried to blame Watergate on alcohol.

There has been enough variety in the commentary on Richard Nixon over the years to suit anyone's political tastes. Noted historian Stephen Ambrose experienced some of that variety with his own views after writing a three-volume biography on Nixon. Earlier in life, Ambrose had thought of Nixon as "a politician who would always lie to advance his personal cause, a man who believed in nothing but himself." Ambrose's wife, Moira, had worked for the Nixon campaign in 1960, but she later turned on Nixon after he failed to end the Vietnam War in a speedy fashion. As Ambrose spent years working on the Nixon biography, he found that his wife's dislike for Nixon grew as she learned more about him. But Ambrose, who along with his wife had been a Vietnam War protestor, "developed a grudging admiration for the man...and deep admiration for many of his policies...and...almost a liking for him."[13]

Nixon might have gained an unlikely admirer in the liberal Ambrose, but the President lost his share of conservatives along the way. Journalists Susan Schmidt and Michael Weisskopf wrote that Special Prosecutor Ken Starr, who later became Bill Clinton's nemesis, was not a fan of Nixon. Starr "saw Richard Nixon as a study in the abuse of power, a politician who bent the presidency and the Department of Justice to serve his own interests instead of the rule of law Starr viewed as sacrosanct."[14]

Others have taken more extreme positions. Author Fawn M. Brodie, whose book *Richard Nixon: The Shaping of His Character* found that character lacking, cited several sources that referred to Nixon personally as "dangerous and wicked," lumping in Gerald Ford's, "the long nightmare of the nation is over."[15] Not only did Brodie misquote Ford, who said, "My fellow Americans, our long national nightmare is over,"[16] but Ford's nightmare was the whole Watergate mess, not solely or even primarily Nixon. While Brodie tried too hard to tear Nixon down, there are those on the other end of the spectrum who have gone too far to rehabilitate his image, like Ann Coulter. It is certainly an understatement to argue, as Coulter did, that Nixon was only guilty of "invoking a single, somewhat legitimate privilege once, telling one lie to the public, [and] allowing one part of an investigation to be delayed for two weeks."[17] Nixon's actions were much more serious than that.

Since the theme here is Watergate, there will be little emphasis on the day-to-day affairs of Nixon's White House. Also, attention to such things as Nixon's handling of racial strife and the economy will be minimal since such things had little to do with the decisions that culminated with the Watergate scandal. However, some non-Watergate topics are relevant to this study. For example, foreign affairs will be covered at length. One of the men featured in this book is Jeb Stuart Magruder, the number two man on the Committee to Re-Elect the President. Magruder admitted that while part of the motivation he and his associates had for their coverup was to stay out of jail, they were also driven by foreign affairs concerns. They believed that Richard Nixon had a realistic plan for an "honorable peace" in Vietnam. But if Democratic candidate George McGovern was able to take advantage of the Watergate scandal to get elected, it would be a "national disaster." As Magruder put it, "We were not covering up a burglary, we were safeguarding world peace. It was a rationalization we all found easy to accept."[18]

Magruder also reasoned that the Nixon administration's efforts to get G. Harold Carswell confirmed to the Supreme Court and the White House's efforts to explain the expansion of the Vietnam conflict into Cambodia helped cause Watergate. According to Magruder, the White House staff was absorbed with how these situations played out, and they learned from these experiences to adopt increasingly drastic tactics to ensure their success in future situations.[19]

Another prominent figure in this work, Bob Haldeman, had multiple rationalizations for the corrupt activities often referred to collectively as "Watergate." Haldeman wrote, "The Vietnam War destroyed Nixon as completely as it shattered President Johnson." Haldeman's point is not totally without merit. As constitutional scholar Michael Belknap noted, Abraham Lincoln, Franklin Roosevelt, and Harry Truman all violated rights during wartime before Lyndon Johnson and Nixon came along.[20] Haldeman believed that Nixon was punished for doing what others had done during wartime, and Nixon's Chief of Staff also pointed out that Johnson was guilty of the same sort of wiretapping that ruined Nixon, but Johnson was not caught.[21] Public knowledge of Johnson's secret tapes, and what they contained, would have increased the negative feelings the nation had for Johnson in 1968, just as attitudes hardened against Nixon when it was discovered that he had secretly taped conversations (and when people found out what was on them). Finally, Haldeman argued that Nixon's efforts to reorganize the Executive Branch contributed to the Watergate scandal. Nixon wanted to revamp a bureaucracy that was bloated and inefficient. He wanted an Executive Branch that actually served the wishes of its Chief Executive. Watergate would have been a small, mostly ignored matter, according to Haldeman, but Nixon terrified the Washington elite by shaking up the status quo. If Nixon had succeeded with his reorganization, he would have been a very powerful force, and Democrats reacted to that threat by using the Watergate break-ins to bring down the President. Also in the process of his attempted reorganization, Nixon and Haldeman alienated many loyal Republican staffers who would have otherwise helped them in their time of need.[22]

There is a certain logic to Haldeman's views, but a couple of other factors also need to be pointed out. One, if the Watergate break-ins had not occurred, Nixon's enemies would have lacked the sword they needed to so fatally wound him. Two, the heavy-handed tactics and arrogance of Nixon and his staff provoked congressional Republicans who could have stopped or at least slowed down the train before it wrecked so badly. Three, even if past Presidents had gotten away with violating the rights of the people that does not give future Presidents the excuse to continue violating rights.

Another foreign policy issue that impacted Watergate was Nixon's breakthrough in relations with China. The breakthrough was used as an excuse for neglecting behavior that got out of hand, and it was used to justify the attempts to coverup the Watergate crimes. Again, the rationale by Nixon and his men was that the work of the Nixon Administration was too important to be thwarted by such a petty thing as a little political espionage.

The story in this book is a story of great successes. The reality that Nixon and his men had reached the top of the mountain is made clear by the number of books written about Nixon and his presidency that have the word "power" in the title. There were books written by insiders, like Bob Haldeman's *The Ends of Power*, John Ehrlichman's *Witness to Power*, and Jeb Stuart Magruder's *From Power to Peace*. There were even more books written by those outside the Nixon Administration that featured this theme. These titles include Leon Jaworski's *The Right and the Power*, Stanley I. Kutler's *Abuse of Power*, Seymour M. Hersh's *The Price of Power*, Anthony Summers's *The Arrogance of Power*, and *Nixon in the White House: The Frustration of Power* by Rowland Evans, Jr. and Robert D. Novak. Nixon and his men wanted power, but in their desire to hold on to it they were corrupted by it. While this is a story of great successes, it is also a story of failures and how these men coped with their fall from the mountaintop.

CHAPTER ONE

Introduction to the White House—1969

How did Watergate happen? It happened because Richard Nixon once lost a close election, so he and his men did not want to leave anything to chance. It happened because he was a man full of anger towards his enemies. It happened because he lacked enough close friends to tell him that his attitude would poison his administration. It happened because his Chief of Staff, H.R. "Bob" Haldeman, reinforced Nixon's win at all costs mentality. As Haldeman described his expectations for his subordinates, "I drummed into them the concept that anything can be done if you just figure out how to do it and don't give up. I wouldn't take 'no' for an answer. They knew they were expected to deliver,"[23] even when the demands were illegal. Watergate happened because Nixon's people had G. Gordon Liddy on their staff, a man who would follow through on what others suggested, and he followed through on his own ideas when they were not shot down. How did Watergate happen? Here is how it happened…

Richard Nixon's Cabinet was sworn in by Chief Justice Earl Warren at eight A.M. January 22, 1969. Nixon chose to have the ceremony so early in the morning to communicate to the American people that his Cabinet would work hard.[24] Nixon also wanted to create the impression that he was going to rely heavily on the Cabinet and work closely with its members. But from the start there was a difference between reality and the image Nixon wanted to convey. Nixon had decided back when he was Dwight Eisenhower's Vice President that the Cabinet should make many decisions, especially domestic policy ones, without bothering the President. Nixon had suggested as much to Eisenhower, and Ike had agreed with him. But Ike was an older President, and his health had been troublesome, so he did not want to do anything that made it look like he was not living up to the typical demands of his office.[25] President Nixon did not suffer from such concerns, which left him comfortable with isolating himself from the Cabinet. Before very long, the people with real power in the Nixon administration were not the Cabinet officials, they were the key members of Nixon's White House staff.[26]

As the Nixon administration prepared for business, the new President did not have a lot of close friends in general, much less close friends with political experience. So, as writer Kenneth Franklin Kurz put it, "Nixon, at least to an extent, surrounded himself with men who told him what he wanted to hear."[27] Without enough friends he could trust, loyalty was the characteristic he looked for in his subordinates, and it was what they looked for in their subordinates. Loyalty was more important than expertise or virtue. The members of Nixon's inner circle were not enthusiastic about bringing on subordinates who outshined them. Nixon's administration had some real talent, but his officials were lacking when compared to other administrations. It started at the top. Bob Haldeman, a public relations expert, became Nixon's Chief of Staff because Nixon trusted Haldeman's loyalty. It helped that Haldeman possessed another attribute that Nixon prized. Nixon told Haldeman that Eisenhower had described a certain kind of man every President needed on his staff. Ike had said that a President needed "his SOB" to play the heavy, and President-elect Nixon decided that among his workers Haldeman fit the bill.[28] Future Watergate casualty Jeb Stuart Magruder got a sample of Haldeman's toughness when Magruder was recruited to work for the White House. One day Magruder, Haldeman, and Haldeman's assistant Larry Higby were walking out of a building about two hundred yards from Nixon's West Coast residence. When Haldeman discovered that his golf cart was not there to take the three of them this short distance, he turned on Higby. Haldeman coldly told Higby that if he could not keep track of the golf carts, then Haldeman would replace him with an assistant who could. As Magruder thought about it then and later, he could not decide if Haldeman was genuinely angry or if he was trying to send the message that if Magruder came to work for the White House, detailed efficiency would be demanded. Either way, Magruder saw that Haldeman "did not suffer fools gladly."[29]

John Dean, who also went to prison for Watergate, described a car ride with Haldeman, Higby, and another aide named Dwight Chapin. Haldeman peppered Higby and Chapin with questions and acted condescendingly to them when their answers did not meet his expectations. While Dean found Haldeman overbearing, Dean thought that Higby and Chapin brought some of the abuse on themselves by acting obsequiously. Higby and Chapin had followed Haldeman from private business to the Nixon campaign team in 1968 and on to the White House. Haldeman had gotten used to pushing them around, and they had gotten used to taking it.[30] Men like Higby and Chapin were not working in the White House because of their experience in government; they were there because they could get things done for Haldeman. If he lost confidence in them, they did not have the credentials or personal contacts to survive in Washington, putting them totally at his mercy.

Haldeman could deal roughly with his people, but despite Nixon's respect for toughness, the President had difficulty being tough with subordinates personally. Nixon knew he needed Haldeman if the President wanted to see his agenda carried out.[31] One way Nixon dealt with his unwillingness to confront employees was through stacked meetings. Sometimes Nixon would call a meeting to discuss a topic with a staff member who disagreed with him. Nixon and Haldeman would arrange it so that everyone else at the meeting would agree with the President. Nixon would have the dissenter speak first then pretend to agree with him. Next the President would have the others give the contrary view, and he would pretend to change his mind to the position he had held all along. It was hard for the mark to maintain his position under such circumstances.[32] A President who would go to such lengths to avoid a disagreement needed a strong willed Chief of Staff.

A typical Haldeman tongue-lashing of a subordinate would include phrases like, "You've done a lousy job on this. You're not helping the President. Now get on the ball or we'll find somebody else to do the job." Then the Chief of Staff would move on to other business. If an aide had messed up too badly, he would simply be fired.[33]

As Haldeman put it, "My primary responsibility was to enable the President to function most effectively."[34] Haldeman had become so good at protecting Nixon's interests and compensating for Nixon's weaknesses (confronting unproductive staffers, etc.) that he had gotten closer to Nixon—professionally, but not personally—than anyone, including Rose Mary Woods, who had been Nixon's devoted secretary for years. Nixon's family did not like Haldeman's ascension because Woods was more approachable, but Nixon had become dependent upon Haldeman.[35] As Attorney General John Mitchell put it, Haldeman was "the President's right and left hands."[36] Another plus for Haldeman was that he was not troubled by the fact that he and Nixon were not close personally. As Haldeman described it, "He didn't see me as a person or even, I believe, as a human being. I was a machine. A robot." Haldeman went on to write, "And I was a good machine. I was efficient, I didn't requite a lot of 'oiling'—and he wasn't good at 'oiling'."[37] There were perhaps no three better qualities Haldeman could have possessed in Nixon's eyes. Haldeman was loyal, tough when it came to implementing the President's will, and Nixon never had to worry about Haldeman's feelings. Despite his unswerving devotion to the President, Haldeman did have a sense of humor about his boss, which Haldeman shared with his old friend and fellow Nixon aide, John Ehrlichman. When talking discreetly to Ehrlichman, Haldeman alternately called the President "The Old Man," "Rufus," "The Leader of the Free World," "Milhous," and "Thelma's Husband." "Thelma" was the given name of Nixon's wife, who went by "Pat."[38]

John Ehrlichman's career experience was, like Haldemnan's, also rather limited, given the position of power he had acquired in the Nixon White House. He was a self-described "zoning lawyer from Seattle" who had spent the 1968 campaign as an advance man who, again in his own words, "was on the road seeing that things ran on time, chasing down reporters' lost luggage, and keeping the candidate in a good humor."[39] So what qualified Ehrlichman to get offered jobs as Attorney General, Director of the CIA, and Chairman of the Republican National Committee? According to Ehrlichman, "The answer was that Richard Nixon had confidence in me. If he hadn't, it wouldn't matter how much training and experience I'd had."[40] Ehrlichman turned down the positions Nixon offered him before suggesting a job as White House Counsel to which Nixon agreed.

What helped Ehrlichman the most was that Haldeman believed in him, and Nixon believed in Haldeman. As Haldeman described him, Ehrlichman "was known for three traits: a sarcastic wit, intelligence, and a love of intrigue." Ehrlichman had a fourth trait that Haldeman relied on-Ehrichman had never lied to him.[41]

Also, as John Dean observed, "Being rattled was not an admired state in the White House," and "many encounters…revealed John Ehrlichman to be unflappable."[42] Ehrlichman was so trusted by the President and Haldeman that Ehrlichman filled in for the Chief of Staff when

Haldeman took time off. Ehrlichman's role on such occasions was to spend time with the President as Nixon ruminated over issues during an average work day, on a presidential vacation, or during a phone call late at night.[43]

Though National Security Advisor Henry Kissinger acknowledged that Ehrlichman could be "very helpful and encouraging," to him, Kissinger also characterized Ehrlichman as "extraordinarily aggressive and even unpleasant" in Ehrlichman's efforts to be a leading man in the White House. Kissinger claimed that Ehrlichman used the investigation of leaks as a way to harass and undermine Kissinger. The National Security Advisor's assessment of Ehrlichman has the ring of truth, but it is undermined somewhat by Kissinger's fundamental misunderstanding of one aspect of Ehrlichman that everyone else saw clearly-Ehrlichman's relationship with Haldeman. Kissinger described Ehrlichman and Haldeman as competitors whose relationship improved when Ehrlichman's power grew in a way that did not overlap with Haldeman's power.[44] It was pretty clear to everyone else that Haldeman was Ehrlichman's patron and close friend, not his rival.

John Ehrlichman would not seem like the prototypical Nixon man. For example, after the Cambodia bombings had inflamed antiwar activists, there were some in the White House who suggested that staffers should meet with some of the angry young people in the country. Two-way communication, it was thought, might lead to more civility. The liberals on Nixon's staff, like Patrick Moynihan, were expected to participate, but surprisingly, Ehrlichman was a leader of this initiative. Also, Ehrlichman, more than the others in Nixon's upper echelon, bristled at the long hours that kept him away from his family. Ehrlichman was not one of those, as Nixon speech writer William Safire put it, who was "secretly pleased to get away from the wife and kids."[45] Ehrlichman's greatest priority was not always just to promote the interests of Richard Nixon.

Some columnists criticized Nixon's choices for some of his key positions, arguing that Nixon's top men were not qualified to help lead the country; they had just done a good job on Nixon's campaign. Ehrlichman countered that the President could always find experts to provide insight on particular issues, but what he needed from his most trusted staffers was "loyalty, versatility, and reliability."[46] Unfortunately, the President did not find an expert to act as a political coach for

Haldeman and Ehrlichman. Such a consultant might have told the pair that the image of arrogant indifference they displayed to outsiders was not a good thing. Media figures Rowland Evans and Robert Novak, who were hardly liberal in their politics, described Haldeman and Ehrlichman as "dangerously distant from the constituencies that a President must take into serious account: Congress, his political party's leaders, the press." And Evans and Rowland were not Monday morning quarterbacks coming up with excuses after the Watergate debacle. They wrote these words in 1971, a year before Watergate.[47] Worse yet, the arrogance displayed by Haldeman and Ehrlichman was not only reserved for outsiders. Caspar Weinberger was a White House staffer who had known Nixon, Haldeman, and Ehrlichman from their days in California. Weinberger observed a change in Ehrlichman after the latter went to Washington. Previously, Ehrlichman had been "open and friendly," but he became "annoyed, distant, and buttoned up" when Weinberger went to Ehrlichman's office on work related matters. Weinberger had to go see him personally because Ehrlichman was not good about returning phone calls. Weinberger had a slightly different perception of Nixon's Chief of Staff. "Haldeman...hardly changed at all. He had always been stern and brusque," though Weinberger also noted that Haldeman "was extremely efficient" and more communicative than Ehrlichman.[48]

One incident that occurred in February 1969 highlighted just how much Ehrlichman had to learn about working for the White House. Ehrlichman was responsible for working out the logistics of a Nixon trip to Europe, which was an assignment Ehrlichman actually had experience with on a national level. Ehrlichman wanted to dictate the guest list for Nixon's dinner in London. The American ambassador, David Bruce, cabled back, "Surely the absurdity of telling the Prime Minister whom he can invite to his own home for dinner requires no explanation."[49] That was a mistake Ehrlichman did not repeat.

One issue that Ehrlichman and Haldeman traded memos on shows not only how wide ranging their responsibilities were but also their rapport and Haldeman's sense of humor. Haldeman wrote to Ehrlichman, "Billy Graham raised with the President today the point that postal rates for religious publications are being increased 400%, while postal rates for pornography are only being increased 25%. Needless to say, the President was horrified to learn about the state of affairs and wants to know what we are doing about it." Ehrlichman replied, "Shall we lower religious mail or raise the rates for porn?" Haldeman wrote back, "You'll have to raise the question w/ RN and BG-I am only qualified to report the horror, not to act upon it."[50]

The two other staff members Nixon had the most faith in at the beginning of his first term were the aforementioned John Mitchell and Henry Kissinger. John Mitchell, Nixon's first Attorney General, was in the words of John Ehrlichman, "Probably the man closest to the President."[51] Ehrlichman had only been offered the Attorney General position after Mitchell had turned it down because of an issue in his personal life. Mitchell's wife, Martha, was in a sanitarium dealing with her alcoholism. Mitchell later changed his mind and became Nixon's AG. Mitchell was perhaps the President's only real friend on the staff besides Rose Mary Woods, but Nixon also appreciated a characteristic his Attorney General shared with Haldeman and Erhlichman. According to Nixon, "There's a man who can do any job-John Mitchell. He's a tough SOB."[52] Next to loyalty, toughness was the thing Nixon prized most among his subordinates. Despite this toughness, Mitchell was considered a father figure to many in the Nixon White House, including Jeb Stuart Magruder and John Dean.[53] Though Mitchell could be quite charming and paternal, he was also ruthless when it came to politics. His combination of toughness and charm endeared him to the President, but many in Washington did not share Nixon's sentiment. There were a number of Republicans who bristled at his heavy handedness and his disregard for returning phone calls.[54]

Henry Kissinger, Nixon's National Security Advisor, had proved his loyalty by spying on the Democrats during the 1968 campaign.[55] Also as Richard V. Allen, Nixon's coordinator of foreign policy research during the campaign, put it, "Henry was a hard-nosed SOB," which was always a plus with Nixon. Additionally, Kissinger, Harvard professor and darling of the Eastern Establishment that he was, could potentially broaden the tent of Nixon's popularity. It helped Kissinger survive in the White House when he won over Bob Haldeman, who found the professor "quiet, deferential, (and) engaging." But more than that, Haldeman saw Kissinger as "a brilliant theorist" who "had a comprehensive, wide-ranging mind, and a precise grasp of the political realities involved in every situation."[56] Kissinger out shined Secretary of State William Rogers so much so that Nixon eventually had Kissinger brief the press on the most important developments in foreign affairs.[57] Speech writer William Safire described Kissinger's White House relations in a way that was similar to the description a Harvard colleague had used years before.[58] Safire wrote, "To the President, he [Kissinger] was more deferential than any of us...to his colleagues on the senior staff he would show the respect of a faculty member to other professors with tenure...to his subordinates he was a slave driver."[59] Another biting commentary on Kissinger was offered by one of those overworked, mistreated subordinates, Robert McFarlane. According to McFarlane, "Not only was Kissinger demanding and dogmatic, a man who did not tolerate rational argument with temperance or any measure of good grace, he was also distrustful, hypocritical, routinely dishonest and abusive to his friends....Fair play was to him just a rhetorical metaphor, and life and especially international politics were a very Darwinian process."[60] Nixon, however, was impressed with Kissinger's grasp of the issues and creative thinking. The President did not want to make him Secretary of State, which is how a President's number one foreign policy advisor would be expected to serve. Nixon wanted foreign policy to be dictated by the White House, so he was not interested in having a strong Secretary of State.[61]

One other man who had Nixon's trust never worked in the Nixon Administration-at least not in an official capacity. Charles "Bebe" Rebozo was a Miami businessman and friend of politicians. Rebozo's qualities were summarized well by Ehrlichman. "Rebozo the garage mechanic, having become the owner of a state bank, a student of real estate and the folkways of the wealthy, can...carry his end of a conversation with anyone with unfailing pleasantness...He is a bartender of some accomplishment...Rebozo is completely loyal to Richard Nixon. And he does not gossip."[62] Bob Haldeman described Rebozo as the only person outside Nixon's family that the President seemed to relax around.[63]

Rebozo was protective of the President's wishes, especially where they dovetailed with his own. In the fall of 1969, Rebozo thought the firm of Vincent Andrews and Company was doing a poor job of taking care of the President's personal funds. Claudia Val, a friend of Rose Mary Woods, worked for Vincent Andrews, so Woods opposed a change. But Woods was no match for either Haldeman or Rebozo, so when those two combined with Ehrlichman to argue to Nixon that such a change should be made, Woods was left disappointed. The money was to be managed by Herb Kalmbach with large portions of it sitting in Rebozo's bank to draw interest.

Another way that Rebozo's influence manifested itself was as a pipeline for suggestions from the President to his staff, even to high ranking officials like Ehrlichman.[64] Again, for as much as Nixon valued toughness, he had a hard time confronting personal acquaintances; he much preferred going through a third party to avoid unpleasant interactions.

Rebozo's protective attitude towards Nixon led the businessman to the same conclusion as the President regarding members of the press: they were the enemy. And, like Nixon, Rebozo was given fuel for his hatred when he found himself the target of investigations by media figures. These investigations would probably not have been launched were Rebozo not a friend of the President. As William Safire described it, to Rebozo's pre-politically correct way of thinking, Nixon and his associates were the cowboys and media figures were the Indians. And for that matter, anybody in the White House who liked reporters, like Safire himself, was an Indian too.[65]

Rebozo's influence was understood within a month of Nixon's inauguration, if not before, when Haldeman sent a memo to Ehrlichman saying that the President wanted Rebozo to set up a fund for contributions from major donors. The money would not be a part of the Republican National Committee's war chest; it would be a part of a secret stash to be used to carry out the President's agenda through unofficial channels. This was not technically illegal,[66] but it did help bring down the Nixon presidency. The fund was ultimately used to pay for illegal activities. Most notably it provided ready cash for the Watergate crew.

The contemporary reader might be surprised that Nixon's first Vice President, Spiro Agnew, was not on the list of Nixon intimates. Nixon had been the first openly politically active Vice President,[67] so one might think that Nixon would make good use of his own VP. Nixon said that Agnew would be an important part of the team, but Agnew soon found himself virtually frozen out by Ehrlichman. Rather than challenge Ehrlichman or confront Nixon, Agnew played the dutiful soldier, ever mindful that it was Nixon who had brought him to prominence.[68] Nixon had quickly grown unimpressed by Agnew's abilities. It was also frustrating to the President that his Vice President did not treat Nixon with the same deference that Nixon had shown Eisenhower. Perhaps if

Nixon had commanded the Allied Forces that had made half the world safe for democracy, Agnew would have shown him such respect. Nevertheless, Nixon had gotten tired of Agnew's meetings with him always including demands for greater perks. Nixon shuffled Agnew off first to Bob Haldeman and, after that relationship soured, John Ehrlichman.[69]

Nixon relied on his staff virtually to the exclusion of all other Washington power bases. Nixon was particularly hostile towards Washington socialites, whose influence with opinion brokers in the media-indeed, some of the socialites were the opinion brokers-should not be underestimated. Nixon used to make faces as he talked about "boring and time-wasting tea parties" thrown by the Washington Establishment. The introverted Nixon was almost always uncomfortable at such parties, but he thought he had to go to some of them earlier in his career. As President, he felt no such burden. He would host parties as his responsibilities dictated and sometimes have gatherings for people he knew or wanted to get to know. But there was no love lost between the President and the in-crowd.[70]

In addition to not liking the socialites, Nixon also had trouble with Congress. His influence with the Legislative Branch was limited because when he took office the Republican Party was not in control of either house. And while it was difficult enough to find willing Democrats to help achieve parts of his agenda, Nixon also had problems within his own party. Nixon had little regard for the Republican leaders in the two houses, and this general lack of respect caused Nixon to occasionally run roughshod over his supposed allies. Nixon's inner circle shared his opinion. John Ehrlichman's attitude is manifested in comments in his autobiography like, "Flashy and bright congressmen are distrusted by the others." Ehrlichman did concede that as he and Gerald Ford, the House Minority Leader, worked together over the years Ehrlichman gained some respect for him.[71] But such disdain for career Washingtonians by Nixon's staffers like Ehrlichman contributed to the attitude that the members of Nixon's inner circle were too arrogant to work well with others.

On Nixon's first Sunday as President, evangelist Billy Graham conducted a worship service at the White House for the First Family and staffers' families.[72] Nevertheless, the media overestimated the amount of influence wielded by Graham on the Nixon administration. *Newsweek* referred to Graham as "the President's Preacher," and *Life* magazine made reference to his "omnipresence." But Graham actually spent less time alone with Nixon than the evangelist had with President Johnson.[73] Jeb Magruder claimed that the religious services conducted at the White House by Graham and others were intended to be more political than spiritual. Magruder believed the services "served as a convenient way to invite certain kinds of people to the White House-the kind who just didn't seem to fit into other occasions-and earn their good will.[74] Later, Graham learned that there were members of the President's staff who were intervening to limit Graham's contact with the President.[75]

The characterization of Graham's influence over Nixon by the media was not only inaccurate; it also turned out to be a big headache for the preacher. In just the first three months that Nixon was in the White House, Graham was flooded with hundreds of requests for favors from people. It was believed that Graham could get jobs and pardons from the President, even though the preacher never did nor tried.[76] One can only wonder what a stronger dose of Graham's morality would have done for the Nixon White House.

Another misconception of the Nixon Administration is that it was overwhelmingly conservative. For example, political observer Charles Ashman once wrote, "Richard Nixon is the ultimate partisan...a one-party thinker...When Nixon promised...a bipartisan Cabinet, it was interpreted by most political observers to mean that he would give a second-echelon administrative job to the most conservative Democrat he could find."[77] Despite the perceptions of Ashman and others, however, Nixon actually veered to the left when he first took office. On the domestic front, aides like Arthur Burns and Democrat Patrick Moynihan were pushing plans to expand welfare assistance and help poor families. Regarding Vietnam, Nixon endorsed the idea of troop withdrawals. After floating such a plan in general terms for awhile, Nixon announced on June 8 that 25,000 military personnel would be brought home by the end of August. Such initiatives were consistent with Nixon over the years—he could be progressive and flexible in his thinking. The reason he is generally perceived as a conservative is that liberals attacked him for his vehement anti-Communism. These attacks by liberals, coupled with Nixon's genuine anti-Communist sentiment, made Nixon a darling of conservatives over the years. When Nixon's policies as President came into the public eye, it created a problem for him. William Safire wrote that

"Many of his public moves were interpreted, correctly…as progressive; this was making him few friends on the left and building much resentment on the right."[78]

The Vietnam War was the biggest concern in America in 1969. If anyone in the country questioned that, their doubts would have been erased at Nixon's inauguration. Thousands of antiwar protestors lined the streets as Nixon's motorcade drove by, chanting things like, "Ho, Ho, Ho Chi-minh, the Viet Cong are going to win."[79] Perhaps the modern reader could better appreciate the impact of such chants if the reader imagined pro al Quaeda chants voiced by thousands of Americans at the 2005 inaugural.

Nixon was supremely confident that he could end the Vietnam War during his first year in office, and he was bitterly disappointed when this did not work out. Henry Kissinger found that the North Vietnamese were slow to negotiate because they understood how much animosity there was towards the war in the United States. The North Vietnamese saw "that it was only a matter of time before the U.S. would have to pull out, no matter what. So why negotiate?"[80] Nixon's policy of Vietnamization of the war called for the United States to continue to provide war materials to South Vietnam and to step up training for the South Vietnamese military, while also downsizing the number of American troops. Nixon wanted the Vietnamese to ultimately have more influence over their own fate. Also, downsizing the American military presence in Vietnam would lower American casualty figures, which could partially mollify protestors. But when the media reported the bombing campaign in Cambodia, critics of the war were outraged, and any benefit the President hoped to get from Vietnamization was lost.[81]

Nixon was already having the FBI tap phones in his first year as President. The effort targeted members of the media and White House staffers who might have been responsible for leaks coming out of Henry Kissinger's offices.[82] Though these taps were not court-authorized, one could argue that they were defensible insofar as the United States was involved in the Vietnam War, so the taps were in the interests of national security. Wiretapping without obtaining warrants had been going on since Franklin Roosevelt was President.[83] Reasonable people could conclude that leaks of government information were treasonous-for example,

Dwight Eisenhower felt this way.[84] As historian Joan Hoff observed, "The United States has never fought a war without violating the rights of its citizens."[85] On the other hand, the fact that it had previously happened does not make it right. This violation of civil liberties had to be stopped at some point, and the only way to stop it was to prosecute those who were guilty of it.

During the first five months Nixon was President, there were more than twenty stories in major newspapers that were based on leaks. Given that the Vietnam War was in progress and Cold War relations with the Soviets were always a matter of concern in this era, Attorney General Mitchell agreed with FBI Director J. Edgar Hoover, Henry Kissinger, and Nixon that telephones of suspected government officials and journalists should be wiretapped. Though the FBI tapped several phones, not a single leak was plugged this way.[86] Since the Nixon administration justified to itself the legitimacy of crossing conventional limits for such behavior, further steps across the line were easier to justify when the leaks were not stopped.

Part of the reason why security leaks were so frustrating was that the government was spending tens of millions of dollars to keep its secrets safe.[87] The other part, and the most important part to Nixon, was the nature of some of the leaks. The Cambodia bombings were something that the Nixon administration was trying to keep secret for a couple of reasons. One, Nixon did not want to give ammunition to the antiwar movement. Two, the ruler of Cambodia, President Sihanouk, had approved of the bombings, but they would be a troublesome embarrassment to him if they became known. It would look like he was acknowledging that he could not control affairs in his country, which would embolden his enemies. The *New York Times*, however, had no such misgivings-it broke the story. Another article the *Times* ran gave the fallback position of US negotiators regarding the Strategic Arms Limitation Treaty (SALT) talks, which made Nixon livid.[88] Nixon later wrote, "even though I disliked wiretapping…it seemed our only chance to find out who was behind the leaks, and stop them." Rather than apologize for his extreme measures, Nixon maintained the need for them in his memoirs. "I can say unequivocally that without secrecy there would have been no opening to China, no SALT agreement with the Soviet Union, and no peace agreement ending the Vietnam War."[89]

Certainly, one could argue that the public had the right to know when it came to the Cambodia bombings, but leaking the American negotiating strategy during the SALT treaty did undermine American security, and Nixon wanted it stopped. Unfortunately for the President, he failed to make a distinction between national security and his own political security. Along with fourteen wiretaps for national security reasons, there were three White House employees who had nothing to do with national security who also had taps placed on them. One of these three had round-the-clock surveillance on him from July 23, 1969 through September of that year. It only ended when the FBI complained that this was occupying ten agents a day, and it had produced nothing. And the President's Attorney General, John Mitchell, was thoroughly involved in all of this.[90] Despite Nixon's defense of wiretaps, he conceded that they failed to uncover any national security leaks.[91]

The illegal taps are hard to defend as a matter of national security since sympathetic judges could have been found, but it gets worse. Nixon decided to tap the phone of his brother Donald to make sure Donald did not use his position as a First Brother to embarrass the White House. John Ehrlichman, who tended towards sarcasm, pulled no punches regarding the President's brother. Ehrlichman wrote, "In another age F. Donald Nixon might have been a patent-medicine salesman or a carnival barker; when I first met him, he was the modern equivalent, a 'consultant'."[92] Nixon wanted Ehrlichman to ask the CIA to put full surveillance on Donald, which Ehrlichman showed no reluctance in doing. Ehrlichman's contact in the CIA vetoed the plan, though, since it is against the law for the CIA to engage in domestic operations. Nixon's fallback plan was for Ehrlichman to get the FBI to spy on the President's brother. The FBI, familiar with this sort of activity since Lyndon Johnson had the Bureau keep clandestine tabs on his own embarrassing brother, conducted its surveillance from May 27 through July 8, 1969.[93] Even though this had become something of a standard procedure, it was an abuse of power by both Johnson and Nixon to have a government office keep tabs on their siblings just to avoid potential embarrassment.

During his first year in the White House, Nixon developed a system that seemed to work well for him as an introvert and someone who hated meetings. Instead of lots of gatherings with task forces and committees, Nixon and Haldeman met and discussed White House affairs, Nixon and

Kissinger plotted foreign policy strategy, and Nixon and George Shultz handled economic strategy. Initially John Ehrlichman would go through Haldeman for guidance from the President, but eventually the Nixon-Ehrlichman team handled domestic affairs.[94] In the beginning, there were a couple of men ahead of Ehrlichman working on domestic policy. Arthur Burns was an economist, but he was too openly opinionated for the tastes of Nixon and Haldeman. Since Burns talked too much for the quiet President, Burns was moved out of the White House and made chairman of the Federal Reserve Board. Patrick Moynihan was a social planner in John Kennedy's administration, and his hiring was intended to demonstrate Nixon's bipartisanship. Moynihan was, along with Burns, a leading voice in domestic affairs, but Moynihan was too liberal for Nixon's conservative supporters. Because he was alienating Nixon's core without offsetting this by bringing in new voters, his ouster was a must. Though the President genuinely liked him, Moynihan was eventually sent off as ambassador to India. Thus, the door was opened for Ehrlichman, and he was ushered through it by his old friend Haldeman.[95]

There was a lot of overlap between domestic affairs and economic policy, though, which prompted John Mitchell to foresee a turf war between George Shultz and Ehrlichman. As Mitchell explained it to John Dean shortly before Dean left his employ, "I see a head-on collision coming between Shultz and Ehrlichman. Ehrlichman is in over his head. He likes to dabble in everything. Shultz is a good man....Shultz can keep the President out of trouble with Ehrlichman's half-baked schemes to cure the ills of the country."[96]

However power and responsibilities were handed out in the White House, Nixon and Kissinger were primarily preoccupied with Vietnam. In October 1969 Kissinger was having a private talk with William Safire when the National Security Advisor shared his frustrations. Kissinger said, "If only the guys who got us into this would give us the chance to get out of it. I wasn't second-guessing Vance and Harriman in 1965 when I told them privately we couldn't win the war-instead I asked them how I could help." Kissinger also commented, "If you were in Hanoi, and you were one of those who wanted to settle, would you get to first base with all these demonstrations in the U.S.?"[97] It was a fascinating question. Conservatives have long maintained that antiwar protesters were an encouragement to the North Vietnamese and helped them to continue fighting. It is interesting to suggest-and logical to conclude-that North

Vietnamese opinion might have been divided. Americans who were demanding that the United States pull out unilaterally undercut those in North Vietnam who were in favor of an equitable settlement. How could the North Vietnamese give up if the United States was about to?

Within the first week after Nixon's inauguration, there was a task force created to help control the flow of news regarding the President. It was called "the Five O'clock Group," and its existence underscored Nixon's obsession with public relations, as did his frequent suggestions for the task force. These suggestions included general ideas like letter writing campaigns and calls to TV stations, and specific ones like telling John Ehrlichman to get somebody to do "an effective job on the RN comeback theme."[98]

PR concerns opened the door for Jeb Stuart Magruder to join the White House staff in October 1969. Haldeman recruited Magruder for the White House because Haldeman saw the need to coordinate Nixon's public relations efforts. The problem was two-pronged. First, Haldeman saw that the different instruments for public relations were not synchronized. There was a Press Office, an Office of Communications, a Congressional Relations Office, a handful of speech writers, and various consultants. Haldeman wanted Magruder to organize these components into one system that could be directed from the top. Once Magruder had set up the system, Haldeman would find someplace on the White House staff for the young man to settle in and make a niche for himself. One important caveat regarding this system was that it needed to be able to circumvent what the White House believed was a liberal establishment and get the President's message directly to the people. The other part of the PR problem was that Richard Nixon was simply not a very charismatic man. As Magruder put it, Nixon "lacked the warmth of an Eisenhower, the charisma of a Kennedy, or the flamboyance of a Johnson." Haldeman knew that there was not much Magruder could do about that, but a better PR system would be an improvement over the current state of affairs.[99]

Magruder quickly figured out one of the keys to success as a Nixon man: the people Nixon respected, for example Haldeman and John Mitchell, were tough managers. Other men had been brought into Nixon's orbit as miracle workers who would solve Nixon's image problem, and when it became clear that they could not produce the desired results, their influence waned. So, Magruder shrewdly presented himself as a manager, not a public relations expert.[100] To read Haldeman's account of the Nixon Administration, Haldeman regretted wooing Magruder even without Watergate factoring into the equation. Haldeman complained that Magruder was "eager but unreliable."[101] This may or may not have been an accurate characterization, but if Haldeman thought this was the case before Watergate, one is left to wonder why Haldeman did not simply fire him, or put him in an unimportant job. Haldeman claimed that Magruder's shortcomings did not matter when he was transferred to the Committee to Re-Elect the President because John Mitchell would be in charge. But after Mitchell was hopelessly distracted from focusing on his job, Haldeman failed to address the issue[102] even though there would be little that was more important to Nixon than his re-election.

Throughout Nixon's first year, his relations with those outside his inner circle were problematic. Barbara Bush, whose husband George was then a member of the House of Representatives, was ambivalent about Nixon. As she wrote in her memoirs, "I respected the President, but he did not make it easy to like him. He just did not know how to deal with small talk."[103]

Stories of Richard Nixon's interpersonal woes are legion. For example, the personality of Bob Mayo, who was Nixon's Budget Director, irritated the President. Nixon did not like Mayo's sense of humor or his mannerisms. By November 1969, the President decided that he would just not see Mayo anymore, not even on matters pertaining to the budget. Nixon would consult other members of the economic team, and if Mayo wanted to offer any input, it had to be filtered through John Ehrlichman. Mayo finally forced a meeting with Nixon in March 1970. Demonstrating his discomfort with personal confrontations, Nixon assembled Haldeman, Kissinger, and Ehrlichman for Mayo's visit. Mayo expressed his concerns about being isolated from the President, pointing out how impractical that was for a Budget Director, and he said that he would not continue past the summer unless changes were made. Nixon said to Haldeman and Ehrlichman after the others had left, "I guess Mayo has got to go." But the President suggested that action be delayed until after July. Nixon wanted to beat Woodrow Wilson's record for keeping an initial Cabinet team together, and Mayo had Cabinet rank. Nixon's willingness to keep a man for four months after determining that the man was not good for his position, displayed both Nixon's overriding concern for good PR, and his lack of respect for the importance of his Cabinet. On the other hand, Nixon did change his mind after a couple of weeks and decided to expedite Mayo's departure.[104]

Secretary of Defense Melvin Laird was another Cabinet official who created problems for the Nixon administration. Laird did not always support the hard line with North Vietnam that Nixon and Kissinger were taking. Laird was interested in his political career post Richard Nixon. Laird believed that the voters of Wisconsin would not support his bid for a Senate seat if he seemed like a hawk on Vietnam, so he leaked to the press his opposition to certain war-related decisions made by the White House. Sometimes Laird would ignore Nixon's directives regarding the conduct of the war. Worse yet, the Army Signal Corps controlled the switchboards at Camp David, which served as a presidential retreat, and Laird used this control of the switchboards to his advantage. Laird had his people listen in on conversations to gain information he would sometimes leak or use in some other way to further his agenda. Nixon discovered that Laird was spying on him, but Nixon felt that Laird was too influential with his former colleagues in the House of Representatives for Nixon to oust him.[105] Because Nixon was unable to get rid of Laird when he wanted to, a couple of characteristics that ultimately hurt Nixon were reinforced: His tendency to not work with his Cabinet and his belief that spying on others was how the game was played in Washington.

On November 3, 1969 Nixon made a speech where he reached out to his "Silent Majority," those people in the country that did not relate to the antiwar protestors and anti-authority crowd. William Safire called it the most important speech Nixon gave in his first four years. It resonated with many listeners, but not with some commentators who followed the Presidents' speech with criticisms, more so than summary remarks.[106] As usual, when Nixon felt attacked, his impulse was to strike back. Jeb Magruder had only been working in the White House for about a month when he got a lesson on the hostility Nixon and his men had for the press. Two days after the President's Silent Majority speech, they were talking about it in a meeting. During the speech, Nixon had referenced his plan to get the South Vietnamese Army to assume a greater role in its self-defense, thus allowing the United States to reduce its number of forces there. Nixon hoped this would undercut the antiwar movement, which had been planning a big demonstration in Washington for November 15. Nixon thought his announcement would cool support for the rally.[107]

Nixon asked Pat Buchanan, the future Cable talk show host and presidential candidate, how the networks had treated the President's speech. Buchanan mentioned a negative report from a newsman whom most of those in the meeting felt was consistently anti-Nixon. Henry Kissinger chimed in, "Well, Mr. President, that man is an agent of the Romanian government." As Kissinger explained it, this newsman was paid by the Romanian government, which was Communist, to provide news reports pertaining to Washington. Providing news service for a Communist government does not necessarily make one a Communist, but this distinction was lost in the heat of the moment.[108]

Nixon, who had been enjoying the meeting up to that point became angry and said, "That's right. That guy is a Communist. Jeb, you're our new ramrod around here. Get the word out on that guy."[109] William Safire once wrote, "I must have heard Richard Nixon say 'the press is the enemy' a dozen times." And "he was saying exactly what he meant: 'The press is the *enemy*' to be hated and beaten."[110]

Though Magruder thought that the media leaned to the left, he knew there were some members that were sympathetic to the Republican Party. He felt that the Nixon White House was a little paranoid and too hostile to the media in general. But as Magruder wrote, "I didn't waste any time soul searching. I'd already seen, in one month in the White House, that those assistants who tried to second-guess the President's judgments didn't last long in his favor."[111] Magruder also saw that those who were soft on the media lost influence with the President. It was the hardliners like Haldeman and Mitchell who the President respected. Magruder wanted that respect, so he spread the word to some friends in the media about the alleged Communist in their midst. Soon, the maligned correspondent was in the White House demanding an apology for being misrepresented. He got the apology through a third party, but Magrauder did not feel too badly. He was doing what he had to do to survive in the Nixon White House.[112]

Another key figure who joined the White House team shortly after Magruder was Charles W. "Chuck" Colson.[113] Colson had been offered jobs by a couple of members of the Nixon administration after the 1968 election. The Secretary of Transportation, John Volpe, was a friend of

Colson's, and Volpe offered Colson a position. Under Secretary of State Elliot Richardson wanted Colson as an Assistant Secretary of State. But Colson decided to gamble on Nixon, figuring that the best job would only come from the President himself. Colson did not want to settle for anything less. After waiting almost a year, Nixon finally reached out to him.[114] Colson became the liaison to special interest groups for the White House, and in that capacity he convinced the President and the Chief of Staff that Nixon could make inroads with certain traditionally Democratic voting groups, like Catholics and blue-collar workers.[115]

In mid-December, an idea circulated in the White House to form a conservative think tank-something that could provide a counter balance to the left leaning Brookings Institute. The proposal suggested that this conservative organization be called "the Institute for an Informed America," and it was to have writers, researchers, PR guys, and film crews. The idea never got off the ground. First, Haldeman and Colson wanted to use the phrase "Silent Majority" in the name of the institute, the term Nixon recently had used. If Haldeman and Colson had gotten their way, then an institution that could have helped provide balance to the public discourse would have instead been perceived as a propaganda arm of the White House, thus diminishing its effectiveness. But Colson was not through yet. In January 1970, Colson suggested that Jeb Stuart Magruder interview a friend of Colson's to be in charge of their proposed institute. Magruder found the man to be intelligent and ideologically conservative, but Magruder was concerned about something. The candidate, Howard Hunt, had a background in the CIA, and Hunt saw this new conservative institute as the perfect vehicle from which to launch secret political operations, which would certainly have represented a shift in the original vision for the project. Magruder was uncomfortable with this new element, but it became a moot point because the institute never got off the ground.[116] Hunt, though, continued to stick around all the way through Watergate.

Nixon relished his political battles, and he had reason to be confident after his first year in office. The death of Mary Jo Kopechne in a car accident seemed to neutralize Edward Kennedy as a presidential threat. Gallup polls showed the President's approval ratings to be hovering in the mid-sixties, despite the wide spread efforts of protestors. Nixon was convinced that by the 1970 elections, "We are going to be able...to 'see the light at the end of the tunnel'" of the Vietnam War.[117] Yet the war would drag on, the protests were becoming ever more passionate, and the economy was flattening. It would be difficult to maintain his popularity, but Nixon enjoyed such struggles. Given the zeal Nixon displayed for political combat, he might have been called "Nixon the Battler," in an earlier century. Ultimately, Nixon took on too many battles, and many critics would say, his worst enemy would be himself, but that would not be clear to the nation for a few more years. By the end of his first year, Nixon had his team in place, and he had developed a blueprint for getting things done that he mistakenly thought would serve him well.

CHAPTER TWO

Completing the Team—1970

The two biggest issues for the Nixon Administration at the outset of 1970 were wrapping up the war in Vietnam and winning Republican majorities in the two houses of Congress in November. Perhaps if Nixon had accomplished either of these objectives that year, the apparent need to break into the Watergate offices would not have manifested itself. But victory in the field and in the voting booth eluded Nixon, so internal tensions mounted.

Though Chuck Colson had struck out in his attempts to enhance his status through the proposed conservative institute, he still found his niche in the Nixon administration, and in Nixon's heart, by January 1970. One Friday morning Colson brought in some Catholic school educators to see the President. They these educators wondered whether or not Nixon was going to honor a campaign pledge to help Catholic schools. It was a frustrating meeting for the President because ever since he had taken office, he had been saying he wanted a staffer to write up an executive order that he could sign to form a commission to study the issue. John Mitchell was not sure it was constitutional for the federal government to subsidize religiously based education. Other key members of the staff thought that any support gained from Catholics would be lost from public school advocates. None of the leading staffers around Nixon wanted to invest themselves in such a dead end project, so nothing had come of it. A few hours after Nixon's meeting with the Catholic educators, he sent for Colson and demanded action. The President said, "Chuck, I want a commission appointed *now*...I ordered it a year ago, and no one pays attention. You do it." Nixon told Colson to do what it took to have an order written up and on the President's desk by the next Monday morning.[118]

Normally, Colson would not have gotten anywhere on such an assignment without the blessing of Domestic Policy Chief John Ehrlichman and Attorney General John Mitchell, whose Justice Department had to clear all executive orders. But Ehrlichman was on a ski trip in Colorado, and Mitchell had gone home by the time Colson was prepared to touch base with him. Colson considered calling Mitchell at home, but since the two men did not get along Colson thought this would be a dead end. Colson worked on the project all weekend and tried to contact Ehrlichman several times to no avail. As Colson put it, "A strictly worded White House staff order required that Ehrlichman pass on all domestic matters. But the President had said Monday morning, and so Monday morning I placed the order on his desk." It made Mitchell and Ehrlichman angry because Colson had successfully poached on their territory,[119] and it made Haldeman frustrated that a staffer had bypassed his tightly controlled system, but Colson had worked his way into Nixon's trust. As Magruder put it, "Colson became the only newcomer to gain the direct access to Nixon that Haldeman, Ehrlichman, Kissinger, Mitchell, Shultz and Connally...enjoyed."[120]

Colson quickly followed up his Catholic schools victory with another big score. He somehow obtained a picture of Ted Kennedy, perhaps the biggest star of the Democratic Party, and a member of the family Nixon was obsessed with, coming out of a Paris nightclub in the wee hours of the morning. The beautiful woman with Kennedy was not his wife. Colson got the picture into one of the supermarket checkout line gossip papers. Because of maneuvers such as these, the President saw Colson as a guy who would get things done.[121] Magruder later wrote, "It was Haldeman's style to order you to do a hundred things by 5 PM in the hope that you might actually do twenty-five of them. For our part, we would rush him a list of twenty-five bold actions we were poised to undertake, when in truth five of them might occur."[122] In such an atmosphere, is it any wonder that Nixon was impressed by Colson, a man who would not just talk a good game but actually back it up with action?

Colson's access to Nixon was a headache for Haldeman at first. Haldeman freely admitted something that many wrote about in accusatory terms—he kept a wall around the President. From Haldeman's point of view, he did not keep the President isolated from others in a selfish attempt to enhance Haldeman's personal status; he did it to keep the President from being buried under an avalanche of unimportant meetings and petty problems. This was what the introverted President preferred. But Haldeman had another motive as well. As Haldeman described it, "the other reason for the wall was my secret. I soon realized that *this* President had to be protected from himself. Time and again I would receive petty, vindictive orders…I'd say, 'I'm working on it,' and delay and delay," until Nixon's mood would change, and he would realize that he had overreacted.[123] Haldeman did not like it at first that Colson had breached the wall because Haldeman felt that Colson catered to Nixon's worst instincts and acted on them. But Haldeman admitted that he came to see the advantage of having Colson around, so the Chief of Staff failed to oppose him and came to agree with his activities;[124] however, the two men never became close personally.

Among others in the White House who did not think much of Colson in 1970 were Jeb Stuart Magruder and, as already mentioned, John Mitchell. Magruder saw Colson "as an evil genius." Magruder believed, like Haldeman, that Colson's "brilliance was undeniable, but it was too often applied to encouraging Nixon's darker side, his desire to lash out at his enemies, his instinct for the jugular." Furthermore, "Colson was one of the men among his [Nixon's] advisors most responsible for creating the climate that made Watergate possible, perhaps inevitable."[125] While this may be true, it is worth noting that when Colson went to jail it was not for a Watergate offense. One is left to wonder if Magruder's desire to minimize his own culpability for Watergate led him, perhaps subconsciously, to shift undue responsibility on Colson. Mitchell hated Colson and believed that Colson's sole purpose for coming to the White House was to drum up business for his legal practice. This was not true, but such a belief illustrates Mitchell's low opinion of Colson.[126]

As Colson's stock was rising in the White House in early 1970, Magruder was still settling in. Haldeman had decided to make Magruder the deputy of Herb Klein in the Office of Communications. Klein had once been a heavy hitter within the Nixon administration; one of those rare individuals who actually had access to the President, but he was eventually held back by Haldeman's wall. Of course, Haldeman generally just did Nixon's bidding, so if Nixon had wanted greater contact with Klein, it would have happened. The problem was that Herb Klein was not nearly as hostile to or distrustful of the press as Nixon, Haldeman, and other key figures in the White House. As a result Klein was variously perceived as soft and/or a friend of the elitists. Either trait would have been enough to get him frozen out. Klein had wanted to be the White House press secretary, but that job went to Ron Ziegler, a Haldeman loyalist. Klein had been put in charge of the newly created Office of Communications, which was supposed to handle long range PR initiatives. But Klein had trouble with this assignment because his strength was press relations, not administration. Therefore Magruder became his deputy and was put in charge of making the Office of Communications run smoothly. It was just as well for Magruder that he landed here instead of continuing his efforts to overhaul the entire public relations apparatus. Magruder and Klein got along well, generally speaking, but Magruder found Ziegler completely uncooperative.[127]

On April 15, Ehrlichman wrote a memo to Haldeman pointing out that the Nixon Administration had done a lot for social programs. In the words of the memo, they were "doing as much or more than Johnson or Kennedy," but they were not getting enough credit for their efforts. The Chief Domestic Policy Advisor believed that people like Spiro Agnew, John Mitchell, and Supreme Court Justice nominee G. Harrold Carswell[128] were leaving a negative impression in the minds of Americans, particularly young people. Haldeman passed the memo along to Magruder and told him to deal with the issue. Magruder suggested enlisting the help of the younger White House staff assistants to reach out to college campuses. Magruder used the opportunity to put in a plug for his friend John Dean, as a young staffer in the Justice Department who would do a good job.[129] This episode is worth noting for several reasons. It shows that not everyone in Nixon's inner circle instinctively hated liberals; Ehrlichman wanted to make it clear how liberal the Nixon administration could be. It is also noteworthy that one of the non-advertising agency guys saw a fundamental problem of the Nixon administration as a PR problem. Finally, it is interesting that people in the Nixon White House went out of their way to promote the careers of individuals like John Dean (and later G. Gordon Liddy) who were ultimately mixed up in Watergate.

Richard Nixon had two major issues to grapple with in the spring and summer of 1970. One was getting the aforementioned Carswell on the Supreme Court. The other was selling the American public on the idea that expanding the Vietnam War's field of operations into Cambodia was a good thing. Getting a Supreme Court justice confirmed is always an important matter for a President, but this one had a special resonance with Nixon. In November 1969, Nixon's first choice, Clement Haynesworth, had been defeated after a withering attack of conflict-of interest charges. The White House believed that Nixon's liberal enemies in the Senate had trumping up these charges solely for political purposes. Nixon and Haldeman could not bear the thought of another Supreme Court nominee being defeated, so several members of the Executive Branch, including White House aides Magruder and Colson, and Justice Department official John Dean were given the assignment of shepherding Carswell through the process. What made Carswell's confirmation difficult—on top of the anticipated liberal opposition—was that Carswell was not an overly impressive candidate. It became impossible for the Nixon men to finesse this fact when one of Carswell's supposed advocates, Republican Senator Roman Hruska, pointed out in a TV interview that there were millions of mediocre Americans, and they deserved a voice on the Supreme Court.[130] As White House staffer Bryce Harlow told the President, "They [the Senators] think Carswell's a boob, a dummy. And what counter is there to that? He is."[131]

As far as Nixon and his men were concerned, the qualifications of the candidate were not the central point. The President's agenda had been thwarted once with Haynesworth; if it happened a second time it would weaken his authority. Pulling the nomination, which became increasingly tempting as some of Carswell's public appearances reinforced the notion of his general deficiency, was not an option. Nixon and Haldeman did not want the President to be seen as backing down on this issue. Nixon was a battler, not a man who publicly second-guessed himself.

The Senate voted against confirmation on April 9. Nixon the Battler had been beaten a second time, and he was furious.[132] To Nixon, the Democrats had crossed the lines of political fairness during this struggle, and the Republicans in Congress had not fought hard enough to support their President's interests. It reinforced Nixon's inclinations to take matters into his own hands and to not worry so much about political niceties (like the Constitution). He would fight harder than the Democrats, and he would not rely on bureaucrats or self-serving politicians to get things done. He would turn to people who could show him results.

On April 30, Nixon announced the sending of ground troops into Cambodia, and the protests roiling across the country only intensified. Nixon compared his plan to choices made by Franklin Roosevelt, Eisenhower and Kennedy. Nixon said, "In those decisions, the American people were not assailed by counsels of doubt and defeat from some of the most widely known opinion leaders of the nation."[133] For antiwar activists, Nixon was contradicting his promise to end the war quickly; in fact, he was escalating it. It was only shortly after this that four protesters were shot and killed on the campus of Kent State in Ohio and two more people were killed at Jackson State College in Mississippi—in both instances by authorities trying to restore order. Nixon and his advisors were surprised by the virulence of the protests. They assumed that all the usual suspects would complain, but Nixon had thought that the Silent Majority of Americans would understand his goals. Namely, Nixon wanted to destroy the North Vietnamese headquarters in Cambodia and their supply efforts along the Mekong River Valley. He believed such actions could hasten the end of the war. But the protesters were incensed, and in their outrage they planned to stage a major demonstration on May 9.[134]

Nixon felt the North Vietnamese had forced his hand by actions they took 16 months earlier. The North Vietnamese had responded to Nixon's call for a negotiated peace with a new offensive in South Vietnam starting in February 1969. The offensive was supported by supply lines that went through Cambodia. When some members of Nixon's staff suggested that bombing raids in Cambodia would prompt congressional opposition and bad press, Henry Kissinger retorted, "What do we care if the *New York Times* clobbers us now if it helps us end the war sooner?" Nixon agreed but waited to see if anything new would develop. He soon decided that the North Vietnamese were not interested in negotiations, and the only way to change their minds was to show them the level of his determination. Unannounced bombing began in Cambodia on March 17, 1969.[135]

Nixon believed that several things justified the decision to bomb in Cambodia and to keep it quiet. One factor was mentioned in the last chapter—Cambodian Prince Sihanouk wanted the bombings kept quiet. Also, according to one estimate, 85 percent of the heavy arms that the North Vietnamese Army was using were shipped into South Vietnam through Cambodia. The North Vietnamese were denying their presence in Cambodia, so as long as the Americans kept their bombing secret, the North Vietnamese could not publicly protest it. Finally, Nixon did not want to fuel the fire of the antiwar protestors, who would be outraged at the idea of Nixon expanding the war instead of narrowing its scope. Nixon's ultimate justification was that Americans casualty figures in South Vietnam had declined.[136] But it had not completely solved the problem even a year later, and Cambodia's political situation had destabilized, so American and South Vietnamese troops were going in to try and finish what American planes had started: the eradication of North Vietnamese forces from Cambodia.[137]

Nixon believed the unrest was causing Henry Kissinger to have second thoughts about the Cambodia invasion, but the President did not share such misgivings. Nixon said to him, "Henry, remember Lot's wife. Never turn back. Don't waste time rehashing things we can't do anything about."[138] But it proved impossible to ignore the reality of the activists as they descended in large numbers on America's capital. The gathering protestors were so great in number and loud in volume that Kissinger could not sleep well in his apartment. He temporarily moved into the White House basement.[139]

In an effort to take control of the situation, Nixon decided to schedule his first televised press conference in three months on November 8. The man who appeared on the nation's TV screens was not Nixon the Battler, but a kinder, gentler Nixon, to paraphrase a later Republican President. Nixon explained the rationale and the early results of the Cambodian operation.[140] He promised that all American troops would be out of Cambodia by July.[141] Nixon promised more troop withdrawals from Vietnam, and he predicted fruitful arms negotiations with the Soviets. He tried to identify with the young protesters across the country by reminiscing about his own youthful protests against Harry Truman. The conference led to more favorable remarks from the press than Nixon often received.[142]

The President was keyed up about his TV appearance, not knowing how well it would play in the press, and he was in a state of anxiety over Vietnam and the protests in general. When he got back to the White House that night, Nixon, an occasional insomniac, got on the phone and logged 50 calls before trying to get some sleep.[143] Nixon phoned long-time friends like Bebe Rebozo and Rose Mary Woods twice and four times, respectively. The President also contacted Billy Graham once and

Bob Haldeman seven times.[144] Nixon did not go to bed until around 2:15 AM, and he was awake an hour later.[145] He got up and went into the Lincoln Sitting Room. Manolo Sanchez, Nixon's valet, heard the music the President had put on, Rachmaninoff's First Piano Concerto, so the valet went out to see if his boss needed anything. Nixon, lost in thought, asked Sanchez, "Have you ever been to the Lincoln Memorial at night?" Sanchez had never been to the Lincoln Memorial at all. When the President heard that, he said, "Let's go look at it now." The thought of the President taking a spontaneous, early morning stroll to a public place where Vietnam War protestors were gathering threw the Secret Service into a panic.[146]

Egil "Bud" Krogh was the White House aide in charge of security for the day. Officially, he was a member of the Domestic Council under the guidance of John Ehrlichman. Krogh had worked on matters pertaining to the Department of Justice[147] and on education issues.[148] G. Gordon Liddy, who first met Krogh in 1969, described him as "young, intelligent, and intense; he was clearly dedicated to Nixon and best of all, open to reasoned argument and suggestion."[149] Jeb Magruder said Krogh was "the hardest working person in the White House;" a man who on more than one occasion worked all night long to get assignments done. Krogh maintained his strength during his long hours with a disciplined regimen of running and lifting weights.[150]

Krogh thought his long hours at the White House had paid off as May 9 began. He had been concerned about what kind of havoc the protesters might wreak, and he had helped come up with a plan to ring the Executive Mansion with 59 city buses. As Krogh had put it, "It was a lot easier to have buses out there than people," as the White House braced for what some were calling a "rebellion."[151]

But Krogh's careful planning would be for naught if Nixon left his secure premises to go visit a hornet's nest. When Nixon walked out of the White House, Krogh heard about it at the Secret Service Command Post.[152] Krogh did not know what to do, so he called his boss, Ehrlichman. Krogh said, "Look, I don't know why the President is down there on the lawn, but this town is filled up with young people who are really geared to expressing their First Amendment rights, and it's probably not a good thing for him to be out and about at this time in the morning."[153] Ehrlichman told Krogh to go to the White House lawn, introduce himself to the President, and ask if he could be of assistance.[154]

Ehrlichman called Haldeman, who tried to catch up with the President but would not reach him until breakfast time.[155] Nixon's aides did not want him to leave the White House premises, but as a junior aide whom the President did not know, Krogh was certainly not in a position to be confrontational. As it turned out, it did not matter. By the time Krogh reached the White House lawn, Nixon and Sanchez were gone.

The President went to the Lincoln Memorial and had time to point out the inscriptions to Sanchez before Krogh showed up. As Nixon and his valet turned to leave, Nixon saw several young people nearby, so he went over and shook hands. Krogh described it as "a surrealistic scene because a lot of these kids were obviously tired and obviously disheveled: they had been driving a long way. This was when fatigue clothes were in and long hair, and here he was, in earnest conversation talking to some of these young people."[156]

Unfortunately for the President, his attempts at conversation backfired. When one of the students said that he had missed Nixon's speech explaining the Cambodia incursion because the student had been traveling to Washington, Nixon said that was too bad because his goals were the same as the students'. He wanted to stop the killing and get out of Vietnam, but students opposed to the fighting found this argument for expanding its scope to be unconvincing. Nixon's rationale was met with silence.[157] The President next tried a different approach to relating to them, saying, "I know that probably most of you think I'm an SOB, but I want you to know that I understand just how you feel." Nixon went on to talk about how he had grown up hating war as a Quaker, and that led him to favor Neville Chamberlain's attitude towards the Nazis instead of Winston Churchill's outlook. What went without saying was that Chamberlain had been naïve to trust the Nazis, and Churchill's desire to fight them was justified by subsequent events. Nixon went on to talk about foreign relations with China, but he felt the young people were losing interest in his comments, so he began to talk about race relations in the United States before moving on to the next group of young people who were nearby.[158]

Nixon began to ask them questions and tried to make small talk. When one young woman said she was from Syracuse University, Nixon commented on her school's football team. And that became a talking point for the media. As the Syracuse student put it to a reporter, "Here we come from a university that's completely uptight, on strike, and when we told him where we were from, he talked about the football team. And when someone said he was from California, he [Nixon] talked about surfing." The *Washington Post* called Nixon's interactions with the students "a dialogue of the deaf."[159] Certainly one *could* interpret Nixon as being patronizing. These young people were spending their time and money—or perhaps their parent's money—to go to Washington to protest a war they thought was immoral. First the President tried to lecture them about it then he wanted to talk about college football. They were upset; they did not want to talk about games or hear excuses; they wanted to talk about putting a stop to the slaughter.

On the other hand, it is also easy to see it from the President's point of view. He had not planned to interact with the youths; he had just stumbled across them. He tried to reach out to them, to show them that in the United States the most powerful man in the country was willing to take some of his valuable time to create a connection with them. His desire to explain and justify his war policy was perfectly natural in the face of the criticism he had received. But given that these people were so opposed to the war that they had traveled to the capital to protest it, there was nothing he could have said to win them over, short of a promise of a complete and immediate withdrawal of American troops. Discussion on the war was at a dead end, so what could Nixon talk about with people who were less than half his age? Never a smooth conversationalist, Nixon tried to create a common bond by discussing one of his passions—sports. Getting mocked in the press for his efforts left Nixon once again feeling frustrated with trying to reach out to his critics or the media.

A few days later, Nixon had Bebe Rebozo's girlfriend sew some little hearts made out of blue cloth. During a trip on the presidential plane, Air Force One, Nixon handed out the blue hearts to Haldeman, Ehrlichman, and Kissinger. Nixon said to the men, "You deserve something like the Purple Heart for all the wounds you have sustained in the line of duty over the past few weeks." The hearts were blue because Nixon's men had been "true blue" in the face of adversity.[160]

The smiles produced by the blue hearts did not last long, though, as Nixon headed to Camp David to brood. Kissinger's stock went down with the President because Nixon believed that Kissinger was losing his resolve. At Camp David, Nixon became increasingly reluctant to take Kissinger's calls. Nixon froze Kissinger out of the wiretapping activities, and the President wanted Haldeman to curb Kissinger's self-aggrandizing press statements. Following the President's lead, the other senior officials grew more distant. Kissinger responded to these slights by skipping Haldeman's eight A.M. staff meetings. Haldeman ordered Kissinger to come to one such meeting when they were discussing why the military had not discovered the Communist headquarters in Cambodia. Haldeman wanted to know what they should say to the press. Ehrlichman, who was also in attendance, later wrote, "Kissinger was horribly offended." The National Security Advisor said, "I do not deal with PR problems." Then he walked out of the meeting.[161]

Nixon's first public appearance on a college campus after the announcement of the Cambodia ground campaign was on May 28 at Neyland Stadium in Knoxville where the University of Tennessee plays football. There was a Billy Graham Crusade scheduled, and Graham invited the President to attend. Nixon was concerned about politicizing the event, but decided to go anyway. Graham tried to establish political unity and balance for the night by inviting Tennessee Senator Al Gore, Sr., a Democrat, but Gore was unable to attend. Tens of thousands of spectators surrounded the stadium, which was filled to capacity. As the Crusade began and Nixon was formally welcomed, 200-300 war protesters began shouting. The majority booed the protesters, but as the service unfolded, the protesters continued. The police made arrests, and some pro-Nixon Tennesseans took matters into their own hands, prompting one of the protesters to shout, "Let's get out of here before these Christians kill us!" But many stayed, shouting "Peace now!" and various obscenities. When it came time for Nixon to make some remarks, he just spoke over the activists. The President received loud applause from the majority at the end of his speech, but the chants and obscenities had continued.[162] These were turbulent times.

After Ehrlichman was promoted from Counsel to the President to Chief of Domestic Policy, a replacement was needed for his old position. Bud Krogh suggested a friend of his, John Dean, who was serving as an associate deputy attorney general.[163] In May, Krogh approached Dean about joining the White House team. Dean had been working for John Mitchell at the Justice Department, and Dean liked his job, but it was not the White House. Like Colson and Magruder, Dean knew the importance of not seeming to be over eager. Dean acted noncommittal with Krogh and waited to see how badly they wanted him. Dean was attracted to the idea of working in the White House, but in his opinion too many talented young men had been turned into gophers, a fate Dean was determined to avoid. Dean's boss, John Mitchell, told Dean that if he stayed in the Justice Department he could expect to move up. Mitchell also expressed a dislike for at least some elements of the White House staff. But Mitchell said he had talked about the matter with the White House, and Mitchell had raised no objections to Dean's transfer.[164]

Dean went to Jeb Magruder to ask his advice about joining the White House staff. Magruder had met Dean in November 1969 and was impressed with the young lawyer's potential. Magruder thought Dean handled himself smoothly and was a rising talent. Magruder listened to Dean express misgivings about the job then replied, "Take it. You can handle the White House, and that is where the action is. Besides, when you're ready to go back to private practice, it won't hurt to have the White House on your resume."[165]

Dean eventually met with Haldeman, and one of the questions Haldeman asked surprised the young lawyer. "Do you believe you can be loyal to Richard Nixon and work for the White House rather than for John Mitchell?" Dean knew that Mitchell and Nixon were close friends, and that Mitchell was completely loyal to the President, so the question threw him. It was another early example of the mutual distrust between Mitchell and Nixon's top White House staffers.[166] Mitchell and Haldeman had actually gotten along well in the past, but the pair did not have much respect for several of each other's top aides, thus complicating their own relationship.[167] At one point Mitchell told the President that Mitchell did not want to deal with anyone in the White House outside of Nixon or Haldeman.[168] Mitchell's feelings of disdain for the White House staff were mutual, so the White House staffers wanted to be sure they could trust one of Mitchell's men who was coming to work with them. Dean assured Haldeman that loyalty would not be a problem and the interview continued. Dean passed inspection with Haldeman, met with Nixon, and started his job as Counsel to the President on July 27.[169] Perhaps unfortunately, Mitchell, whom the President and Haldeman trusted, and Bud Krogh, whom Ehrlichman trusted, vouched for Dean, so the White House skipped the normal background check on Dean. Such a check would have revealed that Dean, who had previously been in a private law practice for less than a year, had left his first firm under less than ideal circumstances. There were accusations of a conflict of interest. An investigation would not necessarily have revealed character issues on Dean's part, but it might have prompted Haldeman to go for a safer choice.[170]

Not everyone was so taken with John Dean, including Gordon Liddy, who was working in the Treasury Department in 1969 when they first met. Liddy wrote in his autobiography, *Will*, that he had been advised to be careful around Dean, who was accused of being an "idea thief." As Liddy put it, "If one mentioned a good idea in Dean's presence, one remotely in Dean's area of official interest, before one's memorandum was out of the typewriter, Dean's would be on the appropriate desk, crediting himself with the idea."[171] Of course, given the different ways these men handled themselves during the Watergate scandal, and the attitudes that festered as a result, it should not be surprising that Liddy had something negative to say about Dean. Magruder continued to like Dean as he got to know him better, believing that they shared the same sense of irony and detachment towards events in the White House. But Magruder acknowledged Dean's more selfish nature. When describing another man, Magruder compared him to Dean, saying that both men were "capable and could be engaging, but" they were "obviously always studying all the angles and trying to manipulate events to [their] own advantage."[172]

Occasionally, Dean's work as a White House legal counsel led him to cross paths with Magruder on a professional level. When Magruder wanted to send a mass mailing out to Nixon supporters and charge it to the government, Dean's office informed Magruder that such an action would be illegal. Magruder did it anyway.[173] Such were the legal and moral compromises of Nixon's men.

Dean's first assignment at the White House had to do with a fledgling magazine called *Scanlon's Monthly*, which claimed in an article that Vice President Spiro Agnew was part of a plot to cancel the 1972 presidential election and repeal the Bill of Rights. When Agnew referred to the magazine's story and evidence as "completely false" and "ridiculous," *Scanlon's Monthly* responded with, "The Vice President's denial is as clumsy as it is fraudulent. The document [which was the magazine's evidence] came directly from Mr. Agnew's office and he knows it."[174]

Dean was expected to file a suit or launch a federal investigation or do something to retaliate against this baseless attack. Dean was a little surprised to learn that Nixon was personally invested in this dispute. The new Counsel thought the President would be concerned with more substantive issues than the nonsense in one article of an obscure, extremist magazine. It was suggested from the upper echelon that Dean should pressure the IRS to investigate the magazine, which Dean thought might be an illegal thing for him to do. He asked a White House veteran, Murray Chotiner, for advice, but Chotiner replied, "You're the lawyer. You're the one who is supposed to give counsel around here." Dean replied that he "was still trying to find the water fountains."[175]

After Dean explained his problem, it seemed pretty simple to Chotiner, who said, "If the President wants you to turn the IRS loose, then you turn the IRS loose. It's that simple, John." When Dean protested, Chotiner grew irritated and said, "It's the way the game is played. Do you think for a second that Lyndon Johnson was above using the IRS to harass those guys who were giving him a hard time on the war? No sir. Nor was Lyndon Johnson above using the IRS against some good Republicans like Richard Nixon."[176]

In the end Dean pointed out to his superiors that an IRS investigation of the magazine would be fruitless because it had not been in existence long enough to file any returns. However, Dean reported that an investigation of the magazine's owners might be worthwhile. Dean had actually handed the assignment off to someone else, limiting his culpability, but as he later wrote, "I had crossed an ethical line. I had no choice, as I saw it."[177] Dean made it clear with this admission that maintaining his integrity was not his top priority, and he was hardly alone in this regard.

Perhaps the White House's descent into the world of serious internal espionage began with the Huston Plan. This plan was the work of one Thomas Charles Huston, a young staffer who dreamed of coordinating all domestic intelligence activities through the White House. The rationale for this was a common theme to Nixon and many conservatives. They believed that many antiwar activities were aided and abetted by enemies in Communist capitals around the world. Thus, such activities might be monitored by the FBI, the CIA, and/or various branches of the military, but these different organizations often times did not work together very well. By February 1970, Huston had proposed an interagency group, which someone in the White House could chair. Huston told Bud Krogh that the FBI and the Justice Department were simply not serving the President's interests. The like-minded Krogh said to Bob Haldeman that the Justice Department was "almost blind to opportunities which could help us."[178]

In July, Nixon temporarily approved the Huston Plan, which in its final form would have done more than coordinate intelligence gathering efforts. The Huston Plan called for electronic surveillance, mail-openings, the employment of informants, etc. in an effort to deal with domestic terrorist groups like the Weathermen and the Black Panthers. While it might seem extreme to contemporary readers to refer to such groups as terrorist organizations, their members talked openly of kidnapping and murder, and sometimes they did more than talk. Nixon rescinded his approval only five days after giving it, and he made no illusions about his thinking. He did not try to gloss over his original decision, nor did he claim to be motivated by civil rights concerns when he changed his mind. He simply noted that J. Edgar Hoover and John Mitchell were both against it. Having the Attorney General against it was bad enough, but as Nixon put it, "I knew that if Hoover had decided not to cooperate, it would matter little what I had decided or approved. Even if I issued a direct order to him, while he would undoubtedly carry it out, he would soon see to it that I had cause to reverse myself.[179]

Critics say that Nixon was not just interested in security issues. They say his primary interest in this plan was the political advantage it could give him.[180] The truth was probably somewhere in between what Nixon admitted and what his enemies accused him of. Nixon was interested in maintaining his political dominance, but he was also frustrated with the inefficiency of the federal bureaucracy. There was a lot of unrest in the nation, and Nixon felt that Hoover had lost his zeal in dealing with it. In his younger days Hoover was willing to break a few rules to get the bad guys, but now, as John Dean had put it, Hoover had "lost his guts."[181] Perhaps, though, it was not his guts that Hoover was worried about losing, but his control over dealing with domestic intelligence. If the White House horned in on this area, the FBI would have less power.[182]

Dean had his own crisis of nerves when Haldeman made it clear that the White House was not done with the plan, and the new Counsel needed to get it moving again. Dean had no idea how to get Hoover to change his mind and support the Huston Plan, and the young lawyer was concerned about his own legal liability if the plan was implemented. Dean went to John Mitchell to talk things over. Dean was thrilled to hear Mitchell say, "John, the President loves all this stuff, but it just isn't necessary." Mitchell and Dean cooked up the idea of creating the Intelligence Evaluation Committee. It would be a study group that could be presented to the White House as an important first step to implementing the Huston Plan, but at the same time it would be presented to Hoover as a meaningless effort to placate Nixon. A disappointed Tom Huston left the White House staff after he realized that his initiative was destined to die a slow death.[183] Once again, Nixon and Haldeman were frustrated as their demands for action were agreed to but not carried out.

Based on his later actions, it is safe to say that there was one Nixon man who would have been a true believer in the Huston Plan: Gordon Liddy. But Liddy was not yet working in the White House. His path did cross with the President in October 1970 because of the Organized Crime Control Act. Liddy, who had drafted an early version of the bill, was in attendance at the signing ceremony. The two men chatted, and Liddy found Nixon to be "warm, engaging, and looking very well." Many people would not have described Nixon thus, but Liddy blamed part of the negative perception of Nixon on TV coverage, where Nixon came across as tense, sickly, and just not telegenic in Liddy's opinion.[184]

As the 1970 congressional elections approached, Nixon decided not to campaign personally; he believed that Vice President Spiro Agnew should be the standard bearer for the party the way Nixon had been when he was Vice President under Eisenhower in the 1950s.[185] Nixon demonstrated how uninvolved with the campaign he was by taking a trip to Europe from September 27 to October 5.[186]

By the time Nixon got back to America, the political races were not shaping up well for the Republicans. Complicating Nixon's problem was the combative Agnew. Some Republicans said privately that they did not want Agnew to campaign for them because he would alienate their constituents. Senator Robert Taft of Ohio said it publicly. When Nixon had one of his men call the Senator to complain about his remarks, Taft hung up on the staffer. Eventually, Agnew was sent off to Native American reservations to win over the Indian vote.[187] Agnew's involvement in the campaign was just another example of how relations between the Republican White House and the Republicans in Congress continued to spiral down the drain.

Meanwhile, Nixon reversed his earlier decision and decided to go out and campaign himself. The President made a stop at an auditorium in San Jose filled with 5,000 supporters. Unfortunately for the President, there were 2,000 antiwar demonstrators outside. When Nixon left the auditorium he was greeted with obscene chants. The demonstrators became even more worked up when Nixon got on the hood of a car and flashed his double V-sign at them. They began to pelt Nixon's entourage with rocks, eggs, and vegetables, and they broke multiple windows out of vehicles in Nixon's motorcade.[188] Once again, Nixon was reminded that the political life was a rough one, as if he needed any such reminders.

Certainly, no one had to tell Chuck Colson that politics were not for the faint of heart. He decided to target Democratic Senator Joseph Tydings, a liberal Marylander with Kennedy connections.[189] Colson ran ads in the *Washington Post* painting Tydings as an extreme liberal. Colson also planted a story with *Life* magazine that accused Tydings of influence peddling, which turned out to be not true. Colson's dirty trick was successful, though, Tydings was defeated. And when rivals within the administration would point out unsuccessful Colson schemes in the future, Colson would sometimes reply, "Yeah, but I'm the guy who got Joe Tydings."[190]

Another target of the White House in 1970 was the aforementioned Al Gore, Sr. of Tennessee. Haldeman sent Colson memos on the efforts to unseat Gore. When Gore's son, the future Vice President, was informed of his impending transfer to Vietnam, the younger Gore told friends that his family believed his transfer was politically influenced. The Gores thought Nixon officials delayed the transfer long enough to cheat the senior Gore out of any election eve PR advantage of having a son in Vietnam. If that was the case, it worked; Al Gore, Sr. was defeated in 1970 by Republican Bill Brock. There has never been any proof offered that Nixon forces conspired in holding up Al Gore, Jr's. transfer,[191] but it is an example of the cynicism with which the Nixon administration was viewed by its enemies.

A Republican casualty of the 1970 elections was George Bush, who was defeated in a run for the Senate. His seat in the House of Representatives had been safe, but at Nixon's request, and in fulfillment of his own ambition, Bush ran for the Senate and lost. Bush then asked the President for an ambassadorship to the United Nations. Bush said he would serve wherever it pleased the President, but Bush did point out that the current ambassador was a liberal Democrat. Nixon had wanted Bush for a different assignment; one closer to the Oval Office, but in the end Bush was offered the job he wanted.[192] If Bush had been more timid, he might have been sucked into the coming Watergate morass, and future presidential politics might have unfolded much differently.

There were mixed opinions regarding the elections. John Mitchell believed that the Republican Party lost the 1970 congressional elections for two main reasons. Richard Nixon was not portrayed as being a statesman-like leader of a political party, and there was not a lone coordinator of a national strategy, which resulted in the Republican National Committee leaders and White House officials not always pursuing the same agenda.[193] While it is true that the White House traditionally only picked a national coordinator when the presidency was at stake, this White House had been much more involved in congressional elections than any previous one, so a coordinator was needed.[194] Despite Mitchell's assessment, Nixon argued that Republican losses were not so bad, especially compared to other administrations during off-year elections. The Republicans had lost nine seats in the House, but they gained two in the Senate.[195] Regardless of how it was spun, Nixon's weak hand in Congress had gotten weaker.

The fact that negative campaigning was a prominent part of the President's failed strategy prompted him to decide that he needed to act more statesmanlike in his 1972 re-election campaign. Unfortunately, it would only be an act. As the President sought to have himself portrayed as someone who was above politics, he encouraged his operatives to gather intelligence and engage in dirty tricks in a more covert fashion.[196] Nixon believed that dirty tricks were just part of the political game. Long time Nixon enemy Frank Mankiewicz is more caustic in his assessment of why Nixon condoned such activities by his people. "Ignorance, hubris, and an unwillingness to accept the American system remain the best reasons to assign to Nixon's reliance on 'dirty tricks.'"[197] It is perhaps an exaggeration to say that Nixon was unwilling to accept the American system, but it is fair to say that Nixon had a fairly cynical attitude about how the system really worked.

Jeb Magruder was hospitalized for gall bladder surgery after the 1970 elections. With his surgery and rehabilitation, Magruder was out of work for a month, and during that time he contemplated his future. Magruder decided to leave the White House, but not Nixon's service. Magruder was falling out of love with his current job, and he was afraid Chuck Colson's power plays would result in Colson becoming Magruder's boss, which was an eventuality that Magruder wanted no part of. Magruder decided that his best option was to work on Nixon's re-election campaign. Magruder believed, accurately, that John Mitchell would be put in charge of the campaign, and Magruder respected Mitchell. But Magruder also had something else in mind. He believed he already had Haldeman's support, and if Magruder cultivated a good relationship with Mitchell, then Magruder thought he would be well positioned to get a plumb assignment during Nixon's second term.[198] How could Magruder fail with Nixon's top two men on his side?

With the November 1970 elections behind him, Nixon began to think creatively in regard to his re-election bid in 1972. Fearful of defeat, he wooed Democrat John Connally into his administration. Nixon saw Connally as a major threat in 1972, so he convinced Connally to join forces with him by becoming Secretary of the Treasury in December 1970. But Nixon's efforts to recruit Connally were not solely the result of shrewd politics; Nixon truly admired the Texas Democrat. Connally's charisma awed the President, who responded by treating the Texan with more respect than he gave most other men in public or private.[199] Perhaps John Ehrlichman put it best when he wrote, "As everyone knows, John B. Connally was Nixon's darling boy. Of all his Cabinet and staff, Nixon saw only Connally as his potential successor." Ehrlichman and the others in Nixon's inner circle had to accommodate themselves to Nixon's respect for Connally. Ehrlichman routinely had subordinates deal with Cabinet officials instead of seeing them personally, but Connally did not tolerate such power plays. And if there was a message from the President, then even Haldeman and Ehrlichman were underlings. Such a message had to be delivered by the President himself. Despite Connally's demand for respect, he could be quite friendly and decent when he did not feel he was being challenged.[200]

John Connally, like the other most important men in the Nixon Administration, had proven his loyalty and toughness. Connally's toughness was demonstrated November 22, 1963 when Connally was shot and received multiple wounds during the assassination of John Kennedy.[201] On top of Connally's physical toughness, according to Haldeman, "Nixon felt Connally was the only politician as tough as himself."[202] In Nixon's opinion, "Only three men in America understand the use of power. I do. John Connally does. And, I guess Nelson [Rockefeller, Gerald Ford's VP and Nixon's former rival] does."[203] Like Kissinger, Connally was also attractive to Nixon because, as a Democrat, Connally was seen as someone who could bring more supporters behind the new administration.

Connally had previously been named to Nixon's Advisory Council on Executive Organization, then Connally got a seat on the Foreign Intelligence Advisory Board in the State Department, then on December 14, 1970 Connally became the Secretary of the Treasury. And Ehrlichman was right: Nixon was so taken with Connally that the President began grooming him as a potential running mate in 1972, but this plan would be scuttled by Agnew's popularity with the Republican rank and file.[204]

Near the end of 1970 the President made a list of things he wanted his staff to focus on as they presented Nixon and his first couple of years in office to the public. The list included:

1. The success of Cambodia—President's courage
2. The "open" White House
3. Dignity and respect—at home and abroad
4. Effective handling of Press Conferences—TV
5. Warmth in personal relations with staff & people
6. Handling of world leaders
7. Takes attacks by Press et al—without flapping
8. Hard work
9. Listen to different views[205]

There are several noteworthy things about Nixon's list. He was so preoccupied with his image that he made such a detailed list. He was so preoccupied with PR that he mentioned the press twice. He was self-conscious enough about his people skills that he wanted his staff to tell the country that he was a warm person. He did not believe that his personal warmth would be manifest enough for people to see it for themselves. Nixon, who had certainly been a hard worker, was now self-conscious enough about his work ethic that he wanted his people to talk about that too, or he was so convinced that he would not get fair press coverage that he felt he needed to make it clear to the public. For Nixon, it was not enough to make decisions and lead the country; he wanted to control the flow of information coming out of the White House. He also wanted to know what his rivals were planning, so he would be prepared in 1972. These desires led to his undoing.

CHAPTER THREE

The Plumbers and the CRP—1971

In 1971 Nixon was still operating by his minimal human contact approach. He preferred to work with one key individual and have that person turn the President's will into reality. But sometimes the President operated through different individuals on the same project. Bob Haldeman described how it worked. Haldeman "was the man for the straight, hit-them-over-the head strategy. Ehrlichman, who loved intrigue, was given the more devious assignments. And Colson was assigned the real underground routes." But this was not a subtle dig at his colleagues. Haldeman pointed out that Nixon "provided the output which all of us, including Colson, Ehrlichman, and myself, were ordered to put into action."[206]

Because Nixon liked to limit the number of people he was exposed to, a lot of power was put into the hands of the few who had regular access to him. Colson would later tell a biographer that he "found it remarkable that there was so much high level work going on that [Colson] was so deeply involved in. There was no trial period or supervised training."[207] Unfortunately, supervised training was exactly what was needed. Nixon's men were clearly dedicated to him. Colson's father described Chuck as "viciously loyal;" several colleagues noted how eager to please John Dean was when it came to Nixon. Tom Huston, architect of the failed Huston Plan, said of several of his coworkers, "If Nixon told them to nationalize the railroads, they'd have nationalized the railroads. If he'd told them to exterminate the Jews, they'd have exterminated the Jews." Such hyperbole might strike one as politically incorrect, but it does make the point that the men were loyal. John Ehrlichman believed part of the problem in the Nixon White House was that the President had a tendency to issue "rhetorical instructions…excesses…you just simply had to know the difference….There were people around that didn't know the difference."[208] Of course, Nixon, Haldeman, and Ehrlichman were

58

responsible for bringing such men into the White House, so this explanation does little to absolve the key players of guilt. They chose their team, and they chose their method of operation, so they had to live with the results of those choices.

In February, the President made another operational choice that had major ramifications on his legacy. Two years to the month after having Lyndon Johnson's secret taping system torn out of the White House, Nixon had his own installed. One rationale for taping was that it would be a nice feature for Nixon's future presidential library, and it made sense. Why not use modern technology to record history for posterity? Nixon wanted more in his library than just a bunch of old papers. The fact that Nixon did not intend for the taping system to be used against unsuspecting visitors is evidenced both by the embarrassing material Nixon himself provided and by the lack of evidence that Nixon ever used the tapes against anybody. When the taping system was installed, the only people privy to its existence were Nixon, Haldeman, and two of Haldeman's aides, Larry Higby and Alex Butterfield. Even Nixon's and Haldeman's best friends John Mitchell and John Ehrlichman, respectively, were left out of the loop.[209] It has been argued that the tapes could have been used in cases where Nixon's visitors said one thing when speaking with him then something else to the press—something Kissinger was accused of doing.[210] But despite transgressions of this sort by Kissinger and others, Nixon never ordered that the tapes be used to trap or threaten anybody.

In March Nixon made a pretty candid observation to a member of the press about the media in general. "It is true that of all the Presidents in this century, it is probably true, that I have less, as somebody has said, supporters in the press than any President."[211] The comment revealed so many aspects of this President. Nixon the Battler was not so tough in face to face encounters. When speaking to a specific member of the media, Nixon could not bring himself to attack, so he started by saying that something was true, then restated it as "probably true," then attributed the idea to someone else. One also gets a glimpse of Nixon the Persecuted—he is the most hated President. Finally, one is left to wonder at what Nixon does with this perception of his treatment. Is it easier to break the rules when you feel the game is being unfairly played against you? For Nixon, apparently it was.

Breaking the rules was precisely what was going to happen at the Committee to Re-Elect the President (CRP), and the problem started at the top. One of John Mitchell's conditions to agreeing to chair the CRP was that he needed to have total power over it. He did not want Chuck Colson interfering with CRP operations. Not only did Colson ultimately interfere, but Mitchell had another problem. It would become hard to maintain the fiction of his ignorance of CRP operations like Watergate when he had demanded absolute power over the organization.[212]

In March Mitchell spoke to Jeb Magruder about leaving the White House and joining the CRP,[213] which would be dubbed "CREEP" by the press. Magruder got Haldeman's blessing to transfer jobs. Not only was Magruder seen as a Haldeman loyalist who would report on the CRP's activities to Nixon's Chief of Staff, but as Haldeman put it, "I saw a chance to reassign him to a position that was less demanding and better suited to him. At the No. 2 post of CRP, he simply would be following the orders of a strong leader, John Mitchell."[214] This was not, however, how Haldeman sold the transfer to Magruder. The Chief of Staff told Magruder, "You've got a great opportunity to build a campaign from the ground up. This is the most important thing we'll be doing in the next two years."[215] As in the last chapter, one is left to wonder about Haldeman's rationale. If Haldeman was so convinced of Magruder's incompetence, then why make him the second in command of something that would be so important to Nixon? It seems that Haldeman is taking ownership of a smaller mistake, a bad staffing decision, to minimize his role in the larger mistake, the Watergate break-ins.

John Dean's wife, Maureen, who later worked with Magruder during Nixon's second presidential inauguration, thought Magruder was too "rank-conscious" in the presence of high-ranking administration officials.[216] Of course this would describe the character of several of the other men who got caught up in Watergate, notably Mrs. Dean's husband. Such youthful ambition is what helped create the yes-men who were responsible for carrying out many of the crimes associated with the Nixon administration.

When Mitchell was setting up the CRP, he decided that other than petty cash all expenditures required his approval. Maintaining control was to be made easier by not using credit cards. Part of what prompted this policy was that Nixon campaign staffers had run up millions of dollars worth of charges in 1968.[217] Thus, the CRP wound up with all sorts of large dollar cash expenditures. Operating under such a philosophy, it seemed like it would be easy to hide big cash pay outs since there would be so many requests for large cash withdrawals coming into the finance department.

During the meeting where Mitchell invited Jeb Magruder to join the CRP, Mitchell had one other, rather delicate matter to bring up. "By the way, Jeb," he said to Magruder, "I have a problem I'd like you to help me out with. My wife, Martha, has become rather well known. She's getting flooded with requests for speeches and interviews. She needs professional guidance. She can help the Administration, if she's used properly. So I wish you'd give her a hand."[218]

In and of itself, this was not an unusual or unreasonable request. Barbara Bush, wife of then-Congressman George Bush was already being sent out by the CRP to help get Nixon re-elected. Usually, she just introduced the wives of other Executive Branch officials down in Texas where these women would speak to the masses about the virtues of the Richard Nixon administration.[219]

Martha Mitchell, though, was not the typical wife of an Executive Branch official. On the plus side, Magruder reckoned her to be at one point "the third most sought after Republican in America, trailing only the President and the Vice President." And she sincerely wanted to help Nixon's cause. Though her husband did not think she was an able speechmaker, she had a good sense of humor and was excellent at informal talks. Her downside was that she had—to put it diplomatically—a unique perspective on things. She was convinced that people wanted to assassinate her and her husband. To be fair, they had received threatening letters, but that hardly made them unique in Washington. Mrs. Mitchell, though, took the threats seriously and rarely went out casually in public. And because of her erratic behavior and history with alcohol, many people were reluctant to invite the Mitchells over for private get-togethers. Martha Mitchell consequently got bored and lonely and often times resentful of her husband's coworkers who came over on political business. This led to late night phone calls to people who did not always appreciate such calls. Sometimes it led to ill-considered calls to journalists. Complicating matters further, she loved to travel on Air Force One because if made her feel both safe and important, but the President could not stand her. Nixon had a hard enough time confronting people he knew much less the wife of one of his best friends, so keeping her away from Air Force One became Magruder's responsibility. All in all, she was a burden to Magruder and the people at the CRP he passed her off to.[220]

She was an even bigger burden to her husband. Bob Haldeman wrote that John Mitchell was so concerned his wife might commit suicide that he would not allow her to be alone. If Mitchell was in a meeting and got a call saying that his wife's company had to leave, Mitchell would leave the meeting regardless of its importance. Thanks to Martha Mitchell and a matter known as the ITT scandal, John Mitchell was giving almost no attention to his responsibilities as the chairman of the Committee to Re-Elect the President.[221]

Though Martha Mitchell has been blamed for Watergate by being a distraction to her husband, Magruder's wife, Gail, saw Mrs. Mitchell as more of a victim than a culprit. According to Gail Magruder, Martha Mitchell was a warmhearted woman with a great sense of humor who was terribly insecure. Unfortunately, she married a cold man whose ambition got in the way of his giving his wife the attention and affirmation she so desperately craved. In general, Gail Magruder believed that the top men in Nixon's administration were so driven to succeed that they neglected their families. In retrospect, Jeb Magruder agreed with her.[222]

Besides their own ambition, something that further greased the slope towards criminal misconduct was a sign hung in the war room of the CRP that read, "WINNING IN POLITICS ISN'T EVERYTHING, IT'S THE ONLY THING." Plus, the men involved at the CRP all knew that intelligence gathering by political campaigns had become standard operating procedure.[223] There just seemed to be too many factors pointing towards going outside the lines for the overly ambitious young men to resist.

Meanwhile, back at the White House, trouble was afoot, involving the aforementioned ITT case. John Ehrlichman told the Deputy Attorney General, Richard Kleindienst, to stop the government's appeal in the case of ITT's attempt to acquire the Grinnell Corporation. Kleindienst ignored Ehrlichman's request, so the President himself called and pressured Kleindienst. The DAG appealed to his boss, John Mitchell, for help. Kleindienst said that unless Nixon backed off, Kleindienst would resign, which, given the circumstances, would have been bad PR for the President. Nixon let it go because Mitchell backed Kleindienst and so did conservative Senator Barry Goldwater, whose support Nixon needed.[224]

Nixon's attempt at an abuse of power failed. Nixon needed to keep Goldwater happy on this matter because the President made him mad with some of the White House's liberal domestic policies, which were needed to appease legislators who were on the fence regarding Vietnam issues. In the White House, almost everything led back to Vietnam.

In May a Harris Poll had Senator Muskie ahead of Richard Nixon 47% to 39%.[225] Concern over this drove Nixon's men to desire an increasing amount of political intelligence regarding the opposition. Their desperation, and Nixon's desire to appear more statesmanlike in 1972, led to a much greater degree of clandestine political activities than would have otherwise been the case.[226] And more seeds were being sown for trouble ahead.

The Pentagon Papers began to get published in the *New York Times* on June 13.[227] At first Nixon did not see this development as that serious compared to other leaks since the Pentagon Papers pertained to foreign policy during the Kennedy and Johnson administrations. Chuck Colson shared this view, believing that the Pentagon Papers would prove an embarrassment to the Democrats since they had controlled the White House, and thus American foreign policy, for most of the years covered by the Papers (1945-1968).[228] But Kissinger, as Bob Haldeman later noted, "really knew how to get to Nixon." Kissinger argued that "It shows you're a weakling, Mr. President." Kissinger said that the Soviets would not respect the U.S., and other nations could not trust the U.S., if individuals in America could take it upon themselves to release secret negotiations to the world.[229] Colson would later testify to the Watergate special prosecutors that it was Kissinger who had gotten the President upset about the Pentagon Papers. According to Colson, Nixon was "near hysteria" regarding this matter, but only because of Kissinger. Ehrlichman who had lost his love for the President after Watergate, also blamed the White House's reaction to the Pentagon Papers leak on Kissinger. Ehrlichman said, "The Pentagon Papers problem was no larger than a bread box on the horizon until Henry got to the President. Henry managed to raise the heat so high that Nixon was giving orders left and right that could only lead to trouble."[230]

Haldeman had a theory for why Kissinger would be so worked up over material that had nothing to do with either Nixon or Kissinger. Haldeman believed it was because the man who leaked the material,

Daniel Ellsberg, had worked for Kissinger. Kissinger felt personally betrayed, so he responded strongly. Included in the Kissinger offensive was an attack on Ellsberg's character. Kissinger said the man was a drug user and sexual deviant who had enjoyed taking potshots at Vietnamese from the safety of a helicopter.[231] One also wonders if Kissinger reacted this strongly so Nixon would not think that Ellsberg was operating under Kissinger's orders. Kissinger's behavior in this episode serves as an example of a characteristic that Colson later ascribed to all the men in Nixon's inner circle. Colson, the former "Hatchet Man," observed that, "everybody thinks the people surrounding the President were drunk with power, but it was not arrogance at all. It was insecurity. That insecurity began to breed a form of paranoia."[232]

Nixon became obsessed with stopping the leaks that were, he believed, hampering his efforts at peace with honor in Vietnam. Hoover was not being as vigilant, so he could not be relied upon. Nixon became convinced that there were leaks coming out of the State Department. He decided that if he could not count on the FBI to stop the leaks, or the State Department to govern itself, the White House would have to get the job done. Nixon ordered Haldeman to have all State Department employees take a lie detector test. Haldeman decided to stall on this project until Nixon gave up on it since there were thousands of employees who would have faced the polygraph.[233]

Nixon told Ehrlichman to put together a Special Investigations Unit to plug the leaks. Because of the nature of their work, the unit was quickly dubbed "the Plumbers." Ehrlichman was a natural choice to oversee the project due to his love of intrigue. Ehrichman picked his man Bud Krogh to lead the team. Its other members included David Young, who had worked for Henry Kissinger; Howard Hunt, an ex-CIA man who was close to Chuck Colson; and G. Gordon Liddy.[234] Gordon Liddy joined the White House staff in June 1971 thanks to the efforts of Bud Krogh and with the full support of John Mitchell. Liddy was supposed to work on issues pertaining to narcotics and guns, but he was immediately put to work with the Plumbers.[235]

The Plumbers worked on some legitimate projects, like declassifying documents from World War Two and the Korean War, but they quickly exceeded legal boundaries. They gained access to IRS files in the course of their efforts to investigate and harass their targets.[236] Hunt created bogus government cables in an attempt to show John Kennedy was guilty of involvement in the assassination of the South Vietnamese leader Ngo Dinh Diem. Hunt was convinced that Kennedy was involved, but he had been unable to prove it after investigating the matter in 1969.[237]

When Daniel Ellsberg was indicted on June 28, the Plumbers were ordered by the White House to keep an eye on the case and make sure Ellsberg was punished. Krogh had plenty of other things to worry about, David Young was in charge of finding out who had leaked information about SALT, and Hunt had not yet joined the team, so Liddy became the de facto point man on the Ellsberg project. Hunt quickly joined Liddy, and the two of them began to follow the Ellsberg case closely.[238]

Perhaps the Plumbers work in the White House seemed okay to those in charge because the Plumbers were not doing anything that was fundamentally different from how Nixon and his inner circle operated in general. Admiral R. Zumwalt, Jr. offered a scathing critique of Nixon, Kissinger, Haldeman, et al, and how they handled international affairs. They conducted a foreign policy of secret negotiations that bypassed their own Cabinet offices. "Their concealment and deceit was practiced against the public, the press, the Congress, the allies, and even most of the officials within the Executive Branch who had a statutory responsibility to provide advice about matters of national security.[239]

Whatever its shortcomings, there was a foreign policy breakthrough in 1971. After about a year and a half of secret negotiations, culminating in a secret trip by Kissinger in July of 1971, Nixon shocked the world by announcing that he was going to visit China.[240] Once again Nixon had refused to submit to the two-dimensional stereotypes that his political enemies tried to saddle him with. Nixon, the supposedly mindless, reactionary, Commie-hater, was reaching out to Communist China.

Nixon was going to recognize the Communist government of China and visit there in 1972. As Nixon later wrote, "It was in the interests of both nations that we forge a link based not on common ideals, which bind us to our allies in Western Europe and around the world, but on common interests." The interest of the United States was to improve relations with China, so China would be less tempted to return to the Soviet sphere of influence. Nixon hoped cordial relations between America and China would force the Soviets to be more accommodating to American interests. China needed leverage against the Soviets because of the Soviet troops on China's border and Soviet missiles aimed at Chinese cities.[241]

Though Nixon was trying to embrace China, he was not forsaking Taiwan, which the Communists claimed was part of their nation, but which was under the control of the Nationalist government that the Communists had ousted from the mainland in 1949. Nixon could stomach reaching out to a Communist power, as long as it helped him against the number one Communist enemy of the United States. But it would have been too much of a *volte face* to embrace the Communist Chinese and betray American allies in Taiwan, so Nixon sent former California Governor Ronald Reagan to Taiwan to assure them of continued American protection.[242] Employing the conservative Reagan in such a fashion was also meant reassure conservative Americans that their President had not gone over to the other side.

John Ehrlichman wanted to be Nixon's advance man for his China trip, and he suggested as much to the President on July 20, 1971. Nixon bounced the idea off Kissinger and Haldeman. Kissinger said he was concerned about Ehrlichman's blunt nature, but the National Security Advisor did not really object, so Nixon told Ehrlichaman it would be okay. Kissinger, however, was not finished with the subject. Haldeman approached Ehrlichman a couple of weeks later and told him that Kissinger had changed Nixon's mind, arguing that since Kissinger and Ehrlichman were of equal rank, it would create protocol issues for the Chinese. Ehrlichman was upset at the loss of such an opportunity, and he was embarrassed since he had already told his family he was going. Ehrlichman's initial response was to demand to hear about the change of plans from Nixon himself. The President had okayed it for Ehrlichman, so the President should personally have to tell him about the change. Ever protective of the President, Haldeman talked Ehrlichman out of pressing his demand. The Chief of Staff pointed out that it would hardly score points with Nixon for Ehrlichman to put him in such an awkward position.[243]

Ehrlichman was willing to give Nixon a pass, but the President's Chief Domestic Policy Advisor did not extend the same consideration to Kissinger. The rivalry between the two men spilled out during a senior staff meeting. Kissinger made it clear to the others assembled that "no one is going to go around me. They are not going around me on intelligence matters or narcotics or the budget or anything else." Ehrlichman shot back that Kissinger was "a bottleneck," and sometimes they did not get his approval on things within his sphere "because if we waited for your sign-off nothing would happen."

Kissinger got mad at that point and replied, "I cannot do everything. I have heavy responsibilities here. I work an eighteen-hour day as it is."

Ehrlichman was mad, too, and likened Kissinger's assertion to animal excrement. Ehrlichman continued, "You get here an hour later than the rest of us, and you're usually the first to leave to go to some Georgetown party. Don't give us that eighteen-hour baloney."[244]

Eventually, the conflict blew over. Ehrlichman and Kissinger cleared the air in Ehlichman's office and reached a mutual understanding, if not an abiding love. Nixon sent Ehrlichman and George Shultz, their families, and their staffs on a separate trip to Asia with stops in Hong Kong, Japan, Singapore and Vietnam. Ehrlichman took it as a consolation prize, calling it "a generous and unforgettable recompense for losing out on the China trip."[245] Unfortunately, it was not really Nixon who was being generous since the trip was paid for by the American taxpayers. It is regrettable that the public had to pay for Nixon's social awkwardness and inability to be direct with his subordinates.

Richard Nixon had always opposed wage and price controls established by the government; such things seemed communistic after all, but his new Treasury Secretary, John Connally, persuaded the President that they would be a good idea. Nixon liked bold initiatives, and Connally convinced him that such an economic policy would qualify. So Nixon announced the controls that summer,[246] and his economic program was popular with the public. The majority that favored the moves was only slight—53% according to a Harris Poll taken 6 weeks after Nixon's announcement—but only 23% of Americans thought the moves were bad with 24% being undecided. Nixon wrote in his memoirs that the long term damage to the economy outweighed the poll bump and short term rise in consumer confidence,[247] but that is not the point.

Perhaps some could argue that this demonstrated that the future Watergate criminals did not have to give in to their culture. Like Connally, they could have remolded that culture. Connally was able to persuade the President to go against his instincts, so perhaps other Nixon men could have done the same. On the other hand, Connally was held to a level of esteem by the President that Nixon reserved for few, if any, others. There was some talk of Connally replacing Spiro Agnew on the 1972 ticket, and

Connally and Haldeman both encouraged such sentiments.[248] The point is that it might be unfair to expect a Jeb Magruder to be as influential on the Nixon culture as a John Connally was.

It was in early August that Liddy and Hunt targeted Daniel Ellsberg's psychiatrist, Dr. Lewis Fielding. The Plumbers knew Ellsberg talked to his psychiatrist excessively, so Liddy and Hunt thought a look through Fielding's records would be worthwhile. Liddy was curious as to whether or not Ellsberg was connected to the KGB. Hunt, operating under Colson's instructions, wanted dirt on Ellsberg in order to publicly discredit the man. It offended the Administration that Ellsberg was being made into a hero by the press, so Colson wanted to besmirch his character.[249]

Liddy and Hunt asked Bud Krogh to get permission for them to break into Fielding's Los Angeles office. Krogh reported back to them that the break-in could take place, but Liddy and Hunt could not personally be involved. Liddy started to lose interest, but Hunt said he knew some Cuban-Americans who could do the job, so the mission proceeded.[250] Hunt's men were all from Miami. Bernard Barker and Eugenio Martinez were involved in both the break-in at the office of Daniel Ellsberg's psychiatrist and in the Watergate break-ins. Felipe DeDiego was involved in the Fielding break-in, but he played no role at the Watergate.[251]

Krogh provided Liddy and Hunt with money for their operation. With an admonishment to not get caught, he sent them on their way to California on September 1. The pair bought all of the equipment they needed then sent their three-man team into Fielding's office. Liddy decided to keep watch since the men had to break a window to get in. The window itself was rather concealed by shrubbery, so that was good news. But because it was so well covered the Cubans would not realize if someone was close by as they were trying to sneak out of the building. Liddy's plan was to draw away anybody who happened by, but if necessary he would use his knife and kill someone, if he felt it necessary to protect his team.[252]

Hunt had been assigned to Fielding's house during the operation, but he drove up that night and told Liddy that Fielding had left, and Hunt had lost him. Hunt, the ex-CIA spy, lost his nerve. He wanted to abort the mission, fearful that Fielding could show up at any time. Liddy pointed out that if Fielding were heading to his office, he would have arrived before Hunt. That placated Hunt briefly, and he left Liddy to go and scout the area. Hunt returned shortly thereafter and wanted Liddy to get the men out. Liddy agreed only to radio the men and check on their progress, but neither he nor Hunt could raise the men. Hunt then said that one of them should go in and get them, but Liddy refused since Krogh had said the two leaders needed to be removed from the operation. As the pair debated their next move, their team showed up. They had gotten into Fielding's office files, but they could not find any information on Daniel Ellsberg.[253]

It has been widely reported that on the trip back from Los Angeles to Washington D.C., the two Plumbers were not as discreet as they could have been, though there is some dispute over exactly who was careless. Frank Mankiewicz, a Watergate writer who worked for both Robert Kennedy and George McGovern, only mentioned Howard Hunt's actions. Hunt, a married man, chatted with one of the stewardesses and later sent her one of his books, which nullified any benefits of using the cover name of "Hamilton." Enclosed with the book was a message signed "Hamilton" on *White House stationery*.[254]

When Liddy called Bud Krogh about the Fielding operation, Krogh was so relieved that his men had not been caught that he was not overly upset to learn the mission had in fact been fruitless. A few days later when Liddy reported in person, he showed Krogh his tools, even the knife Liddy would have used if events had called for it. Krogh was stunned that Liddy was so ready to kill and questioned him on it. Liddy said that he would have killed but "only if there were absolutely no other way. But yes, I would, if necessary to protect my men. I gave them my word I would cover them." Krogh was shaken up, but the only thing he said to Liddy was "Hang on to those tools and things, we may need them again later on." Liddy had talked about murder, and there was no vocal, moral outrage from a colleague in the White House who had more authority.[255]

William Safire sent a memo to Haldeman in 1971 that was copied to John Dean. Safire began his memo asking, "Why don't we make more of the fact that ours is a scandal free Administration?"[256] If Safire had spent time around G. Gordon Liddy, Safire would not have written such a memo. In September, Howard Hunt told Liddy that Daniel Ellsberg was supposed to speak at a fund-raiser in Washington, and Chuck Colson wanted to discredit him. Hunt and Liddy came up with a plan to drug

Ellsberg, but only enough to make Ellsberg incoherent during his speech. Hunt was confident that with his contacts from his CIA days and within the Cuban community in Miami, he could work out the logistics for this operation. Liddy and Hunt went through Colson for their approval, and they got it, but it came too late for the operation to work.[257] Given that such things were sanctioned by those higher up, is it any wonder that Liddy and Hunt did not think twice about illegally wiretapping the Watergate Building?

Another issue handed to the Plumbers involved the Brookings Institute. It was believed by the White House that top secret government files had been copied and this material was being stored at the Institute. It was also believed that there was evidence there as to the identity of some of Daniel Ellsberg's fellow conspirators in the theft of such documents. The question for Liddy was how could this evidence be obtained? Liddy and Hunt figured that they could firebomb the building—at night of course to avoid needless fatalities—and send in a team of Cubans dressed as firefighters to pull out anybody in the building and get the desired materials. The Plumbers' superiors vetoed the plan, but not because of the arson or wanton endangerment. It was decided that a used fire engine, which would have to be abandoned at the scene, was simply too expensive.[258] Yet again, there were no moral boundaries placed on the Plumbers.

The Plumbers were disbanded by late September,[259] but Krogh was not done with Liddy. Nixon was frustrated by J. Edgar Hoover's leadership of the FBI, and the President wanted feedback on what was happening there and what he could do about it. Because of Liddy's background with the Bureau and the fact that he still had contacts there, he was a logical choice for writing up a report with a recommendation on what Nixon should do. Liddy submitted his report in October with its suggestion that Hoover should be eased out of office. Nixon did not follow Liddy's recommendation, but the President was nonetheless pleased. Krogh told Liddy, "The President says it's the best memo he's seen in years and wants it used eventually as a model on how to write a memo for the President." Ehrlichman called Liddy and said, "Gordon, I thought you'd like to know your memo on Hoover came back with A+'s all over it. Good job."[260]

Unfortunately for the career of Richard Nixon, Liddy and Hunt were not through helping the President. In the fall of 1971 the White House and the CRP were interested in setting up some kind of intelligence operation. It would be run out of the CRP, and John Mitchell suggested that a lawyer should be in charge, which made since given that campaign espionage could raise certain legal concerns. The decision was also made to make this new lawyer the General Counsel for the CRP to help deal with election law questions. Magruder wanted something resolved because he was feeling pressure from Chuck Colson to start getting good information on the Democrats. John Dean and Bud Krogh both blocked efforts to have their deputies recruited for the position. Krogh suggested G. Gordon Liddy, describing him as a good lawyer whose work the President liked, and Korgh pointed out Liddy's FBI experience would make him good at the intelligence work.[261]

Dean and Krogh met with Liddy in Krogh's office. Dean and Liddy talked about the Republicans' need for a first rate intelligence operation with offensive and defensive capabilities. When Liddy commented on how much such an operation would cost, he was assured that money was no object when Dean replied, "How's a half a million for openers?"[262]

Much has been made of Liddy's personality and his willingness to embark on a plan to burglarize Democratic headquarters. It is easy for some to dismiss him as crazy or a Nazi, but he provides a logical rationale for his activities in his autobiography.

The riots and violence of the past summer with its attempts to shut down the government of the United States; the wholesale theft of top-secret documents

by Ellsburg and the support for those taking such extreme measures by the traditional backers of the Democratic Party among the media—*The New York Times, The Washington Post,* and the networks—made it plain that we weren't

in for a campaign in '72; it would be a war....But it would be an undeclared war and what I would be doing was clearly illegal.[263]

Liddy decided in Krogh's office that day that while he was wiling to go to war for the President, he was not willing to do the same for John Dean. Liddy was conscious of the fact that junior staffers sometimes invoked the names of superiors to get things moving, even when those superiors knew nothing about the matters in question. Liddy said he would get on board if Krogh cleared it with Ehrlichman, who was the supervisor of both Liddy and Krogh, and if Dean cleared it with John

Mitchell. Dean said, "Fair enough" and promised to get back to him.[264] Dean was impressed by Liddy, so the White House Counsel sent his name up the food chain. Ehrlichman, Haldeman, and Mitchell all signed off on Liddy joining the CRP.[265]

Dean got away from the White House for awhile in the fall to visit Europe, and it gave him time to think. He was by his own admission a driven man. He wanted success, but he felt that he had risen as high as he was going to go in the White House; Ehrlichman would always be between him and the President. Dean decided he would find a well paying job in Europe. He even started taking French lessons and began fielding job offers. When Dean broke the news to Haldeman, the Chief of Staff pointed out that Dean would not have gotten such good job offers if it were not for his association with Nixon. "The same offers will be there after the election, probably more," Haldeman argued. "You owe it to the President to stay through the election. Then you can leave if you want." By balking at Dean's departure and arguing that great awards awaited, Haldeman appealed to both Dean's vanity and his ambition.[266] Haldeman seemed like a shrewd manager at the time, but if he had let Dean leave, events certainly would have turned out differently.

When Dean and Liddy had showed up in Magruder's office on December 3, Magruder thought he was conducting a job interview, but Dean quickly made it clear that this was not the case. Dean said, "Jeb, the Attorney General thinks Gordon is the ideal man to be your General Counsel." Magruder was annoyed that the decision was taken out of his hands, but Liddy seemed qualified and Dean raved about him, so Magruder acquiesced.[267]

As it turned out, Liddy was less than thrilled with Magruder. Krogh told Liddy that Magruder was a nice guy, but Liddy was not impressed. Magruder was in charge at the CRP until John Mitchell moved over from the Attorney General's office. Liddy did not want to be ordered around by a man like Magruder who was neither a lawyer, nor an intelligence operative, so Liddy entered the relationship determined not to give any ground to him.[268]

Liddy joined the CRP staff on December 13, 1971 and went to work as the General Counsel and chief intelligence gathering officer. His first meeting with Jeb Stuart Magruder as an employee of CRP did not go well. Liddy was expecting to have a million dollar operation over the next eleven months. He told Magruder that was what Dean had promised him.[269] Dean later claimed that he had casually suggested to Liddy that he might have half a million.[270] Liddy, however, wrote that when Dean suggested that figure, Liddy said he could get started for that amount, but it would take just as much to finish the job, to which Dean said, "No problem."[271] Both men's figures were a lot more than the four to five thousand a month Marauder had in mind. Rather than derail Liddy's train right there, Magruder instead said, "Gordon, a million dollars is a lot of money. You'd better get a plan together for the Attorney General that will justify that kind of money." Liddy promised he would.[272]

After talking about Liddy's intelligence gathering responsibilities, Magruder changed the subject. Magruder warned Liddy about an assistant of Haldeman's named Gordon Strachan. Magruder described Strachan as a young, inexperienced, and low ranking official who would try to use his connection with Haldeman to over inflate his own importance. Magruder's advice for handling Strachan was "If he calls, just say yes to what he asks, but put him off. Try not to give him anything. It's nothing intentional, but he's just unreliable."[273]

Liddy described his reaction in his autobiography. "I'm not with this guy three minutes and he's poisoning the well of another guy in the White House I don't even know....Magruder had been a Haldeman staffer and so was Strachan....Magruder, now removed from proximity to Haldeman, was afraid Strachan was going to move up at his expense. I wasn't going to get involved in that crap." Liddy said that it would be best if he did not share the details of his work with too many people, but he added, "If I get orders from a competent authority to give something to this Strachan guy, I'm going to have to do it. You guys'll just have to work that out yourselves." Liddy noted that the meeting ended with some tension, and relations between the two men only got worse.[274]

Their next conflict occurred when, as part of his introduction of Liddy to the office personnel, Magruder said, "Gordon will also be in charge of 'dirty tricks.'" Liddy was irritated by what he saw as a "gratuitous security breach." Afterwards, Liddy said to Magruder that Magruder was jeopardizing Liddy's intelligence services with such remarks, and Liddy took exception to having his work characterized as nothing more than "dirty tricks." Liddy left Magruder and called John Dean, whom Liddy told to get Magruder under control.[275] Dean placed a call to Magruder and pointed out that "it was less than prudent to announce that Gordon Liddy was handling dirty tricks."[276]

Shortly after starting work at the CRP, Liddy happened to see Bud Krogh on the steps of the Old Executive Office Building. Liddy remembered a meeting that he and Krogh had been in with the State Department. Liddy had suggested at the time that the United States should start executing foreign drug smugglers. The Start Department officials were quite disturbed, but Liddy's impression was that Krogh was intrigued by the idea. Remembering the meeting, and mindful of Krogh's support of Liddy's career, Liddy patted the White House staffer on the back and said, "Bud, if you want anyone killed, just let me know." In response to Krogh's smile, Liddy said, "I'm serious." Krogh lost his smile and said, "I know you are. I'll let you know."[277]

Krogh and Magruder were not the only two men who were concerned about Gordon Liddy. Dean saw Liddy at the White House and noticed that Liddy had a big bandage on his hand. Liddy shrugged off Dean's questions, but the White House Counsel persisted, so Liddy said he had burned his hand with a candle flame to impress potential operatives. To Liddy it made perfect sense. He was asking people to get secrets and keep secrets, so he needed to show them that he was tough enough to keep secrets, too. It did not, however, make perfect sense to John Dean, who called Bud Krogh as soon as Liddy left Dean's office. Unfazed by Dean's story, Krogh called Liddy "a romantic" and said simply that "Gordon needs guidance. Somebody should keep an eye on him."[278]

Dean was frustrated at his colleague. "Bud, this guy is a strange bird. Why didn't you tell me this before? I can't watch him." Dean suggested that Krogh had recommended Liddy so highly to get him out from Krogh's area of operations. One reason this occurred to Dean was because it was the kind of thing he had done to other people. Dean transitioned from frustration to damage control, suggesting that Krogh call Magruder and warn the CRP man to watch Liddy. Dean followed that up with a call himself. It turned out that Magruder had heard the story behind the burn, and he characterized Liddy as simply a "weird guy."[279]

There were other tensions between the Nixon men. John Ehrlichman and John Mitchell butted heads over where the authority of one man ended and the other man began. Increasingly, Ehrlichman tried to undermine Mitchell, whom Ehrlichman perceived as lacking in competence. Mitchell commented to his friends, "John [Ehrlicman] is getting too big for his britches." What spared the personally non-confrontational Nixon from a conflict he could not ignore was the fact that Mitchell had gotten bored with his job as Attorney General, which was why he was taking over the President's re-election campaign.[280] Still, the tensions between the two men would later make the complicated Watergate problem a little bit worse. With the CRP team up and running, and the mutual friction between members of it and the White House staff, everything was in place for the pivotal events of 1972.

CHAPTER FOUR

Trouble—1972

During its first term, the Nixon administration did progressive things, such as hire Barbara Hackman Franklin, who worked as a staff assistant to the President. Her job was to come up with a list of women who were qualified for policy-making and management positions in government. It was the first time such a job existed on a President's staff. By 1972 there were three times as many women in policy-making positions making at least $28,000 as there had been heretofore.[281] Also, as Ehrlichman told John Dean and another White House staffer, "the President appears truly interested in appointing the first woman to the Supreme Court. Haldeman says he keeps coming back to it. The President thinks it could have significant political benefits in '72. And I agree with him."[282]

Nixon was frustrated that his efforts seemed to do little to mitigate liberals' disdain for him, so PR concerns continued to preoccupy the White House. Such was Nixon's concern over public relations that even inner circle member John Ehrlichman lost the freedom to speak with the press on his own initiative. Ehrlichman had to clear requests for interviews with Press Secretary Ron Ziegler. Haldeman told Ehrlichman that the President decided this because Ehrlichman had gotten too chummy with members of the media perceived as liberal.[283] Ehrlichman had been warned to stay away from such individuals, and when he would not, he was disciplined.[284]

Even at his most optimistic, Nixon was not planning on winning over a majority of liberals; he knew he would have to beat their candidate, whomever that would be. Ted Kennedy was the man who struck the most fear in the White House, but Kennedy publicly stated that he did not have the experience in either foreign or domestic affairs to run for the presidency in 1972.[285] And perhaps he was concerned that not enough time had elapsed from the incident at Chappaquiddick. George McGovern was considered a strong candidate. He was a genuinely great listener, which helped people connect with him, but over time many supporters and media figures grew frustrated over how little McGovern would reveal. As another Democratic presidential candidate, Eugene McCarthy put it, "Talking with George McGovern is like eating a Chinese meal. An hour after it's over, you wonder whether you really ate anything."[286]

The man who seemed to have most of the support within the Democratic establishment in January 1972 was Edmund Muskie. He felt the country did not trust Nixon and wanted to create a contrasting image of himself, hence his slogan "Trusty Muskie." He spoke in the primaries about how Nixon had failed to live up to his promise to bring the country together, and Muskie promoted the idea that he could be the unifying presence that the country needed.[287]

The White House was also worried about the other end of the political spectrum, where George Wallace sat. According to White House insiders, it was not so much the South that they worried about because Nixon was solid down there. Nixon's men were worried about the North, where Wallace might take enough votes away from Nixon that some states might swing Democrat.[288]

Just months before the Watergate break-ins, and Nixon's subsequent involvement in the coverup, Billy Graham still had an over inflated view of Nixon's moral code. Graham said, "I am certain that he has brought a sense of ethics to the Presidency that has been largely derived from the Christian faith as believed and practiced by his parents."[289] Graham later said, "Early in 1972, Mr. Nixon asked me if I had any advice for him in the campaign. I said, 'Yes. Let others run your campaign and you just keep on being a good President.' In hindsight, I wonder if that was good advice."[290] While some have suggested over the years that Nixon was reasonably innocent of wrongdoing, and it was his aides who made bad choices, it simply does not describe the working relationship that Nixon had with his men. As Ehrlichman once said, "There shouldn't be a lot of leeway in following the President's policies...When he says 'jump,' they [Nixon's Cabinet] [should] only ask how high." Richard Whalen, a former speech writer for Nixon, saw Ehrlichman and Nixon's other aides as servants who followed the plans that Richard Nixon masterminded.[291]

January 27, was a big day for G. Gordon Liddy—he was going to present his plan for intelligence gathering, GEMSTONE, to the future head of the CRP, John Mitchell. Liddy considered the meeting a formality since he was convinced it was what the White House wanted, so he was eager to get the last green light he would need to get things started. John Dean was in attendance representing the White House, and to Liddy's great disappointment, Jeb Magruder was there, too. Liddy did not want Magruder around, not just because Liddy disliked him, but also because Liddy felt that the more people there were who knew about his plans, the greater the possibility existed to compromise his operation.[292]

The meeting took place at the Justice Department since Mitchell was still the Attorney General, and he had not yet moved formally over to the CRP. One reason Magruder admired Mitchell was because of the AG's lack of pride. Mitchell's chose to meet in a small office, not the big, ceremonial Attorney General's office.[293]

Liddy's plan for dealing with violent demonstrators was creative, to say the least. Because Liddy saw these demonstrators as organized urban guerrillas with homemade bombs and dangerous intentions, he had no qualms with radical actions against them. Liddy's plan for dealing with these individuals was called DIAMOND. It called for identifying the leaders in a demonstration before things turned violent. Liddy would have a trained team kidnap the leaders, drug them, and take them to Mexico where they would be held until after the November elections. Without their leaders, the demonstrators would be effectively neutralized.[294]

Magruder had not reviewed Liddy's plans ahead of time, which was in contrast to Magruder's standard procedure when taking a division head in to meet with Mitchell. Magruder was simply caught up in other things on this occasion. While Magruder appreciated Liddy's self-confidence in his abilities to pull off his exotic plans, Magruder was shocked by their content. John Dean was disturbed, too, saying later that he found Liddy's proposals "mind-boggling."[295]

Liddy thought he was delivering what he was supposed to, so he was quite disappointed when he saw Magruder and Dean both staring at Mitchell trying to gauge his reaction. Liddy thought they were acting like yes men, wanting to know what the boss thought, so they would know what to say. Liddy expected as much from Magruder, but he was disappointed in Dean; Liddy thought Dean would be speaking up in favor of Liddy's plans. Liddy pressed on, reasoning that Dean and Magruder were too young to really comprehend the dangers of organized violent protests, but Mitchell would understand. Liddy rattled off a series of other code words and the plans associated with them, occasionally eliciting a question or comment from Mitchell, but getting nothing out of the other two. Among other things, Liddy wanted to use prostitutes to get information out of Democrats at their national convention, and sabotage the air conditioners at the convention, which was being held in the summer in Miami.[296] Liddy also suggested some espionage involving the Democratic National Committee's headquarters, which was located in some offices at a place called Watergate. Liddy's price tag came close to the one million dollars he was expecting to get.[297]

After Liddy wrapped up his presentation, Mitchell fiddled with reloading his pipe, buying time while he gathered his thoughts, a common practice by the old lawyer. He finally said, "Gordon, a million dollars is a hell of a lot of money, much more than we had in mind. I'd like you to go back and come up with something more realistic." Liddy acknowledged his orders and began to pack up to leave when Mitchell added, "And Gordon? Burn those charts; do it personally."[298]

Magruder took Mitchell's complaint about the money to be an "understated way of expressing his displeasure with the more extreme aspects of the plan."[299] Dean, too, thought it was clear that Mitchell was not taking the plan seriously. At one point in Liddy's discourse, Dean caught Mitchell's eyes and shrugged. Mitchell winked and offered a small, brief smile in reply.[300] Of course, given Liddy's clearly demonstrated toughness, his psyche could have handled much blunter condemnation, but none of the other three men chose to explicitly say that Liddy's objectives and methods were too extreme.

John Dean had a different version of this meeting. According to Dean, he objected when Liddy presented the plan to use prostitutes at the Democratic National Convention. Dean also credited himself with giving Liddy the advice to destroy the charts.[301] The evidence, however, seems to be stacked against Dean. Magruder did not mention Dean's objection in his account, even though Magruder made it clear that everyone besides Liddy was uncomfortable with GEMSTONE. Liddy complained in his autobiography that Dean and Magruder let him down, but Liddy wrote that he was disappointed by their silence, not by any objections. Liddy made clear his personal dislike of Magruder, so it is not that he was afraid to attack someone in print, which Liddy would have done if he had gotten blindsided in the meeting. Regarding the destruction of Liddy's charts, Magruder and Liddy had no incentive to lie about who suggested it, but Dean did. If he wanted to inflate his importance and create the impression that he was trying to subtly warn the others that they were treading on dangerous ground, it might explain why he would massage the facts.

As Liddy and Magruder cleaned up after Liddy's presentation, disassembling visuals and returning a borrowed easel, Dean claimed he went over to Mitchell and whispered, "Unreal, and a little frightening." Mitchell smiled and replied, "I'd say that's a fair assessment."[302]

The three younger men shared a car as they left the Justice Department after the meeting. Liddy made no effort to hide his displeasure with his colleagues. "Thanks for all the help," he said sarcastically. He confronted Dean about promising a dollar amount that Mitchell had just said was too high. Liddy pointed out, "I've got top people committed and standing by on the basis of a budget of a million, in good faith. What's going on?"[303]

Magruder intervened. "Mr. Mitchell sees more of the picture than any of us. It may be that contributions aren't up to what they were expected to be by now and there just isn't the money for intelligence and dirty tricks they thought would be available. These things happen in campaigns. You've got to be flexible. You're going to have to cut out the most expensive stuff." Dean agreed.[304] As Magruder described the ride back to the office, he wrote that both Dean and he were trying to encourage Liddy, who was visibly deflated. Magruder said, "Cheer up, Gordon. You just tone the plan down a little and we'll try again."[305] Noticeably absent from this is any sense of moral outrage at the illegalities Liddy was advocating.

Liddy was frustrated, but he agreed. "All right, but I want a figure I can rely on. I've got to tell my people something. I want to know exactly what budget to plan for." They had arrived at the White House, so Dean avoided responding, but Magruder said that Liddy should plan for half a million.[306] Again, Dean's account differed from Magruder's and Liddy's, and again they had no obvious incentive for making up what was said, though Dean did. Dean maintained that they rode to the White House in silence.[307]

A week later the four of them met again. Magruder had reviewed Liddy's plans in advance this time and was pleased that Liddy had cut down on the use of prostitutes and sabotage. The new plan called for surveillance that included illegal wiretapping. A prime target for such attention was Larry O'Brien, the Democratic National Committee Chairman and the most effective critic of the Nixon administration.[308] Dean had wanted to skip the meeting because as he put it, he "didn't want to know what Gordon Liddy was doing." But Dean felt he could not avoid it because he was responsible for keeping the White House abreast of what was going on at the CRP,[309] and the White House was most definitely interested in intelligence gathering plans.

After Liddy presented his revised plan, and Mitchell said he would think about it, there was again some discrepancy in what happened. Dean claimed that when he, Magruder, and Liddy left Mitchell's office, Dean said that Liddy should not present such plans to Mitchell again; they should go through Magruder. And Dean added that he, too, wanted to be kept out of the loop.[310] If it had happened that way, it certainly would have minimized the culpability of Mitchell and Dean. But both Magruder and Liddy claim that Dean suggested in front of Mitchell that the Attorney General should be removed from such future discussion with Liddy, and neither Liddy nor Magruder mention Dean's request to not know what was being planned.[311]

Dean left Magruder and Liddy alone, at which point Liddy unloaded on Magruder. Peppering his remarks with curse words, Liddy asked why he was "being put in the position of a salesman for something somebody has already ordered?" Liddy went on to point out that the professionals he had picked for his operations would be alarmed by such indecisiveness, and they would reconsider their involvement. Magruder promised Liddy that decisions would be made soon.[312]

Dean claimed, "I was troubled by my unwillingness to confront Liddy or Magruder directly." When he told them he did not want to be a part of their future discussions, he acknowledged that his discomfort with the operation was ambiguous. Yet Dean went on to claim that he mustered up the courage to go tell Haldeman that Liddy's covert operations were a bad idea, even though he believed the idea originated with Nixon and Haldeman. According to Dean, Haldeman replied, "You're right. You should have nothing to do with Gordon Liddy." It strains credibility that Dean could not bring himself to be more candid with the little fish, yet he could tell one of the biggest fish exactly what he thought about Liddy's plans.

Haldeman's version is different from Dean's. According to the Chief of Staff, he could not remember a meeting with Dean where they agreed to "turn off" Liddy's illegal operations. But over a period of several months, Dean "reminded" Haldeman of their meeting so many times that Haldeman thought it must have happened. It was not until years later, according to Haldeman, that he checked his visitors log and realized the meeting had never taken place.[313]

Magruder had a difficult time moving things forward because Mitchell was so busy. Mitchell finally stepped down from the Attorney General's office and moved over to take official charge of the CRP, but the ITT scandal was taking huge chunks of his time, and according to Magruder, neither he nor Mitchell thought that Liddy's activities were a high priority.[314] When Liddy did get his answer, it was once again a negative.

Though Liddy was having trouble getting his work approved, Republican efforts to sabotage the Democrats were proceeding on other fronts. Chuck Colson had convinced Nixon to approve a write-in campaign for Ted Kennedy in the New Hampshire primary. Kennedy was not a contender, but Colson thought that if he could make it appear that Kennedy was interested, it would create animosity between Kennedy and Muskie, which could only help Nixon. Colson's people duped Democrat Robin Ficker of Maryland, who really did want Kennedy to run, to put his signature on a letter for the Republicans to use. The CRP mailed out approximately 165,000 of these letters at their own expense to New Hampshire Democrats, but Republican involvement was kept secret,[315] which was illegal.

Back at the CRP one of the other assignments Liddy had, besides setting up an intelligence operation, was to write legal opinions concerning some of the states' primary election laws. According to Liddy, Magruder had told him that Liddy's work was too hard to understand, and it needed to be simplified. Liddy told Magruder that it was written for a lawyer, John Mitchell, and Liddy assured Magruder that a lawyer would understand it.[316] And the mutual antipathy the two men had continued to grow.

As G. Gordon Liddy was planning the capers that would end Richard Nixon's presidency, Nixon was worried about something on the other side of the world, and for once it did not primarily involve Vietnam. Nixon left on his historic trip to China on February 17 after two years of complex diplomacy.[317] From the point of view of the President, this trip was about more than just sightseeing or good PR (for a change); it was really a continuation of the strategy developed by Nixon and Kissinger that they referred to as "linkage." Linkage was the term used for the doctrine of marrying arms negotiations to Soviet activities. The United States could use the Soviets' desire for an arms agreement to pressure the Soviets regarding certain hot spots around the world where the Soviets were involved.[318] It was hoped that forging better relations with China would make the Soviets more accommodating towards American interests. And "real progress" was made on arms control talks with the Soviets after Nixon's visit to China, Nixon critic Anthony Summers conceded.[319] From China's point of view, not only was the U.S. useful for helping to keep the Soviets in check, but the U.S. could also work to forestall any potential Japanese imperialism that might rear its head.[320]

Nixon's visit to China was successful at fostering improved relations between the two countries. Perhaps Nixon was hyperbolizing when he called his visit with the Chinese "the week that changed the world,"[321] but if it was an overstatement, it was not by much. Despite the improvement in relations, though, there were fundamental differences between the policies of the two powers that could not be ignored. The Communist Chinese government wanted the United States to fundamentally alter its policy towards Taiwan by denouncing their defense treaty, breaking off diplomatic relations with the island, and removing all American military personnel from there.[322] But Nixon had no intention of complying with these demands. The shared anti-Soviet attitudes could only bring the U.S. and China so close.

In late February, Magruder found Liddy in front of some elevators in their office building. According to Liddy, the taller Magruder rested his arm on Liddy's shoulder and spoke to him in a loud enough voice to attract the attention of everybody in the vicinity. Magruder brought up the issue of the legal briefs again, saying "Gordon, I'm not really satisfied with your work on the primaries. You're just going to have to redo it."[323] Magruder's version of the story is a little different. He alleges that it took place in March, and Liddy had not done all of the work in question, which was causing Haldeman and Mitchell to give Magruder some grief. Magruder wrote that he put his hand on Liddy's arm and asked about the reports, which prompted an angry response. Magruder said, "Well, the delay is causing me problems. If you're going to be our General Counsel, you've got to do your work."[324]

Liddy claimed that he replied, "Jeb, if you don't take your arm off my shoulder, I'm going to tear it off and beat you to death with it."[325] Magruder claimed that Liddy yelled, "Get you hand off me or I'll kill you!"[326] While disagreeing on the exact verbiage, the message is pretty consistent.

Magruder quickly pulled away, lowering Liddy's opinion of him even further. Liddy was convinced that Magruder only survived in his job because, as Liddy put it, "He was Haldeman's boy."[327] Magruder believed that Liddy was only interested in doing the spy stuff, not the General Counsel responsibilities that were also important to the campaign. And Magruder was convinced that Liddy's problems with Magruder stemmed from Liddy's perception of Magruder's relative youth and inexperience. Liddy did not want to be ordered about by a young man with basically a PR background.[328]

A few minutes after Liddy yelled at Magruder, the CRP's number two man decided that the two of them needed to clear the air. Magruder had Liddy report to him for a meeting that was also attended by another CRP manager named Fred LaRue. Magruder said, "This isn't working out, Gordon. I can't work with people who talk about killing me. We've got to make a change."

"That's fine with me," the ex-FBI agent responded. "I'm sick of [messing] around with a punk like you."

"Maybe you should go work for Stans," suggested Magruder. Maurice Stans was the chairman of the CRP's Finance Committee.

"That's fine with me. I respect Stans. He knows the score."

The work for Stans, though, only covered the General Counsel responsibilities; it did not cover Liddy's intelligence gathering. There was some discussion over whether or not to turn that over to Liddy's associate, Howard Hunt. Magruder failed to resolve the issue, concluding the meeting with a vague, "We can decide that later."

Liddy later called Dean and had him intervene with Magruder to keep Liddy in charge of intelligence. Dean phoned Magruder and argued, "Jeb, you don't want to let your personal feelings about Liddy get in the way of an important operation." The congenial Magruder acquiesced.[329]

However, the dislike between the two men was a growing problem. Magruder vented to Liddy one day about a journalist, saying "Gordon, you're just going to have to kill Jack Anderson." Liddy decided he was tired of listening to such complaints, so out in the hallway he approached

Magruder's assistant. Liddy told the young man that Magruder had just ordered Liddy to kill Anderson. The assistant was horrified and ran in to see his boss. Liddy let several elevators pass as he waited for the assistant to rush back out and assure him that Magruder was just kidding. Then Liddy pretended to be mad and said that such orders should not be kidded about. To Liddy, it was just a way to needle Magruder.[330] To Magruder, it was another example of how hard it was to get along with Liddy. Magruder felt that he could not even blow off steam without Liddy turning it into something weird.

The government's continuing antitrust suit against ITT became both an opportunity for Ehrlichman to make a power play against John Mitchell and a scandal for the Nixon administration to deal with then and later. One of Mitchell's subordinates in the Justice Department was pursuing the case despite the fact that the President wanted to settle. Ehrlichman used this to show that John Mitchell was not making his department answerable to the President of the United States. As if that was not a big enough headache, on February 29, a newspaper printed a memo allegedly written by ITT lobbyist Dita Beard. She claimed that the Administration would drop the lawsuit if ITT provided a $400,000 contribution in money and services to the Republican Convention that was at that point slated for San Diego. The White House believed the memo was a forgery, and Beard later denied writing it, but it led to a round of hearings and difficult questions for Administration officials who apparently were not guilty in this matter, but had violated the law during other activities.[331]

There are a couple of interesting side notes regarding the ITT Scandal. One, the White House had sent Beard's memo to the FBI for analysis, and the agent in charge of taking care of it was Mark Felt.[332] In the late spring of 2005, it was revealed that Felt was the source known as "Deep Throat" who was used by Bob Woodward during his and Carl Bernstein's investigations of the Watergate Scandal. Two, The ITT story was broken by Nixon nemesis Jack Anderson, a widely read columnist. The young reporter working for Anderson who confirmed the story with Dita Beard herself was Brit Hume, who later went on to serve as one of the Goliaths of Fox News.[333]

John Dean claimed that the ITT Scandal uncovered an example of pre-Watergate corruption by Nixon that dated back to the Hiss case.

According to Dean, Nixon said to Chick Colson, "The typewriters are always the key." Nixon was drawing a parallel between the Hiss case and the ITT scandal. The President went on to say, "We built one in the Hiss case." But both Nixon, who had reason to lie about it, and Colson, who did not, have denied that this conversation ever took place.[334]

G. Gordon Liddy did not care about the ITT Scandal; he had a mission to complete. Liddy grew impatient waiting for his operation to be approved. If he was going to make a difference in winning this election for Nixon, he had to get started. Liddy had another problem, too. The office gossips at the CRP were saying that Mitchell would return to his New York law practice after the election. Liddy had hoped to gain the confidence of someone from Nixon's inner circle, so Liddy's future would be secured during Nixon's next term. Mitchell was a good candidate, but he was leaving. Liddy figured he could kill two birds with one stone. He got Howard Hunt to introduce him to Chuck Colson. Liddy candidly told Colson that Liddy wanted to work for him after the election. Next, Liddy tried to explain to Colson the difficulties with getting GEMSTONE approved, but according to Liddy, "Colson didn't want to hear a thing about GEMSTONE and cut me off with "All you need is a decision, right?" When Liddy answered in the affirmative, Colson called Magruder on the phone and said, "Gordon Liddy tells me he can't get a decision out of you people on an intelligence program. I don't want to get into a debate on the merits; it just seems to me that after all this time somebody ought to be able to make a decision. Let's get on it."[335]

According to John Dean, this phone call was pivotal. Dean claimed that he had put a stop to Liddy's plans, as Dean later put it, "I was unaware that Liddy had gotten to Colson who intervened on his behalf with Magruder and Mitchell. Hindsight is always clearer, unfortunately."[336] But Colson was not Magruder's boss. The decision to authorize Liddy's plan was not made until a month later, and Colson was not a part of that final equation.

John Mitchell finally stepped down as Attorney General in mid February. It was a disappointment for John Ehrlichman that he did not get the chance to succeed Mitchell. Instead the AG job went to Mitchell's friend Richard Kleindienst.[337]

Down in Key Biscayne, Florida on March 30, John Mitchell tried to relax in a villa rented by Bebe Rebozo. Mitchell was supposed to get almost two months of rest before officially taking over as the head of the CRP on April 13. But Mitchell was preoccupied with his wife's increasing alcohol consumption and eccentric behavior, and the ITT situation troubled him, too. The Senate was conducting committee hearings on the ITT settlement, and concerns had been raised about Mitchell's conduct. Recently his hands had begun shaking and even his friends wondered if Mitchell was getting too old for his work.[338]

In Florida Mitchell was unable to relax because business had been piling up for the CRP; decisions needed to be made. Mitchell had to meet with Jeb Magruder and another key aide, Fred LaRue to talk CRP business. Magruder had two briefcases full of material for Mitchell to handle. Magruder saved GEMSTONE until last. He claimed that Mitchell approved a modified version of the plan after about ten minutes of discussion. Watergate researchers Len Colodny and Robert Gettlin pointed out that "Mitchell consistently denied he ever discussed an illegal break-in with anyone and insisted that he never granted an approval." The researchers believed him and assumed Magruder's recollection is false. But the researchers' premise was that John Dean was the sole mastermind of the break-ins, and this impacted their interpretation.[339] To believe that Mitchell never discussed a break-in, one must believe that Dean, Magruder, and Liddy all lied about their first two meetings with Mitchell, and Magruder lied about the third one. Not only did Mitchell approve of the plan, though; it also had the blessing of a higher authority. Decades after the fact, Jeb Magruder claimed that he heard Mitchell and Nixon talking on the phone about it that day.[340] According to Magruder, during his meeting with Mitchell, the former AG told Magruder to call Haldeman. When Magruder did, Haldeman said he was putting Nixon on the line, so Magruder handed the phone to Mitchell. After a brief conversation, Mitchell hung up and told Magruder to give Liddy $250,000 to fund his operations.[341]

March 30 was also the day that Howard Hunt officially went off the White House payroll, according to a White House memo. This separation between the White House and Hunt might have been more convincing to Watergate investigators if the White House staff had removed his name from their phone directories and made Hunt clear out the safe he kept in the White House, but the staff failed to do so.[342]

The same day that Mitchell was approving Liddy's latest illegal scenario and Hunt's tenure at the White House ended, the North Vietnamese launched another assault, sending 120,000 more troops across the Demilitarized Zone into South Vietnam.[343] Secretary of Defense Melvin Laird believed the United States should not do anything special to turn back this latest assault, but Nixon did not agree. He ordered air strikes and naval bombardments of the North. The war weary Senate was not impressed. They voted to weaken presidential power to make war without congressional approval.[344]

Late in April Magruder asked Liddy the fateful question, "Gordon, do you think you could get into the Watergate?" Liddy told him he could do it, but Liddy said he thought it was kind of early in the election year process to be bugging the Democratic National Committee's headquarters. Magruder asked if Liddy could put a bug in Larry O'Brien's office. O'Brien was the DNC Chairman. Liddy said, "For that, it's a bit late."[345] Liddy thought it was early for the DNC headquarters in general because most of the people at the DNC would be focused on preparations for the Democratic National Convention, which would be down in Miami in July. There did not seem to be much incentive for going after the Watergate. When Magruder mentioned O'Brien, Liddy was hesitant because O'Brien would already be spending most of his time in Miami, and Liddy had actually been focusing on an approved operation down there. But Magruder persisted and Liddy agreed. Magruder skipped over this late April meeting entirely when he wrote his books on Watergate, but according to researchers Colodny and Gettlin, Magruder later said the pressure to go into the Watergate Building came from John Dean.[346] It seems unfair, however, to put too much of the burden on Dean. In an April 2006 interview, Magruder pointed out that Liddy had suggested the Watergate break-in, and, again, Mitchell had okayed it after consultation with the President.[347] And as Magruder wrote in his first book on Watergate, "I think Mitchell came close to rejecting the Liddy plan…It was…made under pressure to please the White House. But nonetheless, the decision was made."[348] On the other hand, Dean's recent explanation, "After personally throwing cold water on Liddy's crazy plans, I thought his illegal activities had been ended,"[349] goes a bit too far in its exoneration of Dean.

Nixon did not have the luxury of just worrying about the election; he was trying to work out the situation in Vietnam. In May he instructed Kissinger and Haldeman to go to Treasury Secretary John Connally and ask his advice on how to handle North Vietnam. Connally told them, "Most important—the President must not lose the war!" Among his further comments, Connally added, "He's got to show his guts and leadership on this one."[350] Nixon's sometimes liberal academician, Kissinger, and his resident Democrat, Connally, were both telling him the same thing: Do not compromise with North Vietnam. There were times when Nixon wondered if he should not run for re-election and instead just focus on the war. When he allowed himself such thoughts, it was with the intention of endorsing Connally as his successor, "on whose advice and moral support Nixon increasingly relied during this period" in the words of Alexander Haig, who served as Nixon's Chief of Staff after Haldeman.[351]

Connally did more than just give advice in his efforts to get the President re-elected. Connally decided to step down as Secretary of Treasury—he was replaced by George Shultz—and campaign for Nixon. Connally efforts were seen as especially important because he was going to target his fellow Democrats. But as is often the case in politics, Connally was also looking out for number one. Connally was creating some powerful enemies among the Nixon faithful. Shultz, an economic conservative, had been against Connally's wage and price control plan, and Kissinger did not appreciate Connally's interest and involvement in foreign affairs. Connally's sacrifice of his job to help the President was a way for the Texas Democrat to avoid a coming two-front war with Shultz and Kissinger.[352] Connally explained his decision to his fellow Democrats by saying that he just could not support McGovern, yet he had talked about leaving the party nine months before McGovern had won the Democratic nomination. Connally was planning to leave the party when Hubert Humphrey was the projected frontrunner.[353]

George Wallace was removed from the presidential race on May 15 when he was shot at an outdoor rally in Laurel, Maryland.[354] Later that night, Nixon phoned Colson and asked about the shooter. "Is he a left winger, right-winger?" The President feared that if the man was some overzealous conservative, then it might ruin Nixon's re-election chances. Wallace himself wondered if in fact there were Republicans behind the shooting. But Nixon's question, which was recorded off of his telephone on the White House tapes, shows that he really did not know who was behind it.[355]

Nixon and Colson wanted to try and take advantage of the situation, so Colson decided to send Howard Hunt to the Milwaukee apartment of the shooter, Arthur Bremer, and plant McGovern campaign literature.[356] Hunt talked it over with Gordon Liddy, and both men were all too aware of the logistical difficulties of such an operation. Armed with Liddy's reinforcement of his own views,[357] Hunt contacted Colson and pointed out that the FBI would have the apartment sealed by that time. Even if Hunt could somehow get in and out, the FBI would be suspicious about the suddenly appearance of Democratic literature. Colson bowed to Hunt's logic and scrubbed the mission.[358]

Nixon's stroke of good fortune with the departure of Wallace from the race almost turned out completely different. According to Bremer's diary, he had shadowed Nixon during the President's recent trip to Canada. Apparently the crazed gunman had decided that one presidential candidate was as good as any other.[359]

In late May, Liddy reported to Magruder that Liddy's team had successfully broken into Democratic headquarters, placed their wiretaps, and photographed documents. Magruder was indifferent; he was interested in results, not progress reports. But Magruder's interest was piqued when Liddy said there was a little trouble with McGovern's campaign headquarters. Liddy had been worried about a streetlight, he said, so he shot it out. Magruder was concerned that Liddy was placing himself too close to the action with such a reckless stunt. Liddy was unfazed. "Don't worry, don't worry," he said, "I just had to go along and make sure everything was done right. I won't do it again."[360]

According to Magruder, McGovern's narrow victory over Hubert Humphrey in California later that week began to indicate what a weak candidate McGovern would be against Nixon in the general election.[361] This is significant because part of the Nixon-Haldeman defense in proclaiming their innocence of the break-in planning was that it was stupid to do something so pointless against such a weak candidate. Magruder's account indicates that McGovern was not perceived as being that weak until after the first break-in had already been planned and executed.

Much later, after Dean decided to cooperate with investigators in an effort to minimize his punishment, Liddy's attitude towards him took a turn for the worse. In Liddy's characteristically blunt style, he wrote, "The self-contradicting testimony of John Dean, former Counsel to President Nixon, deceived all as he betrayed his client to save his own worthless skin."[362]

Liddy also went a step further; though, he argued that Dean did not just lie to minimize his limited part in the Watergate scandal, Dean pushed for one of the break-ins to save himself from embarrassment. There was a prostitution ring that operated out of a building near the Watergate. Allegedly, the people in charge of the ring developed connections within the Democratic National Committee. Maureen Biner, Dean's girlfriend and future wife, was well acquainted with the woman in charge of the ring. Dean was afraid that the Democrats might have had records of this relationship, so he pushed for the second break-in where the burglars got caught. Liddy was first presented with this theory in a book by Colodny and Gettlin entitled *Silent Coup: The Removal of a President.* So to Liddy's way of thinking, Dean caused them to get caught then betrayed them to protect himself.[363]

The publisher of *Silent Coup* eventually settled out of court on a $250 million libel suit filed by John and Maureen Dean. Watergate researcher Keith W. Olson described the allegations of Colodny and Gettlin as being without substantiation."[364] Alexander Haig described *Silent Coup* as "inexhaustibly zany."[365] An admittedly limited look at the evidence leaves plenty of room for doubt. There is no real proof that Dean was the one who ordered the second break-in, only evidence that was circumstantial at best. And knowing a pimp does not make a woman a prostitute any more than knowing a defense attorney makes one a criminal. But Liddy grew to hate Dean and assumed the worst. All that is known for sure is that Dean broke some laws and betrayed a President who broke some laws.

Whatever the genesis of the plan, Liddy decided to send his team in for a second operation. There were five actual burglars. Liddy picked James McCord, Jr. to handle the electronics of the operation. In addition to being the security chief for the CRP, James McCord also served as a bodyguard for John Mitchell's wife Martha.[366] Liddy had not wanted to use anyone who worked for the CRP, but he was feeling the time crunch, and Hunt had not been able to find anyone else who was suitable.

Besides, McCord was an experienced, ex-CIA operative, so Liddy thought he was a safe choice. Bernard Barker was also on Liddy's team. Barker had served in the Cuban secret police before Castro took over then Barker joined the CIA where he got to know Hunt during the Bay of Pigs operation. Virgilio Gonzalez was the team's locksmith. Eugenio Martinez was yet another experienced ex-CIA man who had been a part of 354 Agency missions to Cuba. The final member of the crew, Frank A. Sturgis, is usually lumped in with the Cubans, but he was actually an Italian American. Sturgis was a soldier of fortune.[367] Hunt, Sturgis, and the Cubans believed that the Cuban government was helping to fund McGovern's campaign—McGovern was advocating normalized relations with Cuba—so the burglars were looking for proof of this among other potentially valuable finds. While it has been argued that this was a lie just to get the team to support the operation, one Watergate author has argued that it would not make sense to have the men wasting their time looking for something that was not there.[368]

The first Watergate break-in had occurred on May 28, a Sunday night. They had tried to break in the night before, but Bernard Barker, the expert locksmith, failed to bring the right tools on his trip up from Miami. He flew down and back during the day on Sunday, and their second entry attempt was successful. They had gotten into the building through some doors on the garage level, which they taped across the lock bolt. They did not tape the lock bolts open vertically because the tape would not have held the heavy bolts in place. Liddy knew it was an old maintenance man's trick, so it should not have aroused suspicion. And it did not, at least not on their first mission.[369]

On June 12, Liddy was back in Magruder's office. One of the break-in team's bugs was not working right, and the intelligence Magruder was getting was not very good. He wanted the defective bug fixed or replaced, but he also wanted something else. In his office, Magruder gestured to the files that contained embarrassing information on the Democrats and said he wanted that type of information from O'Brien's files. Liddy understood that, as he later wrote, "The purpose of the second Watergate break-in was to find out what O'Brien had of a derogatory nature about us, not for us to get something on him or the Democrats." Liddy believed that photographing all of those files in O'Brien's office would take hours, but those were his orders. Further pressure to go back in came from the White House. Gordon Strachan, an aide of Haldeman's, called Liddy and told him that the intelligence gathered heretofore was unsatisfactory. Liddy told Strachan that there were already plans under way for another break-in.[370]

After looking over the material picked up by the Watergate eavesdropping equipment, Strachan had already commented to Magruder about Liddy, "This idiot is just wasting our time and money." John Mitchell met with Liddy and Magruder and told Liddy, "This stuff isn't worth the paper it's printed on. Liddy replied, "There's a problem. One of the bugs isn't working. And they put one of them on O'Brien's secretary's phone instead of O'Brien's phone. But I'll get everything straightened out right away."[371] Liddy was going to orchestrate another break-in, and John Mitchell and Gordon Strachan in the White House knew it.

When Liddy later informed Hunt that a second break-in was necessary, Hunt protested on several grounds. Hunt was uncomfortable because of the difficulty of successfully breaking into the Watergate in the first place, the scope of the second mission, and the fact that O'Brien would soon be spending a lot of his time in Miami because of the upcoming Democratic Convention down there. Hunt was also concerned that a second Watergate break-in might conflict with plans to break into McGovern's headquarters.[372]

Richard Nixon once remarked to Haig, "Al, this country is so big and strong, and it has so many smart people in it, that it runs itself; the President's job is to try and keep the government out of it." Haig believed his boss, but perhaps Nixon did not believe himself. Nixon's men, some of them a part of the government, were not "out of it;" they were putting themselves into the middle of the process by breaking into the Democratic National Committee's headquarters. Again.[373]

For the second break-in, Liddy and Hunt waited across the street from the Watergate. James McCord had gone in the building through the lobby. He went downstairs to the garage and opened a door that went outside. The door was locked on the outside but not on the inside, So McCord taped it open. It was a common technique by maintenance crews that want to minimize fumbling around with keys. By taping the door locks, McCord and the rest of his team would be able to gain admittance to the building later without being detected. When they went back later that night, they discovered that the tape had been removed. At that point, Hunt wanted to abort the mission. McCord wanted to get it over with. He said that the tape might have been removed by a mail carrier, so he could just go back through the lobby and open the door because there was nothing to worry about. But McCord did not press the issue that strongly. It was Liddy's decision, and he decided to proceed with the mission.[374]

Magruder was troubled when he later found out that McCord taped the door bolts horizontally, which showed the tape on both sides of the door, making it easy for a security guard to spot. In Magruder's opinion, "We had to conclude that either McCord was an incredible bungler or he was a double agent."[375] Bob Haldeman likewise complained about the tape job and suggested it was a deliberate effort to get the burglars caught.[376] But Judge John Sirica later agreed with Liddy that there was no other way to tape doors so that the locks would stay open than the method used by Liddy's team. The door taping provides no proof that Liddy's team was set up from the inside.[377]

Shortly after 2:00 AM, Liddy and Hunt heard a transmission over their radio that there were flashlights spotted as security guards were sweeping through the floors of the Watergate, but they were not typical security guards. One of the guards was wearing a cowboy hat, another was dressed in a sweatshirt, a third was dressed in what one of Liddy's team members described as "hippie clothes." Liddy and Hunt hastily gathered their equipment and exited their hotel room after receiving the following radio message from one of the burglars: "They got us."[378] The burglars were caught. Now there was nothing left but the coverup.

CHAPTER FIVE

The Early Years—1912-1945

Before covering what happened after the Watergate burglars were caught, the beginning of each our subject's story will be described here except for Bud Krogh and John Dean. These two were barely in elementary school during the years covered in this chapter, so information on them will come later.

The oldest among Nixon and his inner circle was Nixon's close friend, Charles "Bebe" Rebozo, born in 1912. Rebozo was the youngest child of a large and poor Cuban family living in Florida. There is some mystery over how large the family actually was. Nixon biographer Jonathon Aitken believed Bebe was one of nine children,[379] but Nixon's daughter, Julie Nixon Eisenhower wrote that the Rebozo family had eleven kids.[380] Bebe overcame meager family assets to become quite a successful businessman. He worked briefly as an airline steward then began to buy and sell boats and real estate among other things, amassing an impressive fortune for himself.[381]

Richard Nixon was born to Frank and Hannah in Yorba Linda, California on January 9, 1913, the same year John Mitchell was born. Yorba Linda was a town of about two hundred in this era, located thirty miles from Los Angeles. Frank Nixon's temper and his love for a good argument were a threat to the success of the family store, which led the family to rush to wait on customers before Frank Nixon could get to them. Despite Frank's combative personality, young Richard had a close relationship with him. The pair liked to analyze Richard's debate team competitions. In the early days of his political career, Richard considered his father to be his number one supporter. Richard Nixon was also close to his mother, who did not like to argue, a welcome contrast from her husband. She was also reticent to talk about her firmly held religious beliefs or her love for her family. Richard frequently referred to her as a saint and admired the sincerity of her Quaker faith.[382] On the day Nixon was inaugurated as Vice President, his mother slipped him a note saying the family was proud of what he had accomplished, but his relationship with God was more important.[383] Richard Nixon inherited his father's combativeness mixed with his mother's private nature. He tried to project an image of his mother's faith-based morality, but the White House tapes later conveyed a morality of a different kind.

John Connally was born in Floresville, Texas in 1917. Floresville was a small town located about 30 miles southeast of San Antonio. Early in Connally's life, his father decided to run for County Clerk, so John and his younger sister were sent door to door to campaign, giving him exposure to political life at a young age.[384]

Slightly more than ten years after Richard Nixon was born in California, Heinz Kissinger was born in Germany in 1923. Heinz would later change his name to Henry when he moved to the United States. His father, Louis, was a teacher, and an Orthodox Jew but not a Zionist, meaning he was not committed to a homeland for the Jews. Louis Kissinger was a loyal German, a politically conservative man who had favored the Kaiser and regretted the monarch's abdication. The reserved Louis' scholarly idealism was offset by his wife Paula's witty, fun-loving nature and her pragmatism. Thus, young Heinz was the beneficiary of a well-rounded perspective on life.[385]

John Ehrlichman and Bob Haldeman were born in 1925 and 1926, respectively, and like Nixon, they were Californians. One difference between Ehrlichman and Haldeman was that Ehrlichman was Jewish, though he tried to ignore and at least at times deny this aspect of who he was.[386] Ehrlichman had an early flirtation with politics that cured him of any aspirations to be a candidate later. In high school he ran for student body president, but he was overwhelmingly defeated by the captain of the football team. From then on he was content to be a power behind the throne.[387] Haldeman's political roots ran deeper. His grandfather was a member of an anti-Communist society. Haldeman was interested in both his education and military service. He excelled in school, later becoming a member of the intellectual group MENSA, and he was an officer in the Naval Reserve.[388]

Richard Nixon had to cope with the early deaths of two of his brothers. His younger brother, Arthur, died in 1925 when Richard was twelve. His older brother, Harold, died when Nixon was in college.[389] Between his cold mother and the loss of two brothers, Richard Nixon was cut off emotionally from literally half his family. Perhaps it explains why Nixon had such a hard time relaxing and opening up, which led to his desire to minimize his contact with people. The deaths of his brothers, the quiet strength of his mother, and his father's combative nature, all left their mark on Richard Nixon. These factors made him tough, a fighter even when the odds were stacked against him, but they also contributed to his win-at-all-costs mentality and to the duration of his futile efforts to stonewall during the Watergate investigations.

G. Gordon Liddy was born in 1930 in New Jersey. While his critics might call him crazy, and his admirers would call him heroic, one thing both camps should agree on is that he was a very intelligent child. He was reading adult books like *The Count of Monte Cristo* and all of Shakespeare's works by his early teens.[390] It was not an easy childhood for Liddy, who described himself as sickly and a coward. Liddy idolized his Uncle Ray, a brave FBI agent, but young Liddy hardly seemed like a candidate to live up to his role model. Liddy's path was altered by two extremely contradictory influences—Adolf Hitler and God. Liddy had been told by the family maid, Teresa, that Adolf Hitler had revitalized the German nation; he had helped it overcome its fear. Liddy decided that if a country could be delivered from fear, so could a little boy. Liddy had been taught in his Catholic Church that people were made in the image of God, and it occurred to him that God was not afraid of anything. With these two ideas in mind, Liddy decided as a six year old that he could face and overcome his fears. He was determined to reach a point where he would not back down from anything.[391] Perhaps it would have been okay if he had maintained some sense of caution in the years to come.

Nixon's higher education began locally at Whittier College. His dream had been to go to Yale, and he had a chance at a scholarship that would have covered tuition, but his other expenses would have been too much for his family because of the Depression-era economy and the expenses related to Harold's tuberculosis.[392]

While at Whittier, Nixon went through a period where his political outlook had—in his words—"a very liberal, almost populist, tinge" to it.[393] However, Nixon had to be able to argue both sides of a topic as a debater, which led to his embrace of a more conservative economic point of view. When he was not studying or involved with the debate team,

Nixon participated in various school plays, which further helped the future politician handle being in front of large crowds in the future.[394]

Nixon got into the law school at Duke because he was such a good student and because of glowing letters of recommendation from two of his professors and the president of Whittier, Walter F. Dexter. President Dexter wrote of Nixon, "I believe he will become one of America's most important if not great leaders."[395] It is noteworthy that Nixon got such support, given all of the stories of Nixon's personality quirks. Nixon did not have the charisma of a Franklin Roosevelt or a Ronald Reagan, but despite the perceptions of some, Nixon could be interpersonally impressive at times.

In November 1934 Jeb Stuart Magruder, named by his Civil War buff father after a Confederate general, was born on Staten Island, New York. Magruder's father was from a wealthy background, but he did not make much money himself. As a result, Jeb Magruder's parents gave their sons exposure to the finer things when those things were not too expensive, and the rest of the time they struggled to get by. As Magruder described it, he "was living kind of a dual existence." But there was not really much that was truly distinct about Magruder's early years. He made good grades, he was a good athlete, and he had his share of schoolboy romances. He started drinking beer and getting traffic tickets, both of which greatly concerned his mother, but he managed to survive high school not too much the worse for wear.[396]

Nixon, however, received yet another tremendous personal blow while in law school. His fiancee, Ola Florence, broke up with him during the summer of 1935, and it took him awhile to concede defeat. Nixon continued to visit her at her parents' house despite her lack of interest in him. When he returned to Duke, he wrote her weekly and continued to refer to their future marriage. In December 1935, she wrote and told Nixon that she was marrying another man and asked him to stop writing her. It took Nixon two months and another request for him to desist writing to make him give up. In his final letter, he compared Ola Florence to his beloved mother. Losing Ola was crushing to Nixon, and it was made all the worse because he bore the pain alone, confiding in no one about his loss. There were those in Nixon's life who later came to believe that a part of his difficulty in getting close to and trusting people came from this traumatic loss.[397]

John Connally started his college career in 1935 when he enrolled at the University of Texas. He took a strong interest in debate, drama, and speech.[398] All three of these interests would help him in his career as a politician, and for that matter these things were also passions of the young Richard Nixon.

Nixon applied for a position with the FBI while still a student at Duke, but he was not hired. As Vice President, Nixon learned that the FBI had planned to hire him but could not because of a budget cut. But for a larger budget in the 1930s, Richard Nixon would have worked, lived, and died anonymously, the Vietnam War would have ended differently, and Watergate would be just the name of a place in Washington few people outside the District had heard of.[399]

A classmate at Duke called Nixon "the hardest working man I ever met.[400] Nixon needed to work that hard. He had won a scholarship to Duke that covered his first year, but then he learned that of the twenty-five scholarships awarded only twelve were renewed for the second year.[401] Nixon had been led to believe when he first applied for the scholarship that as long as he maintained a B average, he would be fine. After arriving at Duke, he learned that it did not matter how well he did; if he was not in the top twelve among the scholarship holders, then he would lose out. This discovery caused a considerable amount of self-doubt, but Nixon rose to the occasion.[402] Nixon worked relentlessly, getting up at five A.M. to study, taking classes, working odd jobs, and then studying until midnight. Nixon even spent many of his Saturday nights studying.[403] Nixon was such a disciplined student that often times when he was studying in the library he would not look up at passing students. One classmate did not think Nixon ever smiled. His serious demeanor and stress over the difficulties of law school earned Nixon the nickname "Gloomy Gus," a nickname he also had in college at Whittier. Despite all this, Nixon did occasionally relax with his friends, going out to eat and watching Duke football games.[404] When he was not studying on Saturday nights, he liked to go to movies sponsored by the student union. Part of the appeal of this type of entertainment was the five cents admission price.[405] Nixon was able to mix with his peers and be enough of a leader in the classroom[406] to get himself elected president of the Student Bar Association at Duke,[407] though there were at least some who credited Nixon's election to respect for his scholastic abilities more so than his personality.[408] Nixon took up playing bridge, but quit after three months when he saw how it was cutting into his study time.[409] Nixon was not in graduate school to make memories.

Nixon already possessed a characteristic at Duke that he later exhibited in the White House—a capacity for making some people instinctively dislike him. What else is one to make of the following quotation by classmate Ethel Farley? "We disliked his 'holier than thou attitude.' He was not unmoral, just amoral. He had no particular ethical system, no strong convictions."[410] How does Nixon project an image of being too holy while at the same time being amoral, without ethics or convictions? The quotation does not make sense, but it does demonstrate an intense dislike of Nixon. Actually, Nixon was still heavily influenced by his Quaker upbringing. For example, his language was rather mild, though not pristine in those days. In fact he was occasionally shocked by the lingual excesses of his peers.[411] Nixon failed to maintain his college-era standards for language, which hurt him as President. One would think this was a non-issue, but Nixon's support in the Bible belt was undermined when transcripts of the President's language on his secret tapes had so many "expletive deleted" notations. People were offended by all kinds of things, not the least of which was the secret taping itself, but the language that once made Nixon blush was offensive to long time friend Billy Graham and others.[412] Consequently, some potential congressional support was lost during the looming impeachment battle because Nixon's language bothered too many constituents in some districts.

Another way Nixon's religion manifested itself at Duke was in the way he treated some of those less fortunate than him. Charles Rhyne was a classmate who was hospitalized for several months. Nixon used to visit him regularly and read the notes he had taken that day in class. Fred Cady was a student crippled by polio. Cady would wait at the front steps of the lecture hall each day, and Nixon would carry him up the stairs.[413] Such acts of compassion seem out of character, given Nixon's later excesses, but they were part of who Nixon was.

Nixon's compassion still occasionally appeared during his presidency. Former presidential aide and convict Chuck Colson wrote about Nixon's softer side, saying that his old boss had trouble pointing out to a secretary that she had misspelled some words in a letter he had dictated. Colson claimed he saw Nixon actually change the wording of the letter to avoid embarrassing the secretary.[414]

Nixon's living conditions back at Duke were pretty rough. For a portion of his time at Duke, Nixon lived in an eight-by-twelve-foot tool shed. He lined the inside with cardboard to help keep out the cold.[415] During Nixon's third year at Duke, he moved into a one-room shack with three of his classmates. For heat, they had a wood burning stove in the middle of the room. They also had body heat since they slept two to a bed. They had no indoor plumbing. Nixon shaved in the men's room at the law library and showered at the gym. Breakfast was a candy bar.[416] Nixon was poor, but not as poor as his living conditions indicated. For example, he saved enough money to go in with a brother to buy a fur for his mother.[417]

Where Nixon had grown up, the citizens prided themselves on their fair treatment of minorities.[418] Nixon's mother had African Americans at the family dinner table, continuing a tradition that went back to a relative who helped escaping slaves on the path to freedom.[419] Thus, Nixon was in for a bit of a culture shock when he observed race relations at Duke. Historian Stephen Ambrose noted that, "Nixon began to learn, and to some extent to appreciate, the southern point of view, not only on race relations but also on the Civil War.[420] However, he spoke out against racism, even though the school and its population were deeply racist in this era. As a fellow student put it, "He was shocked and disturbed at the prevalent North Carolina treatment of the Negro population as an inferior group." Another student noted Nixon's "very strong moral convictions" on this subject.[421] There was nothing to be gained by this outsider coming into North Carolina and speaking out against inequality. One might think that Nixon was playing it safe speaking out from a more liberal-minded arena on the campus of Duke, but Nixon was getting into arguments with his classmates. One of his fellow students thought that Nixon's steadfastness on this issue made him "the man least likely to succeed in politics."[422] At the same time, though, he developed a respect for the South, and as he put it, he "felt strongly that it was time to bring the South back into the Union."[423] Nixon said, "I learned in those years to understand and respect them [southern whites] for their patriotism, their pride, and their enormous interest in national issues."[424]

The first break-in associated with Richard Nixon actually occurred while he was a student at Duke. During his second year in law school, Nixon and two friends decided to break into the dean's office to find out their end-of-the-year grades because the school was late in posting them.

Nixon himself climbed through the transom over the door and let the others in then they rifled through drawers until they found their grades. To Nixon it was no big deal.[425] One is left to wonder if Nixon's break-in at Duke shaped his character or merely reflected it. Nixon is generally not blamed for ordering the Watergate break-ins, but his attitude regarding them is worth noting. Nixon wrote in his memoirs, "My confidence in the CRP was undermined more by the stupidity of the DNC bugging than by its illegality." Nixon argued, correctly, that political espionage and buggings were not uncommon,[426] but they were still illegal. For Nixon, breaking into an office and obtaining information was no big deal. This kind of amorality is disturbing in a law student and in a President. If Nixon had been caught while at Duke, his outlook might have been different later, and he might have projected a different moral tone for his administration. Or, to be fair, it might not have mattered much at all.

The hard work and grit it took for him to survive at Duke reinforced Nixon's tenacity and his instincts as a fighter. But Nixon's resentment and jealousy towards the Eastern establishment, which most historians believe had its genesis in the Alger Hiss case, could be said to have its antecedents here. To have to work so hard while watching other students with money and connections coasting—relatively speaking—their way through law school was tough for Nixon.

Charles W. Colson was born in the early 1930s. Colson's father had dropped out of high school to take care of his family when his father died during the post World War One flu epidemic. After Colson's parents were married, Colson father went to night school for the next twelve years, eventually earning a law degree. The hard work and achievements of his father and the advice the man gave inspired young Colson. "Work hard, study hard; nothing comes easy in this life. Tell the truth—always—lies destroy you." Chuck Colson later wrote, "I'd always tried to follow that and always did with him."[427] Too bad Colson, like so many, fell short of his boyhood ideals. But at least in Colson's case he learned from his mistakes.

At the age of fifteen, Henry Kissinger along with his father, mother, and younger brother Walter left Nazi Germany and journeyed to the United States. As Jews, they were only allowed to take one trunk worth of personal items and a few pieces of furniture out of Germany. The impact of having his world turned upside down by the Nazis was felt in many ways by Kissinger. One old friend said, "It made him seek order, and it led him to hunger for acceptance," even where such acceptance would seem unlikely. For example, Kissinger would try to impress Nixon with hard line attitudes regarding the Vietnam War, while at the same time trying to appeal to anti-war faculty members at Harvard. Nazi rule and the subsequent Holocaust prompted Kissinger to reject his Jewish faith. Also, according to Kissinger biographer Walter Isaacson, "Kissinger…like Nixon…harbored an instinctive dislike of colleagues and outsiders alike."[428]

Working hard had led to political success for Nixon in school, but it did not translate so easily to success outside of academia. Though he was a loner throughout his life, he was elected student body president at Whittier College and at Duke Law School. He did not win these elections through personal popularity, as is often the case in such elections, he won them through hard work. But the equation of drive plus talent minus personality led to difficulties getting a job in New York, which is where Nixon wanted to go.[429]

After failing to land a job in New York City, Nixon returned home, and got a job with the legal firm of Wingert and Bewley. He took the Bar exam in 1937 and was convinced he failed. He was so nervous that when his letter arrived at his parents' house, Richard Nixon shut himself off in the bathroom, so his parents would not see how great his disappointment would be. To his great surprise, he passed, and as he later wrote, "If we had been a drinking family, we'd have had a drink, but as it was, we celebrated in milk."[430] Nixon worked so hard throughout his life because he worried too much whenever there was the possibility of failure. Such a mindset helps to explain how the Watergate break-ins could occur when Nixon was so far ahead in the polls.

After he had been at his law firm for a year, Nixon was so successful that they changed their name to Wingert, Bewley, and Nixon.[431] One of the law partners, Tom Bewley, later said of Nixon, "I don't remember that he ever lost a case." That was Nixon did lose a few, but the quotation does make the point that Nixon was quite a good lawyer,[432] which contradicted historian Stephen Ambrose's assessment that "Nixon was not much of a success as a lawyer." Nixon did good work, according to his contemporary, but he was too ambitious to spend his life practicing law in a small town.[433]

His ambition led to a whirlwind of activity. Nixon registered as a Republican on June 15, 1938.[434] He became president of four different civic organizations and the chairmen of two others before he was thirty. He became the youngest member of Whittier College's Board of Trustees, a group that included Herbert Hoover's wife. He used all of the contacts he was making to create public speaking opportunities for himself. To further impress people, he learned the music used by these different organizations, and he would play their tunes on the piano when he would visit them.[435] As Stephen Ambrose wrote, "He had time for many activities, but with the single exception of going to the Whittier College football games on Saturday afternoon, he chose only those activities that would lead to either self-improvement or career success." The number one partner in the law firm, Jeff Wingert, noted all of Nixon's activities and remarked, "That boy will be President of the United States someday if he wants to."[436] Despite the ample evidence of Nixon's difficulties relating to people, he obviously had a talent for inspiring support. In addition to all of the activities Nixon was involved in, he also participated in the theater where he met his future wife, Pat Ryan.

1938 was the year John Mitchell graduated from Fordham Law School. Though Mitchell had been born in Detroit, he grew up in New York where he received an undergraduate degree at Fordham University in 1935 before getting his law degree. Years before Mitchell developed a reputation as a tough-minded politician, he demonstrated a different kind of toughness. He played semipro hockey throughout his college and law school days.[437]

The year 1939 was an important one for John Connally. He had gone on to law school after capping his experience as an undergraduate at the University of Texas by winning the student body presidency. While in law school, fate smiled upon him. A newspaper editor named Sam Fore asked Lyndon Johnson, who was then in the House of Representatives, to find a spot for Connally, who was from Fore's hometown. Johnson hired Connally onto his staff, and Connally made his way to Washington. It would have been exciting enough just to be working for any Congressman, but Johnson was a man on a mission to succeed.[438] As Johnson rose through the ranks, so did Connally. When Johnson ran for re-election in 1940, Connally was his campaign manager.[439]

The death of Texas Senator Morris Shepherd in April 1941 prompted the need for a special election, and Lyndon Johnson threw his hat in the ring. This was going to be a bigger, more hotly contested race than

Johnson's last campaign, so he thought he needed more firepower to manage it. As a result Connally shared campaign management responsibilities with two other men. Johnson was behind in the polls and desperate, so he and his staff leaders decided to raise as much money as they could. There was a federal law that said a Senate candidate could not spend more than $25,000 on a given campaign, but by some estimates Johnson spent more than $500,000. It almost worked. Johnson went from having only 9.3 % support in the polls to almost winning. It actually looked like he would win when the votes were starting to be counted, but his opponent barely squeaked ahead. Some of his supporters wanted Johnson to contest the fishy results of the election, but Connally and one of the other campaign managers advised against it. They could not afford to have Johnson's operation exposed to scrutiny.[440]

When Germany attacked the Soviet Union on June 22, 1941, Richard and Pat Nixon, who had been married for exactly one year and one day, were on a cruise. Nixon's reaction was to hope that the Soviets were victorious and Hitler was defeated. While Nixon disagreed with the Communist system, he did not yet have the passionate hatred for it that he would later develop. Hitler was the bigger threat.[441]

In October 1941 an incident occurred that Gordon Liddy is rather well known for. The family cat had killed a rat and left it on the back steps of their house. Liddy had feared rats as a child, but he had coped with that fear. To prove to himself that he still was not afraid of the little creatures, Liddy picked up the dead rat with his bare hands. He was going to bury it when another idea occurred to him. He started a small fire in the backyard, cooked the rat, and ate it. It was not very tasty, but that was not the point. Anyone who could eat a rat had definitely mastered his fear of them.[442] While the incident would later provide fodder for his critics, Liddy demonstrated that he was a young man of considerable discipline.

Nixon took a pay cut and moved across the country to Washington D.C. in December 1941. He took a job with the government, serving as an assistant attorney for the Office of Price Administration. Nixon worked there for eight months, dealing primarily with the rationing of car tires and rubber.[443] Nixon's later disdain for governmental bureaucracy found its genesis here.

As both a government employee and a Quaker, Nixon could have stayed away from the fighting in World War Two, but he did not choose this option. He actually went out of his way for combat. He joined the

Navy and was initially stationed at an unfinished Naval Air Station in Iowa. He stayed there for awhile before applying for and receiving sea duty in the Pacific. Nixon was still rather removed from the war. He served in the South Pacific Combat Air Transport Command (SCAT) where they helped load and unload cargo and transport planes. Nixon spent his time learning how to play poker and giving free hamburgers and beer to flight crews.[444] According to Nixon, it was not until he got into the Navy that he learned how to drink coffee.[445]

The outbreak of war put the final touch on Lyndon Johnson's inclination not to make a run for a Senate seat. John Connally had said such a run was not a good idea at the time, and it is a measure of Connally's influence that Johnson was leaning in the direction of Connally's advice when the war started. Both Johnson and Connally decided to accept commissions in the Navy.[446]

Another of Nixon's men who was in the Navy during World War Two was John Mitchell, who commanded squadrons of torpedo boats. One of the boats under his authority was the PT-109 on which a young lieutenant named John F. Kennedy served. Years later, Mitchell liked to amuse Nixon and others by referring to Kennedy as "just one of the junior officers."[447] During the war Mictchell received shrapnel wounds in the line of duty that caused his hands to shake for the rest of his life.[448] Before his World War Two stint in the Navy, Mitchell had joined the law firm of Caldwell and Raymond. Mitchell established himself as an expert on municipal bonds before becoming a partner in his Manhattan firm in 1942.[449]

In the Navy, Richard Nixon's became increasingly successful at poker. Some historians have estimated that Nixon won as much as $10,000 during the war.[450] One of his fellow officers, Jim Stewart claimed, "I know for a fact he sent home $6,800," which would be equivalent to over $45,000 by the 21st Century. And Stewart believed that Nixon later accumulated an even larger sum than that. Another officer, James Udall, said, "Nick [Nixon's World War Two nickname] was as good a poker player as, if not better than, anyone we had ever seen....We watched him closely and made the prophecy that he would succeed in whatever civilian career he chose." Actually, poker allowed Nixon to do just that—his winnings help fund Nixon's first congressional race.[451]

The year 1943 was significant for a couple of Nixon's men in particular. John Erhlichman went to war that year at the age of 18. He served in the Eighth Air Force as a navigator, and flew 26 missions in Europe.[452] In March Henry Kissinger joined the Army. One benefit for him was that immigrants got nationalized when they joined the service. From Kissinger's point of view, it also rescued him from a life as an accountant.[453]

Kissinger was sworn in as an American citizen at Camp Croft, South Carolina. Life in the army impacted Kissinger in many ways, not the least of which was it helped acclimate him to the United States. Instead of being a part of a Jewish American or German American subculture, he was thrown in with people from across the United States. Kissinger's intellect qualified him for the Army Specialized Training Program, which allowed him to study engineering at Lafayette College in Easton, Pennsylvania. He might have gone on to become a successful engineer, but the army cancelled its program in April 1944 due to the demand for troops. The opportunity for learning, however, resonated with Kissinger more deeply than it ever had before. The fire was lit that would take him to Harvard and the White House.[454]

Kissinger made a friend in the Army, Fritz Kraemer, who ended up having an enormous impact on Kissinger's life. Kraemer got Kissinger reassigned from the General Infantry to serve as a translator. Later, Kraemer helped Kissinger get picked to oversee the occupation of captured towns, which was a logical choice, given that Kissinger spoke German fluently. Later still, Kraemer helped Kissinger become part of the Counter-Intelligence Corps. When Kissinger considered going to Harvard, Kraemer encouraged him to do so.[455]

Despite the concerns of the war, Nixon went to the trouble of casting an absentee ballot for Republican Thomas Dewey in 1944.[456] But by this time, those war concerns were not so immediate. Over the summer Nixon had been transferred to San Diego. By January 1945, Nixon was on the move again. He was sent east to help deal with Navy contract terminations. Over the next several months, the Nixons lived in Baltimore, New York, Philadelphia, and Washington.[457]

The Nixons celebrated the announcement of the victory over Japan in Times Square.[458] That day, known as V-J Day, was August 14, 1945, and there was at least one American who did not celebrate. Gordon Liddy was still a teenager, and he was upset that the war was over before he had a chance to test himself and demonstrate his bravery. He was depressed for almost a month.[459] Maybe if Liddy had been able to prove himself during

World War Two, he would not have been as zealous to prove himself later. Ultimately, Nixon and his men were as defined by the things that did not happen to them when they were young as they were by the things that did.

CHAPTER SIX

Introduction to Politics—1945-1952

One of the interesting things about the American presidency is that it is not a closed system—there have been a variety of paths to the White House. John Kennedy and George W. Bush had doors opened for them by their fathers. Bill Clinton got there through his own hard work, and it was a path he committed himself to while still a teenager. Richard Nixon did not have an influential father or the advantage of a virtual lifetime of preparation. He was in his thirties before he considered running for a national office, and serious consideration about the presidency was still years away. This chapter focuses on Nixon's introduction into politics, and it begins to show the movement of some of Nixon's men into his orbit.

Nixon was invited to consider a career in politics by Herman Perry in the fall of 1945. Perry believed that Democratic Representative Jerry Voorhis was vulnerable, but Perry did not think any of the Republicans then contemplating a run could unseat him. Nixon was young, articulate, and a World War Two veteran, so Perry thought Nixon could win the job.[460] Perry was a banker, leader in Whittier, and the father of one of Nixon's friends. He sent a letter to Nixon to gauge the young man's interest, which read, "I am writing you this short note to ask if you would like to be a candidate on the Republican ticket in 1946. Jerry Voorhis expects to run—registration is about fifty-fifty. The Republicans are gaining. Please airmail your reply if you are interested." Nixon really had not considered such a career, but he was ambitious, and he and Pat had some money in the bank that they were planning on spending on a house. The decision was made—the house would wait.[461]

When Nixon ran against Voorhis, Nixon claimed he avoided personal attacks. The future President observed, "I have no personal quarrel with my opponent." They simply had "two divergent fundamental political beliefs."[462] But many others would disagree with Nixon's recollection.

After Nixon's first debate with Voorhis, an old friend and fellow college debate team member, Osmyn Stout, was quite critical of Nixon's performance. Stout alleged that "he gave these half-truths, innuendos, and built up the crowd and then by inference pointed out that Jerry Voorhis represented that kind of thinking." Stout went up to his friend after the debate and said, "Why are you doing this?" Nixon replied, "Sometimes you have to do this to be a candidate. I'm going to win."[463]

Nixon won this election primarily from two things. One, it was Vorhis who actually called on Nixon for a debate. This was a mistake not only because Nixon had spent years as a debater in school but also because it raised the status of the relatively unknown Nixon to that of the incumbent. Voorhis had little to gain and much to lose by a debate, ergo suggesting it was a major blunder. Two, Nixon simply worked harder than his opponent. Nixon spent ten months traveling throughout the district, meeting people and giving speeches. Voorhis only spent two months campaigning.[464]

While Nixon was working on getting elected, Bob Haldeman and John Ehrichman were getting to know each other as classmates at UCLA. Haldeman was reportedly the campaign manager for the unsuccessful bid of Jeanne Fisher for student body vice president. It has sometimes been reported that Fisher was the future wife of Ehrlichman.[465] Actually, this was untrue; Haldeman worked for Jane Wilder, whom he described as an "ultraliberal" and who later became a leader for the Students for Democratic Action.[466] The confusion is not that significant yet it occurred partially because Haldeman and Ehrlichman were already getting closely associated with each other in this time period. When Ehrlichman was a junior at UCLA in 1947, he became friends with Haldeman. The two young men, both eagle scouts, became close friends who went on double dates together with their future wives, also UCLA students. Ehrlichman and Haldeman were not exactly carbon copies—Ehrlichman was a little older and more outgoing than his friend.[467] But a bond between the two men was formed that took them to the White House—and out of it—together.

Congressman Richard Nixon got in the spotlight in early 1948 thanks in large part to the Subversive Activities Control Bill, also known as the Mundt-Nixon Bill. According to Nixon, experts had been heard in subcommittee meetings in the House, and most of these experts agreed that the American Communist Party represented a threat to the United

States. The ACP received support from the Soviet Union—the Cold War nemesis of the U.S.—and the American people needed to be kept safe. Perhaps the two most significant parts of Mundt-Nixon were that "it noted that anyone who wanted to establish a totalitarian government in the United States under a foreign power was guilty of a crime [and] the party and its related organizations had to register with the U.S Attorney General."[468]

This bill epitomizes Nixon's record. Well meaning people from both sides of the political divide can look at it and make vastly different interpretations. Proponents, and Nixon himself, argued that this bill was not an attack on the Bill of Rights; it was a defense of national security. It did not outlaw the American Communist Party. The party could, as Nixon put it, "operate as a legitimate American political party above ground and without foreign connections." However, if the party tried to impose totalitarianism in America, that would be against the law. The Communist Party argued, though, that there were already laws against criminal activities like espionage and sabotage. No member of the American Communist Party had ever been convicted of arguing in favor of such things in America, so they should not be targeted by this legislation. Furthermore, if they registered their names, as this bill required, they could be targeted for police harassment and blacklisting. Thus, they argued, Nixon's proposed law was extreme and mean-spirited and a violation of the Bill of Rights.[469]

During the debate over Mundt-Nixon, some of the mail Nixon received was cruel. For those who say that Richard Nixon was a mean-spirited, dirty fighter, it should be noted that Nixon did not just dish it out; sometimes he received it, too. A lawyer from Fort Worth, Texas wrote to Nixon regarding the bill and likened the Congressman to Hitler. The lawyer went on to write "millions, like me, already hate you without even knowing you."[470]

G. Gordon Liddy graduated from prep school in June 1948, already supremely confident in the power of his will. So important to him was his inner strength that "Will" became the name of his autobiography. By Liddy's own admission, because of his personal successes up to this point, he "had gone beyond desirable self-confidence to the excess of arrogance. Having conquered physical and psychological weakness in myself, I was contemptuous of others not as strong, figuring that if I could do it, so could they." His confidence in the power of his will became even greater after a rather bizarre incident one evening that summer after gradation. While reading, he was struck with "indescribable pain" in his head. After barely enduring this for an indeterminate amount of time, Liddy heard a snapping sound, and his head suddenly began to feel better. Afterwards, Liddy felt that he had conquered his great fear of pain.[471] Years later, Liddy would use this fearlessness of pain to try to impress people, to demonstrate the strength of his resolve.

While Liddy was graduating from prep school, and Bud Krogh and John Dean were still in elementary school, John Connally was heavily involved in politics. Connally was still a major player in the career of Lyndon Johnson. In 1948 Connally was trying to help Johnson get elected to the Senate. One unique campaigning idea Johnson and Connally came up with was using a helicopter to get around the state more quickly and to generate public interest. Johnson was deceitful in paying the costs for the helicopter in order to avoid campaign spending limits laws, which provided another lesson for Connally on how serious operators survived the world of politics. Even with his effective campaigning and publicity, Johnson engaged in voter fraud to claim his victory in the election, and Connally was there for it.[472]

Nixon began to make a name for himself with his anti-Communist rhetoric, and his thinking on the subject was not fundamentally different from President Truman's, who privately talked about "Reds" and "parlor pinks." Such thinking was more than just political demagoguery. The FBI's J. Edgar Hoover speculated that there were 100,000 Communists in the United States.[473]

Nixon was easily re-elected to the House of Representatives in 1948. The Democratic Party leadership had wanted Voorhis to run again and try to reclaim his seat, but he was not interested. The Democrats were left with the relatively unknown and inexperienced Stephen Zetterberg, who was no match for Nixon.[474]

A few months before Nixon's re-election, Nixon gained national exposure thanks to the investigation of Alger Hiss. One man who noticed Nixon for the first time was Nixon's future Chief of Staff, Bob Haldeman.[475] Despite the political benefits to be had with national publicity, though, the future President had actually been willing at one point to hand the case over to the FBI. Nixon believed that only the FBI was "capable of fully investigating the espionage angles of the case."[476] But it was the House Un-American Activities Committee that ended up with the responsibility of dealing with Hiss. Nixon was the most junior member of the committee, but he was the only lawyer on it,[477] and this fact along with his experience as a debater, made him the best-equipped committee member to deal with the intelligent, smooth-talking Hiss.

The case revolved around Whitaker Chambers, who had only testified before the committee because someone else had named him as a Communist. Chambers admitted that he had been a Communist, but he had renounced his beliefs. Chambers named other members of an underground Communist movement he had been in while in Washington. One of those named was Alger Hiss, an official in Franklin Roosevelt's State Department who had helped put together the United Nations Charter. Hiss denied a Communist background or knowing Chambers. The story is a complicated one, but in the end Hiss was revealed as a former Communist and a spy.[478]

In the 1990s, two former members of the KGB said as much. In 1998, the *New York Times*, which at that point leaned solidly left, admitted, "Hiss was most likely a Soviet agent."[479] Author Anthony Summers cited the testimony of the Soviet spies and the *Times* editorial, yet went on to add that "as things stand…the newly available data from the old Soviet Union are not proof that Hiss was rightly convicted, at least not the sort of proof that history requires."[480] Summers' standards for history seem a little high when even the *Times* admitted that Hiss looks guilty. Besides, Hiss was actually convicted of two counts of perjury when he denied knowing Whittaker Chambers, and Hiss was blatantly guilty of this.[481]

After the end of the session when Hiss finally acknowledged that he knew Chambers, Chairman McDowell closed by saying to Hiss, "That is all. Thank you very much." Hiss snootily replied, "I don't reciprocate."[482]

Nixon later wrote, "I should have been elated. The case was broken. The Committee would be vindicated, and I personally would receive credit for the part I had played…Politically, we would now be able to give the lie to Truman's contemptuous dismissal of our hearings as a 'red-herring.'" But Nixon actually experienced what he termed a letdown. Though Nixon found an explanation for his feelings here,[483] this became a common facet of Nixon's personality. He relished the battle, but sometimes he did not know how to handle himself after the battle was over. It was almost as if the struggle was more important than the cause, so he did not know how to enjoy his victories.

When Hiss was convicted, Secretary of State Dean Acheson reiterated his long standing support for him, prompting Nixon to call Acheson's speech "disgusting." Well known anti-Communist Joseph McCarthy asked if this meant that Acheson would "not turn his back on any other Communists in the State Department?" Truman supported his Secretary of State, but Nixon observed that the nation did not support the Truman administration on this issue.[484]

In June of 1949 Chuck Colson, voted most likely to succeed by his high school classmates, gave his school's valedictory speech. He won a full scholarship to Harvard, which was the only way he could afford to go to such an expensive school. Ultimately, though, Colson opted for Brown University in Rhode Island. As much as Colson wanted to be good enough to get a full ride to Harvard and thus win acceptance by the Boston elite, he wanted to be able to thumb his nose at the establishment even more.[485] Colson believed that his father's difficulties at having a successful law practice stemmed from the fact that he was not a Harvard man with Harvard connections. Colson relished the opportunity to say that he was one man who was too good for the elitists.[486] Part of the reason why Colson later became so close and influential with Richard Nixon was because of their mutual commitment to hard work and their mutual disdain for the Eastern establishment.

Colson's scholarship to Brown required him to join the Naval Reserve, which gave him something else in common with Nixon, though in Colson's case he would do his active service with the Marines. Full of youthful bravado, Colson regretted that the Korean War ended before he had a chance to graduate college and go fight.[487]

By 1950 Richard Nixon was a rising star in Washington. A *Newsweek* article on the Republican Party referred to Nixon as the "most outstanding member of the present Congress." Raymond Moley, who had been a member of Franklin Roosevelt's brain trust, characterized Nixon as a moderate conservative with a bipartisan foreign policy.[488] It is interesting to note that Moley, who was part of the Democratic establishment, did not see Nixon as a right-winger.

During Nixon's race for a Senate seat against Helen Douglas in 1950, both sides fought rough. Douglas called Nixon a "peewee"[489] and said that she "despised Communism, Nazism, and Nixonism." She went on to draw even more explicit connections between her opponent and Italian fascist Benito Mussolini. She also called Nixon a "pipsqueak" and coined the name "Tricky Dick." For his part, Nixon accused Douglas of wanting Communism to thrive in the United States and said that Douglas was "pink right down to her underwear."[490]

The McCarran-Wood Bill, which was only slightly different from the Mundt-Nixon Bill, became an issue in the Douglas-Nixon race. Douglas was one of only 20 Representatives who voted against McCarran-Wood, such was its popularity and such was the intensity of anti-Communist sentiment in the country. Afterwards Nixon's people hammered away at the theme that Douglas was soft on communism. Part of the attack came in the form of over 500,000 copies of the Pink Sheet, a flyer that compared Douglas' voting record with that of Vito Marcantonio, a Congressman from New York whose voting record was applauded by the American Communist Party. The Pink Sheet exaggerated the closeness of the two voting records, but it was a devastating attack on Douglas, who underestimated its impact. She said, "I wasn't nearly shocked enough when I saw the Pink Sheet. I just thought it was ridiculous, absolutely absurd."[491] Unfortunately for Douglas, many California voters thought it was ridiculous and absurd too, but they also thought it was accurate.

Support for Douglas eroded badly as the election season progressed. Hollywood friends Ronald Reagan and his future wife Nancy Davis not only switched sides but actually held fund-raisers for Nixon. Nixon's ardent anti-Communist message resonated with Reagan. Harry Truman sent in several well-known Democrats to drum up support for Douglas, but Nixon made a campaign issue of outsiders trying to influence how Californians voted. Truman's efforts probably did not hurt Douglas in the election, but they did not help either.[492]

In the last month before the election, Douglas forces tried to counter the Pink Sheet with a rather extreme flyer of their own. It read, "THE BIG LIE! HITLER INVENTED IT. STALIN PERFECTED IT. NIXON USES IT...YOU PICK THE CONGRESSMAN THE KREMLIN LOVES!" Such efforts did not sway the voters of California, though; the election went to Nixon who beat Douglas by 680,000 votes.[493] It seemed like a curious approach by Douglas in the final days, drawing parallels between Nixon the strident anti-Communist and the Kremlin, but it was a measure of Douglas' desperation.

On April 11, 1951, Truman's dismissal of Douglas MacArthur from his post as commander of UN forces in South Korea became public. Richard Nixon joined in the chorus of politicians who condemned the move. Though MacArthur had been grossly insubordinate to Truman, MacArthur was still very popular. Nixon publicly called for MacArthur to be reinstated at once. It was ridiculous to think that Truman would reconsider his decision because Richard Nixon demanded it, but it did put Nixon on the right side of the issue with the majority of Americans.[494]

Four individuals who became very important to Richard Nixon entered his life circa 1951. This was the year that Rose Mary Woods joined his staff.[495] Nixon first caught the attention of Woods during his tenure on the Herter Committee in 1947. Perhaps surprisingly to some, it was his scrupulousness that she admired. He was meticulous about his expenses when many others in national government work tried to get rich or at least live beyond their means while in office. But the thrifty Nixon kept track of every little thing, and it all looked above board[496] to the woman who had been put in charge of bookkeeping for the committee. Rose Woods became a close friend of both Richard and Pat Nixon and later their two daughters.[497] Woods stayed with Nixon all the way through the Watergate scandal and Richard Nixon's resignation from the presidency.

It was also around this time that the friendship between Nixon and the famous evangelist Billy Graham began. They were introduced in the Senate Dining Room by one of Nixon's fellow senators, Clyde Hoey of North Carolina. Surprisingly, Graham, the North Carolina preacher, already knew Senator Nixon's California family. Nixon's mother had become interested in Graham's ministry, and she and her husband had gone to a Billy Graham Crusade in California. The elder Nixons had met with the preacher, and he remembered them. After Graham and Nixon had struck up a conversation in the dining room, the Senator asked Graham to go golfing, which the two men did that same day.[498]

The third significant person Nixon met during his first year in the Senate was Bebe Rebozo. Nixon met Rebozo through Senator George Smathers, who was an old high school classmate of Rebozo. Smathers had introduced Rebozo, who was fairly wealthy at this point, to several politicians, including John Kennedy and Lyndon Johnson. Nixon was the only one who became friends with Rebozo, though it did not seem a likely friendship at first. After his initial meeting with Nixon, Rebozo wrote in a letter to Smathers, "Don't ever send another dull fellow like that down here again. He doesn't drink whisky; he doesn't chase women; he doesn't even play golf." But Rebozo slowly began to respect Nixon, noting, "He had a depth and a genuineness about him which didn't come through because of his shyness." Rebozo also came to consider Nixon "a kind of genius."[499] The Nixons became frequent guests of Rebozo down at his home in Key Biscayne, Florida. Rebozo developed a warm bond with Richard and Pat Nixon by being nice to their kids, and by knowing when to be warm and entertaining and when to give them their space. Rebozo also endeared himself to the Nixons by safeguarding their privacy from the prying eyes of the media.[500] Smathers later said, "I think Bebe brings out the mystic in Nixon. It's a profound relationship. Two men who separately trust nobody yet when together they trust each other absolutely."[501]

The fourth significant person Nixon got to know in 1951 was World War Two hero Dwight D. Eisenhower. Nixon had seen Ike in a parade not too long after the Victory in Europe in 1945, and the pair had met at a luncheon hosted by Herbert Hoover, but in December 1951 Nixon and Ike were able to talk at length. Nixon was impressed by Ike's personality, and it did not hurt that the General praised Nixon for his handling of the Hiss case.[502] Little did Nixon realize how much he and Eisenhower would be seeing each other in the days ahead.

The year 1951 was also a significant in the life of John Ehrlichman. He received a law degree from Stanford. He had a job offer from a Los Angeles law firm, but a vacation to Seattle convinced him that LA was not the place for his family, so they moved up there where Ehrlichman worked briefly for his uncle before opening his own law partnership.[503]

By 1951 Henry Kissinger had begun a project that would increase his visibility for the power brokers of the country. Kissinger was a graduate student at Harvard, and his mentor helped him start something called the Harvard International Seminar. Kissinger got to know many prominent and powerful Americans both by inviting some of them to speak at his seminars and by soliciting donations from others for his program.[504]

The question of whom the vice presidential candidate should be in the 1952 election was thoroughly debated among Republican leaders. About thirty men, including governors, senators, Republican National Committee leaders, and Ike's personal friends/advisors, attended a meeting chaired by Herbert Brownell in Eisenhower's hotel suite at the Republican National Convention. Several possible choices were tossed into the ring and rejected. One of the names they discarded was that of Bill Knowland, the senior senator from California. Knowland was considered damaged goods because he had managed the campaign of Earl Warren, and they had provoked the ire of Ike's advisors by refusing to concede even after things were hopeless for Warren's candidacy. Finally Thomas Dewey ended the debate over the second spot on the ticket when he pitched Nixon's name. Nixon had made a name for himself with the Hiss case, and Nixon was a talented and hard working campaigner, which was something the ticket needed since Ike did not want to campaign much. Nixon was also seen as offering a strong balance to Eisenhower. Ike was older, Nixon was youthful; Nixon was from the West Coast and Eisenhower had spent the last several years on the East Coast; and Nixon had been in the Navy, while Ike had served in the Army.[505] While not too much should be made of the Army-Navy balance, it is worth noting that someone's specific military service would have been of more interest back in 1952 when so many Americans had fought World War Two and there was still a draft in place.

Eisenhower was seen as a man who could bring the country together, but Nixon's role would be important because he could bring the party together. The Republican Party was divided between Eastern, somewhat liberal thinkers who wanted an active foreign policy; and conservatives primarily in the West and Midwest, many of them presently or formerly isolationists who hated Communism. Nixon could draw support from both wings of the party. His staunch anti-Communism resonated with conservatives, and his economic policies were compatible with Eastern Republicans. Plus, Nixon tirelessly worked fundraising dinners for Republicans across the country.[506] Nixon and the Republican Party needed Eisenhower, but to a degree that might surprise the modern reader, Eisenhower and the Republican Party also needed someone like Nixon.

Despite the logic of a Nixon vice presidency, that did not mean all the Republican leaders were thrilled about it. Bob Taft described Nixon as a man who seemed "to radiate tension and conflict." Historian David Halberstam believed, "Everything with Nixon was personal. When others disagreed with him, it was as if they wanted to strip away his hard-won veneer of success and reduce him to the unhappy boy he had once been."[507] Nevertheless, the party leaders felt they were stronger with Nixon than without him.

One issue that left unexplored was the compatibility of the two men who would lead the Republican ticket, and ominous signs appeared almost instantly. Herbert Brownell called Nixon's room and said, "We picked you. The General asked if you would come see him right away. That is, assuming you want it!"[508] Nixon was elated, but the phone call had caught him off guard. Nixon had not been able to sleep the previous night because of the intense heat and lack of air conditioning. At the time of the call, it was almost 100 degrees in Nixon's room. He would have benefited from a shower and clean clothes, and a shave would not have hurt either.[509] But his new boss wanted him "right away," so he went immediately to see Eisenhower, a man who had come out of a career where men were closely inspected on how squared away they were. The appearance of the rather grubby looking recruit did not impress the General, nor did Nixon's chipper "Congratulations, Chief!" Nixon, normally so painfully reserved, simply could not contain his enthusiasm. He threw his arm around the shoulder of Ike[510] who generally disdained such physical contact—a fact Nixon was not aware of until later.[511] For his part, Nixon was surprised by how formal and stiff Eisenhower was.[512]

On July 11, 1952, the day when Ike agreed to have Nixon as his VP, Mrs. Nixon was eating lunch with some friends when she found out. There was a movie playing on the restaurant's TV, and it was interrupted by the announcement of the newly-formed Republican ticket. Pat Nixon was so shocked that her bite of her BLT sandwich fell out of her mouth. She had recently agreed, reluctantly, to support one more campaign if her husband was chosen by Ike, but the announcement was still a surprise, and not an altogether pleasant one. She hated the fact that she would have to spend so much time away from her daughters, but she felt like she needed to support husband one more time.[513] As Pat Nixon hurried over to the Convention Hall to be with her husband, one of her dining companions, Helen Drown, said to her, "Oh honey, you're going to be in the history books now."[514]

The differences in formality between Nixon and Eisenhower, basically a generation gap, were realized time and again. An early manifestation of the gap was seen in Yankee Stadium shortly after the convention. Nixon was watching a game with Herbert Brownell, who described what happened. "Someone hit a homerun. Nixon jumped up, stood on a chair and yelled his head off...as if he was a high school kid...I was embarrassed to put it mildly. I could hardly believe he could be so raw and brash."[515] Nixon was often times stiff and uncomfortable around people, and on this day, one of the rare times he let his guard down, he was foiled by his perfectly natural—though perhaps overly enthusiastic—love of sports.

Eisenhower tried to bond with Nixon through one of the General's favorite past times—fishing. Things started off poorly when Ike arrived dressed in his fishing gear, and Nixon showed up wearing a suit.[516] Eisenhower wanted to teach Nixon the basics of fly-fishing, but, as Nixon put it, "It was a disaster. After hooking a limb the first three times, I caught his shirt on my fourth try. The lessons ended abruptly. I could see that he was disappointed..."[517] Even after they spent more time together, the two men remained somewhat distant. Friendship usually came easily to Ike, but Nixon had trouble trusting people and relaxing around them, which made him a hard man to like.[518] One can only wonder at how things might have been different for them, and for Nixon's career, if they had been able to connect in a leisurely way.

Nixon did most of the dirty work in the campaign. While Ike tended to stay above the fray, Nixon focused on "Korea, Communism, and corruption." Nixon lumped in President Truman with Ike's opponent, Adlai Stevenson, and said they were "traitors to the high principles in which many of the nation's Democrats believe." Truman took it personally that Nixon called him a traitor, and years later Nixon was one of the few men Truman genuinely hated.[519]

Liddy's mind was not yet on politics in 1952. He graduated from Fordham and the Reserve Officers Training Corps and joined the Army Reserves. Liddy went through his 90-day training at Fort Bliss in El Paso, Texas without any trouble until the end. He won a sit-up contest among the young officers but almost died afterwards because in his competitive zeal he had ruptured his appendix. Liddy missed his window for going to Korea. He was instead assigned to an antiaircraft unit with the job of protecting New York City from Soviet attack.[520]

Things started out smoothly enough for Nixon in the campaign of 1952, but he ran into trouble on September 14. Nixon had just finished taping an episode of Meet the Press when one of the reporters, Peter Edson, asked him, "Senator, what is this 'fund' we hear about? There is a rumor to the effect that you have a supplementary salary of $20,000 a year, contributed by a hundred California businessmen. What about it?"[521]

Such a charge was especially sensitive since Ike's campaign theme was a "Crusade to Clean up the Mess in Washington," which centered on allegations of Democrat corruption. But Nixon explained that the money was not a supplemental salary; it funded political activities. Dana Smith, Nixon's finance chairman from his 1950 campaign, was in charge of the fund, and the money was all kept in one bank where it received regular audits. Nixon thought the fund would not be an issue, but it became one as newspapers from around the country began to call for Nixon's resignation from the Republican ticket.[522] Leo Katcher, a screenwriter, had written in the *New York Post* about "the existence of a millionaire's club devoted exclusively to the financial comfort of Senator Nixon, GOP vice presidential candidate."[523] Even though Katcher had gotten his facts wrong, other newspapers jumped on the bandwagon.

Part of Nixon's frustration over what came to be called the "Fund Crisis" was that there was much comment on Nixon's fund, but the media paid less attention to the fund used by Adlai Stevenson. This was especially galling to Nixon because the money in his fund was not accessible to him, and it just paid gas and postage for his political outreach, whereas Stevenson did have access to the money, and it was used for some of his employees' personal expenses. The *Chicago Tribune* broke the story of Stevenson's fund, but for whatever reason the heat stayed on Nixon.[524] Perhaps what kept the pressure on the aspiring VP (other than some media bias against him) was that his fund problem led to speculation over what Ike would do with him. As his party's leader, Stevenson's fate was not in question, so his fund issue seemed less relevant.

Nixon was also frustrated by Eisenhower's response. Ike had his people investigate Nixon's fund, which was not unreasonable since Ike really did not know Nixon. But after a team of accountants had determined that the fund was okay, Eisenhower still resisted embracing his vice presidential candidate. When reporters asked the General if he considered the matter resolved, he said, "By no means." He wanted Nixon to somehow further prove his financial integrity. Eisenhower wanted Nixon to provide evidence that his finances were in order. The General asked the assembled reporters, "What was the use of campaigning against this business of what has been going on in Washington if we ourselves aren't as clean as a hound's tooth?" It looked like Nixon was going to be considered guilty until proven innocent, and it angered him.[525]

As the Fund Crisis came to a head, Nixon described himself in his book *Six Crises* as "edgy and short-tempered," but rather than apologize for this, Nixon thought his emotional response was not only typical but appropriate. If he were not feeling this way, Nixon reasoned, then he "was not adequately keyed up, mentally and emotionally, for the conflict ahead."[526] Of course the downside to such thinking is that it failed to take into account the feelings of the subordinates, friends, and family members who felt Nixon's wrath. The danger here is that such subordinates would be tempted in the future to not deliver bad news or commentary that would inflame the boss' passions.

Nixon decided to deal with the Fund Crisis by getting on TV and explaining things to the American people. He would describe the fund and lay out his personal finances for all the country to hear. About an hour before he was supposed to leave for the TV studio, he got a call from Tom Dewey, who was traveling with Eisenhower's entourage. Dewey said that Ike's top advisors had "asked me to tell you that it is their opinion that at the conclusion of the broadcast tonight you should submit your resignation to Eisenhower." Dewey did not share their sentiments, he said, but it was his job to pass the word to Nixon. After overcoming his sense of shock well enough to speak, Nixon asked what Ike thought about this. Dewey made it clear that Ike had not weighed in, but given that these were his closest men, they were probably not speaking without his approval.[527]

Dewey wanted to know what Nixon was going to do, and the candidate finally exploded, "Just tell them that I haven't the slightest idea as to what I am going to do, and if they want to find out they'd better listen to the broadcast. And tell them I know something about politics, too!"[528]

A particularly interesting part of the speech Nixon gave that night was where he said, "It isn't a question of whether it was legal or illegal, that isn't enough. The question is, was it morally wrong?"[529] Too bad such a question was not raised during the planning for the Watergate break-ins, the coverup, and other issues.

Nixon went on to turn the tables on his Democratic rivals. Stephen Mitchell, the Democratic National Committee Chairman, had said, "If a fellow can't afford to be a Senator, he shouldn't seek the office." Nixon mentioned this during his broadcast and pointed out that Stevenson had inherited a lot of money from his father, but Nixon identified himself with "the common people," a phrase he borrowed from Abraham Lincoln. Nixon put himself on the side of the majority of the viewers, and contrasted himself with the supposed elitists who were running the opposition party. To further connect with his audience, Nixon said that he had received the dog "Checkers" from a supporter and given the dog to his daughters. "I just want to say this right now," Nixon added, "that regardless of what they [his critics] say about it, we are going to keep it." It was the kind of presentation guaranteed to make partisan critics roll their eyes, but for the partisan supporters, the non-political, and most of the moderates, it was quite stirring.[530]

After giving his speech, Nixon was described as being "in a complete emotional daze." Nixon had walked toward the main TV camera as the broadcast was ending, and he was so swept up in emotion that he bumped into it. One of the cameramen, who had been so moved he was openly weeping, had to catch the Senator. Nixon thought he had bombed the speech, saying to his producer friend, Ted Rogers, "I'm sorry, Ted, I loused it up." But Nixon was wrong; the speech was a hit. And as the Nixons left the theater that night they were cheered on by Bob Haldeman and his fellow Young Republicans.[531]

Eisenhower's response to Nixon's performance during the Checkers Speech was summed up by a comment the General made to an associate right after Nixon's broadcast. Ike said, "I would rather go down in defeat fighting with a brave man than to win with a bunch of cowards." But Nixon did not hear that or related comments, so he got frustrated at the thought that his future was still in doubt, and he considered resigning. The misunderstanding was eventually resolved, and when the two men met up, Eisenhower greeted Nixon by saying "You're my boy."[532]

Despite the fact that the Checkers Speech had saved Nixon's career, keeping the door to the vice presidency open and leading to the White House one day, it was still a humiliating experience. Nixon wrote, "I regarded what had been done to me as character assassination." His wife Pat took it even harder. Twenty-six years after the fact, their daughter had asked Pat Nixon about the episode for a biography Julie Nixon Eisenhower was writing on her mother. Pat Nixon responded, "Do we have to talk about this? It kills me."[533]

This time period became doubly difficult for Pat Nixon as her relationship with her husband began to change. One of Nixon's old press secretaries, Jim Bassett, who was in 1952 working for the *Los Angeles Times*, observed that Senator Nixon was becoming increasingly cold towards his wife. Richard Nixon would occasionally lash out at her behind the scenes but in front of friends, but he was always quick to praise her in public. Pat Nixon might have been a moral compass for her husband in the White House, but decades before then, her influence on him was already waning.[534]

Though Eisenhower's overall handling of the Fund Crisis was a disappointment to Nixon, the General perhaps went a long towards making up for it in August at the Republican National Convention. Eisenhower told Nixon, "Dick, I don't want a Vice President who will be a figurehead. I want a man who will be a member of the team."[535] And Eisenhower was good to his word. Nixon would learn from many valuable experiences over the next eight years.

John Connally was involved in Democratic politics during the election of 1952, mainly working to promote the interests of Lyndon Johnson. Johnson had told Democratic Senator Richard Russell that Johnson would support Russell's bid for the presidency. In exchange, if Russell failed, then he would support Johnson's quest for the vice presidency. Johnson did not think Russell could win the top spot, but if Russell did decently, then he would have more clout on the convention floor, and he would be of great assistance to Johnson. Thus, Johnson urged his people, including John Connally, to "hustle for Russell" at the convention.[536] In the end, neither Russell nor Johnson got what they wanted, but the political education of John Connally had continued. By the time the general election rolled around, Connally might well have decided to go with the candidate with the strongest hand. Though Connally publicly denied it later, there was a widespread belief that he had helped the Eisenhower-Nixon ticket win in Texas in 1952.[537]

Jeb Magruder started his higher education at Williams College in 1952. Magruder had chosen a small, liberal arts school in New England. If Magruder had possessed as intense a personality as Richard Nixon, Magruder might have developed the same prejudice towards the rich Eastern Establishment. Magruder was made very conscious of his lack of sophistication or prep school grace during his time at Williams. Magruder bristled at the unfairness of the fraternity system towards minorities and the socially awkward. But rather than harbor deep resentment towards the in-crowd, Magruder simply joined a second class fraternity and kept his mouth shut. Magruder was not that committed to acceptance and success in college any way. By the end of his second year, he had sacrificed his grades at the altar of poker and women.[538]

The same year that Magruder started college, Bud Krogh met John Ehrlichman for the first time. Ehrlichman was already practicing law in Seattle, and Krogh was just a 13-year-old kid. The two were connected by several personal bonds. Ehrlichman's uncle and aunt were friends of Krogh's parents, and Ehrlichman's wife was friends with Krogh's sister. Another thing that connected John Ehrlicman and Bud Krogh was religion—both men were Christian Scientists.[539]

With the exception of John Connally, Bob Haldeman, and perhaps Henry Kissinger, none of Nixon's men yet saw themselves with futures in politics. Richard Nixon, however, was rising fast with many formative experiences just around the corner.

CHAPTER SEVEN

The Vice Presidency, Part I—1953-1956

John Adams, the first Vice President of the United States, referred to his job as "the most insignificant that ever the invention of man contrived or his imagination conceived."[540] John Nance Garner, Vice President for Franklin Roosevelt from 1933-1941, allegedly once complained that his office was not worth "a warm bucket of spit." And the only "alleged" aspect of the quotation is whether or not Garner used a stronger word than "spit." As Nixon later paraphrased Charles G. Dawes, the Vice President "had only two responsibilities—to sit and listen to United States Senators give speeches, and to check the morning's newspaper as to the President's health."[541] The office has increased by leaps and bounds in recent decades, becoming as historian Carl Luna once wrote "more of a deputy presidency.[542] Vice Presidents even gained an office in the White House when John Kennedy gave one to Lyndon Johnson.[543] Nixon helped pave the way for Johnson, his successor to the vice presidency, by being extraordinarily active during Nixon's two terms as Vice President. Because of the combination of Eisenhower's age, health, and lack of background or interest in politicking, Nixon wound up with plenty to do. Nixon's experiences as Vice President brought him into contact with several of the men who figured prominently in his eventual rise to the presidency. Also, the Vice President's experiences with communism and the inner workings of the Executive Branch and the Republican Party impacted the big dreams he would later have for these institutions when he became President.

Richard Nixon's ascendancy to the vice presidency at the age of 40 made him the second youngest man ever to fill that position.[544] Nixon's vice presidential inauguration took place on January 20, 1953, a sunny day that was milder than typical January inaugurals have been. The celebratory parties were tedious for Nixon, who was seldom comfortable at such events, but some respite was found in the intimate family dinner he had the night before his big day. He seemed, alongside Eisenhower, on top of the world. The Checkers Speech had saved his career, the Democrats had been beaten, and future nemesis John Dean was just another thirteen-year-old kid. At his inauguration, Nixon carried in his wallet a note his beloved mother had given him. Hannah Nixon had expressed pride in her son, but at the same time she urged him to keep his relationship with God as his number one priority.[545]

A second note was in his wallet, also; a message Nixon himself had written at his wife's urging. He promised to retire from politics in 1956 when his term as Vice President ended. Interestingly, the two notes were so important to Nixon that he always carried them with him for the next four years, but he failed to honor either of them. He was to run in four more elections after 1952. And given the corruption of the White House during his presidency, it does not seem that he fully honored his mother's desire either.[546]

As he assumed the vice presidency, Nixon only had one member of the team in place that would serve him in his own administration, personal secretary Rose Mary Woods, but he was ready to do battle nevertheless, and it would be a battle. The Republicans held a majority of one in the Senate and were the minority party in the House of Representatives. Dwight Eisenhower was the first Republican President since January 1933. From Nixon's point of view, it was time to clean house after twenty years of Democratic philosophies and appointees in the Executive Branch. Nixon also believed, correctly, that Joseph McCarthy was not one hundred percent wrong about government workers' connections with communism. McCarthy, though still a popular figure in the heartland in early 1953, was controversial among the media and many politicians, including the leadership of the Republican Party. He had many supporters, but there were a rising number of people, including Ike, who believed that he went too far. For awhile Nixon tried to act as a peace maker between McCarthy and the Republicans he was offending. Nixon was a good choice for this role since the Vice President could understand both the attitudes of McCarthy and his critics. But after Nixon had put out a few fires,[547] Ike had something else in mind for his Vice President, which was probably just as well. McCarthy eventually lost his credibility and alienated too many members of his own party, Nixon included, by attacking the U.S. Army.[548] McCarthy's fall from influence prompted Ike to remark to his Cabinet, "Have you heard the latest? McCarthyism is McCarthywasm."[549] Nixon could not have saved McCarthy, but the VP might have gone down with him. Perhaps Nixon's political instincts would have led him away from McCarthy in time, but Ike's intervention did not hurt.

In the spring of 1953, Ike had suggested that the Vice President should take a long trip to Asia including the Middle East. This would be the first of multiple trips Nixon took on behalf of Eisenhower. Eventually, Nixon would travel more than any American leader before him.[550] His first overseas trip as Vice President was certainly logical from a foreign policy standpoint. As Nixon put it, "Eisenhower knew Europe and its leaders better than almost any other non-European in the world. But he did not know Asia or the Middle East well, and he was never one to overestimate his experience or knowledge."[551] While this was true, it was also true that Ike and Nixon were not that close, and Ike had others whose insights and knowledge he would trust more. Sending someone of the Vice President's political rank on a long trip halfway around the world was a nice diplomatic gesture to the countries visited, and it also served the purpose of getting the frequently polarizing Nixon off the radar for some time.

Demonstrating both his disdain for big parties and the cultural elite, and his strong personality, Nixon informed the embassies ahead of time that he was only bringing one dinner jacket, and he wanted to meet a lot of different types of people in the countries, not just the dignitaries, so the formal affairs would have to be kept to a minimum.[552]

It was during this trip that Nixon traveled throughout Vietnam, meeting with Vietnamese politicians and French military officers. Trouble with the Communists was a major concern, but Nixon became convinced that the French had neither trained nor inspired the Vietnamese majority to fight them. Nixon believed the answer to this problem was for the United States to try to keep the French in Vietnam until the war against the Communists was won.[553]

In Burma, Nixon encountered a group of Communist demonstrators. After he faced down the leader of the demonstrators, Nixon decided he had figured out how to deal with Communist aggressors. Nixon was convinced that Communists viewed polite behavior as weakness; therefore the only way to deal with them was to always be firm.[554] He would have this viewpoint reinforced several times throughout his life.

In 1954 Jeb Stuart Magruder began a 21 month stint for the Army in South Korea. He served as an enlisted man after washing out of Officer Candidate School at Fort Sill, Oklahoma. Magruder and several other candidates got caught skipping study hall, which seems like a minor thing, but Magruder noted that they had skipped several times. Magruder and his father both tried to talk the commanding officer into showing some mercy, but the punishment stuck.[555]

Magruder's first assignment in South Korea was to help guard the Demilitarized Zone where the enemy occasionally engaged in sniper fire. The poverty of the South Korean people made an impression on young Magruder, as did the attitude of the people towards the dictatorial rule of South Korea's leader, Syngman Rhee. When Magruder returned to the United States to finish college, he had developed a passionate interest in political science.[556]

Perhaps the most significant event going on in the world in 1954 occurred in Vietnam where the Communist forces of Ho Chi-minh defeated the French colonial army at Dien Bien Phu. The French signed a peace agreement that allowed them to get out of Vietnam and divided the country into northern and southern regions. The United States favored the anti-Communist South Vietnam, which was saddled with a corrupt dictatorship. The USA's ally was not a poster child for democracy, but the American policy of containment sometimes required such alliances to be made.[557]

That summer Communists were also on the move in Guatemala. Eisenhower decided to send a contingent of Naval and Marine forces offshore just in case the pro-American regime needed help. One of the young Marines involved in the operation was Chuck Colson, future hatchet man for Nixon. The government held, so American intervention was not needed. But while there, contemplating the possible end of his life as he looked at the starry sky one night, Colson found God in an agnostic sort of way.[558] It would take the Watergate scandal and the specter of jail time to prompt Colson to crystallize his thoughts on the subject of Christianity.

1954 was also the year G. Gordon Liddy left the Army. Liddy was an ambitious, intelligent man who had no idea what to do with himself. He took an aptitudes test, hoping to find some direction, but the test indicated that Liddy was best suited to edit scholarly publications. Liddy did not think this was a worthy profession for a man of action like himself. Surprisingly, he considered trying to make a career as a singer.[559] Unfortunately for the Nixon administration, he chose differently in the end, going to law school and then joining the FBI.

In the congressional elections that year, Nixon was called upon to be the administration's chief campaigner. Eisenhower generally avoided campaigning during these elections because of his age—the President was 63 that year—and health issues, and because of Ike's general aversion to politicking. Nixon hammered away at the Democrats as the party that was weak on communism and weak on corruption in the federal government, but strong when it came to government controls and regulations. Despite his efforts, the Republicans lost their majority in the Senate and went down even further in the House.[560] However, as Nixon biographer Jonathon Aitken pointed out, "West of the Mississippi, where Nixon had done most of his campaigning, the GOP broke even on House seats and gained one Senate seat. There was hope for the future here, for the West was the fastest growing region of the country."[561]

Despite the positive spin that Nixon might have put on his efforts, he was tired of playing the role of Eisenhower's attack dog. He was getting savaged in the press, the Democrats were taking his bruising political style personally, and Ike would push Nixon to be more and more extreme then express discomfort with Nixon's comportment. Nixon, far from being obsessed with fighting his way to the presidency, was strongly considering turning his back on politics. Nixon's frustration was so great that he actually made a list of reasons why he should get out. The list included his wife's great discomfort with the whole political atmosphere, the fact that he took the issues and the battles waged over them much too personally, and the reality that he really hated the social obligations of his vocation. But he also wrote down reasons for staying in, which included his belief that sometimes politicians need the job and sometimes the job needs them. Nixon felt the job needed him.[562]

Even when Nixon tried to get away from the troubles of work, there were times when things did not go smoothly. He went on a fishing trip in 1955 with Bebe Rebozo down in the Florida Everglades, and he was bedeviled by his almost legendary physical awkwardness. He managed to fall out of the boat not once but twice. The first time, he fell in the water because he had gotten his fishing line caught in a tree. He tried to yank the line loose and lost his balance. The second time, he fell in the mud when his boat turned too sharply.[563]

Nixon almost became President in September 1955. Eisenhower had suffered a heart attack at 2:30 A.M.[564] after a day spent traveling, working, and playing 27 holes of golf. Nixon was speechless when he learned of Ike's condition. The Vice President, who had just returned with some friends from a wedding, finally pulled himself together enough to say that a lot of people have recovered from heart attacks. After he got off the phone, he sat by himself for several minutes, repeating the phrase, "It's terrible!"[565] Nixon was so distraught that he did not even think to tell the people he was with what happened. He called his good friend Bill Rogers, who was the acting Attorney General, while the AG was on vacation out of the country. Later that night Nixon wound up at Rogers house—after avoiding reporters en route—and asked what the Constitution said the Vice President's role should be if the President was incapacitated. Rogers replied, "I'm sorry, I don't have the vaguest idea." Both men were embarrassed,[566] and they should have been. It was within the purview of both of their jobs to know the answer to such a question.

They should have known that the Constitution had no answer to this question. The 25th Amendment deals specifically with the problem of an incapacitated President. This Amendment calls for the Vice President to assume the responsibilities of the President until such time as the President is fit to resume his duties. Unfortunately for Nixon, the 25th Amendment did not go into effect until 1967. This being the case, Nixon's problem during Eisenhower's convalescence "was how to walk on eggs and not break them...What I had to do was to provide leadership without appearing to lead."[567] Nixon had to project a reassuring presence to the United States and its allies; they needed to see that the leading power in the free world was not rudderless. Yet Nixon did not want to come across as if he was usurping the throne while the king was indisposed since, constitutionally speaking, the "throne" was not available for the taking. A power grab would have been unseemly under almost any circumstance, but it would be especially so at this point, given how much more personally popular Ike was than Nixon.

Nixon dealt with Eisenhower's absence from Washington, an absence which stretched for almost two months, by contacting the Cabinet members and getting everyone to provide assurances that any quarreling would be kept quiet and there would be no jockeying for power. Nixon was less successful with Ike's Chief of Staff, Sherman Adams, who showed up at the White House and said, "It's quite a surprise to come back here and suddenly find yourself the President."[568] Such audacity is explainable; as Ike's close friend and Chief of Staff, Adams had gotten used to issuing orders in the President's name, whether Ike had actually given the orders or not. Still, while it is not surprising that Adams had been exercising such power for quite some time, it was a rather indelicate thing for an unelected person to say in a democratic country.

Despite Adams' overbearing attitude, Nixon refused to be drawn into a power struggle. He made clear that he was not the "Acting President" through gestures of both substance and style. During meetings with the Cabinet and the National Security Council, he facilitated discussions, but he did not treat those assembled like he was the new boss. And he never sat in Ike's chair. Nixon continued to play second fiddle so well that at the end of a Cabinet meeting on September 30th, Secretary of State John Foster Dulles said, "I realize that you have been under a very heavy burden during these past few days, and I know I express the opinion of everybody here that you have conducted yourself superbly."[569] Sherman Adams, who had returned to Washington with the idea of preventing Nixon from trying to fill the power vacuum, eventually conceded that the Vice President "leaned over backward to avoid any appearance of assuming presidential authority."[570]

Special Assistant on Disarmament Harold Stassen was the so-called "Secretary of Peace" because of the nature of his work on weapons negotiations and his Cabinet-level status as an advisor. Stassen called Nixon shortly after news of Eisenhower's heart attack became public and pledged his support for Nixon if Ike was unable to run again in 1956. Stassen figured he could continue his work more smoothly if the country transitioned from Eisenhower to Eisenhower's Vice President. But this became a moot point when Ike bounced back and decided to run for a second term.[571]

Eisenhower was not back at work full-time until November 11, but in the entire time he was out, he never sent Nixon a note of appreciation or encouragement.[572] This was unusual since notes from Ike to others were rather common, and the President had wanted Nixon to grow as a leader. But in the opinion of some of Ike's key advisors, a Nixon who had grown politically was not necessarily a good thing for the Republican Party. High ranking Republicans like the aforementioned Harold Stassen and others did not view Nixon as the inevitable future for their party in 1960. Back in 1952 those Republicans who did not care for Nixon were not worried about him since he was stuck in the insignificant role of the vice presidency. But Nixon had been very prominent over the last four years, and during Ike's convalescence, Nixon was actually, dare they admit it, statesmanlike. Thus, Nixon was a threat to the dreams of moderate and liberal Republicans and to those Republicans who simply thought that Nixon's political baggage and/or his personality made him unelectable as President.

Some of the pressure and discomfort Nixon experienced came straight from the top. Ike invited Nixon to the White House on December 26, 1955 to have a talk before the President headed to Florida. Ike said that while he was down there, he would be discussing the future of the party's ticket with his close friends.[573] A couple of things are worth noting here. Though Ike was soliciting Nixon's input, Nixon was clearly not one of the President's closest friends, nor was Nixon one of his key advisors. Also, Eisenhower and his men would not just be talking about Ike's status; they would be talking about Nixon's future, and the VP would not be there to argue his own cause. Nixon was still viewed as very much the junior partner.

Eisenhower wondered aloud whether or not he should run for the presidency again. Nixon vigorously encouraged Ike to serve for another four years. Unfortunately for the Vice President, Ike did not reciprocate those feelings toward another Nixon run. Eisenhower was disappointed that Nixon was not viewed as favorably in the polls as the President had hoped,[574] so Eisenhower suggested to Nixon that the younger man might prefer a Cabinet position in the second term rather than the vice presidency. Ike encouraged his VP to spend some time and think about it. Ike pointed out in one of his autobiographical works that he really was trying to help Nixon. Martin Van Buren was the last sitting Vice President to be elected straight to the presidency, and that happened back in 1836. Ike felt that Nixon had done a great job in the vice presidency, but a great job in the right Cabinet post might help him more. Several Cabinet secretaries had become President. Eisenhower wrote that he did not realize at the time Nixon was hurt by the suggestion to change roles; it was supposed to be a positive thing.[575] But Eisenhower also saw that Nixon was not very popular. Ike said to his Secretary of State John Foster Dulles that Nixon deserved the public's support, but he had not gotten it, and this lack of support helped prompt Ike to think that maybe Nixon was better off serving in a different capacity. Ike had first begun dropping hints indirectly in December 1955 that Nixon should serve elsewhere, and these hints, inevitably, made their way from the White House to the press. While speaking to the press at the end of February 1956, Ike said that he had "tremendous admiration for Mr. Nixon," and "I am very fond of him." But the President also told the press that he would not choose a Vice President for the next term until Ike himself had been nominated.[576]

The media questioned Ike again about Nixon's future on March 7. The President at first defended him, saying, "I will promise you this much: if anyone ever has the effrontery to come in and urge me to dump somebody that I respect as I do Vice President Nixon, there will be more commotion around my office than you have noticed yet." But rather than putting the issue to rest, the President went on to breathe more life into it. He said, "I have not presumed to tell the Vice President what he should do with his own future...The only thing I have asked him to do is to chart out his own course, and tell me what he would like to do...I am not going to be pushed into corners here and say what I would do in a hypothetical question that involves about five ifs."[577] While this was not exactly a kiss of death, Eisenhower's answer avoided any overt endorsement of Nixon for the vice presidency during the next four years. And Eisenhower persisted over the next few months in his fence straddling. While Ike was gently nudging Nixon along the path, the President's public neutrality on the vice presidency should not necessarily be viewed as an overall unfavorable position on Nixon. As Special Assistant to President Eisenhower Arthur Larson noted, Ike did not believe that a President should dictate to his party whom his running mate should be. That was the responsibility of the Republican National Convention. As Larson made clear, the lack of an early and clear endorsement of Nixon was not a cold calculation on the part of Eisenhower, it was simply a manifestation of his political philosophy.[578]

Nevertheless, the *lassiez faire* attitude from his boss put Richard Nixon through a unique kind of hell. As Pat Nixon described this time of uncertainty, and the implied lack of favor from Eisenhower, it left the Vice President "more depressed than I ever remembered."[579] And given the darkness of Richard Nixon's depressions, that was really saying something. Likewise, Nixon's appointments secretary, Dorothy Cox, described the Vice President as being "dreadfully wounded and hurt" by this situation.[580]

The Republican Party chairman at the time, Len Hall said that though both men genuinely respected each other, he acknowledged there was "not much dialogue" between them.[581] Eisenhower wanted what was good for the party, and in Eisenhower's view that meant positioning the party in the center and reaching out to moderate Democrats. This move to the middle was more difficult with Richard Nixon, the champion of the right flank, on the ticket. But Ike had helped keep Nixon out on that flank when the younger man wanted to come back in, and the President felt some responsibility for Nixon's situation. Ike truly did want what was best for Nixon. If Nixon had assumed a different role in the next term, then Nixon would be better able to re-mold his image. If the two men had been closer personally, maybe this would have been communicated more effectively. Ike tried to have Len Hall explain it to Nixon with the instructions for his party chairman to be "very, very gentle." But Nixon wasn't buying. Hall later told Eisenhower, "I never saw a scowl come so fast over a man's face. But beyond that, we got no response at all. He was so uptight when he heard the suggestion [to switch jobs during Ike's second term], he just stared at the ceiling."[582]

Nixon had little to say that day to Len Hall, but he became more animated after hearing the continually noncommittal press conferences of the President. Nixon wrote up a statement that he would be withdrawing from the Eisenhower administration altogether. When word of this got to the White House, Len Hall and presidential aide Jerry Persons intervened and urged Nixon to reconsider.[583] Nixon argued that it was impossible for a Vice President to "chart his own course," and if Ike wanted him to continue on in the vice presidency, the President needed to say so. Hall urged patience and cited Ike's lack of a political background as a reason for such an unusual stance by the President.[584] Nixon was further convinced not to give up by his wife. In a surprise move, given her profound dislike of politics, Pat Nixon encouraged her husband to hang on. She did not want her husband's meteoric career to burn out so dramatically. As she told her friend, Helene Drown, "No one is going to push us off the ticket."[585] She had been in favor of retiring from politics, but she preferred to take the elevator down from the top, not the shaft.

Nixon again spoke to Eisenhower about the vice presidency, and the President said he would "be happy" for the two of them to run for another term together, but not until after the President repeated his suggestion of a Cabinet post. Though Eisenhower kept hammering away at the idea of Nixon serving in a Cabinet office during the next term, and Ike kept trying to spin it as a move that would be good for Nixon, there was another possible scenario that the Vice President had to factor in to his thinking. As Eisenhower said to a friend, "The thing Dick may have figured was that 1960 didn't matter much, and in the event of my—er—disablement [or death], he'd take over and at least have the presidency for *that* long."[586] And of course, Nixon would have all of the advantages of an incumbent in 1960.

Nixon might have been motivated by such thoughts, but there was more to it than that. He believed that if he quit the ticket it would not be enough to make liberals vote for Ike. Conversely, under whatever circumstances Nixon did not stay on as Vice President, it would look like he was ousted. Nixon was convinced that such a move would alienate conservatives. Nixon felt his position on the ticket was a continued necessity to keep the party conservatives loyal to Eisenhower with his moderate tendencies.[587]

The politically savvy Nixon decided to go to the delegates who would cast votes at the Republican National Convention, and he got commitments from enough of them to make his re-nomination inevitable. This tactic enabled Nixon to approach Eisenhower from a position of political strength.[588] On April 26, 1956 Nixon met with Eisenhower and said, "Mr. President, I would be honored to continue as Vice President under you. The only reason I waited this long to tell you was that I didn't want to do anything that would make you think I was trying to force my way onto the ticket if you didn't want me on it."[589] Ike got on the phone and called his press secretary, saying, "Let's get an announcement out right away."[590] Eisenhower instructed Nixon to be there in the briefing room when the announcement was made, and the President added to the press secretary, "And you can tell them [the press] that I'm delighted by the news."[591] This would hardly seem like the response of someone who was looking to throw Nixon overboard, but it was an example of one of Ike's strengths as a leader. When confronted with the inevitable, one might as well make the best of it, and that was what Eisenhower was doing here. He would have preferred a less controversial running mate, but when the switch was no longer an option, Eisenhower embraced the situation. Though Eisenhower said of Nixon, "He knew of my high regard for him,"[592] Nixon had been deeply stung by Ike's seeming lack of strong support, again.

Though it would seem that the VP question had been settled there were some members of the Republican Party who were not quite ready to let it go. One man who was still uncomfortable was Harold Stassen, who had earlier expressed his support for Nixon. The political views that led Stassen to believe that a disarmament agreement with the Soviets was a realistic goal and compelled him to be conciliatory and trusting towards the Soviet Union made Nixon his polar opposite. Stassen was a believer in the progressive side of the Republican Party, but Nixon had risen to political power by beating the anti-Communist drum, and Nixon's association with Eisenhower almost forced him to become a caricature of himself. Eisenhower, a moderate by nature, wanted to be above political posturing, thus Nixon had to do both the mudslinging and all of the outreach work to the passionate anti-Communists among the electorate. Nixon played the good soldier, but it helped make him the lightning rod to the political left that he was.

Stassen went from thinking of Nixon as an acceptable substitute for Ike to viewing Nixon as more trouble than he was worth. Thus, Stassen was behind some of the talk of dumping Nixon from the ticket in 1956. What made Stassen's challenge especially frustrating for the Vice President was that it came in July; two months after Ike had supposedly settled the issue.[593] Stassen met with the President on the subject in the midst of tense negotiations Ike was worried about involving Gamal Abdel Nasser of Egypt. Special Assistant Arthur Larson met with Ike right after the President's meeting with Stassen. After a few minutes of agitated silence, Eisenhower asked, "Art, have you ever been Nasserized and Stassenized on the same day?"[594]

Despite his irritation, Eisenhower was slow to respond to this latest challenge against Nixon, not because he agreed with Stassen necessarily, but because of other factors. Ike thought it was too isolated to pay attention to at first, then when it became more of an issue, Eisenhower was away in Panama. Rather than supporting Stassen, Eisenhower suspended Stassen without pay once the President had returned.[595] To a degree, Ike's hand was forced when 180 of the 203 Republicans in the House of Representatives signed a letter endorsing Nixon.[596] But Stassen's choice, Governor Christian Herter of Massachusetts, still asked Ike what he thought of a Herter vice presidency. Eisenhower offered

Herter both the carrot and the stick, saying that he was interested in having Herter involved in the administration's foreign affairs, but that would not be an option if Herter challenged Nixon. Herter decided to be the one to nominate Nixon for the vice presidency at the Republican National Convention. It was a smart move by Herter—in 1957 he was made Under Secretary of State, and in 1959 he became Secretary of State.[597] At the Republican National Convention, Nixon was voted in for another campaign by a margin of 1323 to 1.[598]

Nixon was not there to enjoy his victory because of the deterioration of his father's health. Nixon left San Francisco, the site of the Republican Convention, and went to Whittier Hospital to find his 78-year-old father clinging to life in an oxygen tent. "You get back there, Dick," Frank Nixon urged his son, "and don't let that Stassen pull any more last-minute funny business on you." Frank Nixon was just a few days from death, and he had the stress of his son's political future weighing on him. Obviously, Harold Stassen had no animosity toward the elder Nixon, but Stassen's actions could be perceived as hastening Frank Nixon's death. Once again, Richard Nixon was reminded that politics was a mean game.[599] Nixon liked politics because he was such a battler, but to a degree he was also such a battler because he liked politics.

Being in the throes of a campaign, Nixon had to deal with his grief quickly. As it turned out, Nixon's responsibilities in the 1956 race were greater than those of a typical Vice President. Eisenhower wanted to keep his own campaigning to a bare minimum again because he still wanted to present himself to the public as presidential and above the political fray. Also, the President's doctors insisted that he needed more rest than usual because of his age and health. This was more than enough of an excuse for Eisenhower to limit his focus to presidential matters and let others slug it out in the political arena.[600]

Complicating matters even further for Nixon, Eisenhower was just too popular for his Democratic rival, Governor Adlai Stevenson, to have much success running against. Stevenson attacked Ike's views on domestic policy, but Stevenson had little substance to offer. Eisenhower believed that many of the New Deal programs, like Social Security, were too popular to attack, so he was not condemning the programs that Stevenson supported.[601] And Stevenson was not going to get anywhere attacking the foreign policy of the World War Two hero either.

Political attacks on Ike might have irritated him personally, but they did not do enough to the polls, so Stevenson chose to focus his campaign on the combination of Ike's health and the likelihood of Nixon's ascendancy. Instead of offering an alternative to the beloved Eisenhower's policies or vision, Stevenson attacked the controversial Nixon, calling the Vice President "this nation's life insurance policy."[602]

It was during this 1956 election that Nixon employed Bob Haldeman, the man who would eventually become his Chief of Staff when Nixon won the presidency in 1968. Haldeman's first meaningful, personal interaction with Nixon came during the Republican National Convention in San Francisco where Haldeman hoped to become an advance man for Nixon.[603] Haldeman was able to arrange a meeting through one of Nixon's secretaries, Loie Gaunt, who Haldman knew from his UCLA days.[604] But this first visit with the future President was not a good one. As Haldeman put it, Nixon "rambled...incoherently" to a degree that convinced Haldeman that Nixon was drunk. But Haldeman later wrote that he believed Nixon was not much of a drinker at all. Nixon's problem was that he would sometimes get overly fatigued.[605] This is certainly believable given the stress Nixon was under at the 1956 convention, his father's poor health and death, and the fact that Nixon was an insomniac.

Haldeman was drawn to support Nixon's cause in 1956, but it was not so much Nixon's ideology as the fact that Nixon was a fellow Californian and a fighter.[606] Haldeman took a leave of absence from his advertising firm, J. Walter Thompson, where he was not quite happy anyway, and went to work for Nixon through the rest of the campaign season.[607] Haldeman went to some lengths in his account of Watergate to point out that he was not overly interested in politics.[608] Perhaps he felt that this would make him seem more human to his critics in the country. But, if true, it might have contributed to part of the later problems in the Nixon White House. If Haldeman was not really committed to any great ideology, then what was he working towards in Washington? He was working for the success of Richard Nixon. The Nixon presidency became his cause. Was there anything else of value that would give his work meaning? Since he indicates that there was not, all of his values and priorities went into keeping Nixon going. Because this was more important to him than anything else, it is easy to see why he would make compromises. Keeping the Nixon administration in power mattered even more than the rule of law. The Nixon presidency became too important to Haldeman. But disaster was still far in the future in 1956.

Haldeman got the job as an advance man, which meant he would go into towns ahead of the Vice President and help handle logistics. Haldeman would make sure Nixon had a place to stay and that local officials would drum up audiences for speaking engagements, etc. Haldeman was successful at his job, which was good for Nixon in 1956 and good for Haldeman when Nixon's stock rose higher in the future.

Murray Chotiner, had been Nixon's campaign manager in 1946 when Nixon ran for his first office, a seat in the House of Representatives. But Chotiner was becoming damaged goods. He ran a tough campaign, which Nixon liked, but it also led to negative publicity and created more impassioned political enemies. In 1956, Chotiner was ordered to appear before a Senate Committee to face charges of influence peddling. By the time the 1960 campaign rolled around, Chotiner was too much of a negative to be associated with Nixon. This was something else that helped open the door for Haldeman.[609]

Eisenhower once again won the state of Texas, it was once again rumored that Democrat John Connally helped make that happen, and Connally once again denied it. But the rumors persisted,[610] and they were reinforced by the close relationship that Nixon and Connally would later develop. If Connally did support the Republicans in this race, he was hardly the only Democrat to do so. As one historian noted, "Farmers, intellectuals, and hard-core Democrats were about all who listened to Adlai."[611]

Eisenhower's reelection in 1956 with 57 percent of the popular vote demonstrated his enduring popularity, but the coattails of the President were not long enough for the Republican Party, which failed to control either house of Congress. It was the first time in over a century that a President had been elected without his party taking at least one of the houses. Eisenhower, who was watching the returns with his Vice President, had an explanation for the Republicans' failure in Congress. "You know why this is happening, Dick," said the President. "It's all those…hardshell conservatives we've got in the party. I think what we need is a new party."[612] So Eisenhower's belief in moderate Republicanism was reinforced by the election, and Nixon's work securing the votes of those "hardshell conservatives" was disparaged.

Eisenhower's election was to a degree at the expense of Nixon, who had been sent out to make partisan attacks on the opposition, while Ike was once again allowed to stay "presidential." Republican Party strategists had believed that their party needed a "hatchet man" who was not afraid to get rough with the Democrats. Eisenhower was not interested in the role, but as historian William Manchester put it, "the Vice President was chosen because he handled hatchets well."[613] Nixon's efforts reinforced his inclinations as a battler and kept him on the edge politically. Nixon was always trying to accomplish something in the partisan wars; he was always trying to get somewhere without ever enjoying the sensation of having arrived. That was a feeling that Ike reserved for himself, and not unjustifiably so, given his status as President and World War Two hero.

Nixon decided after seeing all of the results of the election—Democrats won 20 new House seats (they were hoping for 50) and two in the Senate—that there had to be a new way for Republicans to improve their fortunes. What they had to do better was public relations work. They needed to become masters of image. Such thinking helped to solidify Nixon's relationship with Haldeman and Haldeman's men.[614]

Life was not quite all about politics for Nixon in 1956. The Vice President's daughter Julie, who turned eight that year, gave her father a poem she wrote. The poem is noteworthy in that it does not fit the stereotype that many have of Nixon as a man with a perpetual black cloud over his head. While Nixon's daughter might be expected to be biased in his favor, it still seems evident from the poem below that the man was possessed with some level of charm.

Handsome and kind, Handsome and kind
Always on time,
Loving and good.
Does things he should,
Humorous and funny
Makes the day sunny,
Helping others to live,
Willing to give
His life,
For his beloved country,
That's my dad.[615]

Hopefully, the poem was an encouragement for a man who had gone through a rough four years. Either way, the worst was yet to come.

CHAPTER EIGHT

The Vice Presidency, Part II—1957-1961

Given all of his travels during his second term as VP, Nixon had less time to spend with his family than other Vice Presidents enjoyed. For example, Nixon took a month long trip to eight African nations in 1957. But, as was the case during his first four years as Vice President, at least he was getting a first rate political education as he prepared for a chance to be Eisenhower's successor.

While Nixon was growing as politician, Henry Kissinger was further establishing himself as a member of academia and a foreign affairs guru. Harvard hired Kissinger as a lecturer, but his job title was rather misleading. Along with a colleague, Kissinger had no responsibility during the 1957-1958 academic year for giving lectures to students. The two professors were supposed to start something called the Center for International Affairs, but Kissinger feuded with his colleague, Robert Bowie, and neglected his work. Kissinger was more interested in working on projects for Nelson Rockefeller, one of Nixon's rivals for power within the Republican Party. A Harvard colleague offered a fascinating characterization of Kissinger that was similar to the description William Safire offered for Kissinger in Chapter One, and it that certainly applied to Kissinger's relationships with Rockefeller and Bowie. Kissinger, said Leslie Gelb, was "devious with his peers, domineering with his subordinates, and obsequious to his superiors." Gelb felt that this was a result of Kissinger's "authoritarian background" growing up in Nazi Germany. Whatever his flaws, Kissinger was brilliant and extremely well connected, and he was tenured in Harvard after only two years, much more quickly than normal.[616]

President Eisenhower's health became an issue once again on November 25, 1957. Nixon was told he was needed at the White House and when he arrived Sherman Adams informed him that Ike had suffered a stroke. Nixon was told, "We'll know more in the morning. Right now he's more confused and disoriented than anything else. It will take a few days before the doctors can assess the damage. This is a terribly, terribly difficult thing to handle. You may be President in 24 hours."[617]

Ike survived, but it was not immediately clear that he would be healthy enough mentally to continue in the presidency. When Ike heard his prognosis, his first words were "This is the end. Mamie and I are farmers from now on." Nixon, now much more experienced and closer to his run for the presidency than he was during Ike's earlier health struggles, took a more active role in filling the gap in leadership. It was at this point that Nixon gave his first White House press conference and began fulfilling other presidential responsibilities.[618]

Though the nation had been sympathetic and supportive during Ike's earlier health difficulties, the mood was different this time. Nixon had more seasoning as a replacement for one thing. For another, the Soviets had just launched Sputnik, the first artificial satellite, which shook the confidence of many Americans in their technological superiority over their Cold War adversary. Strong leadership was needed, and it was looking increasingly like Richard Nixon could handle it. Many newspapers called on the President to resign. This aroused Eisenhower's competitive instincts. He talked about dying with his boots on and progressed quickly. Soon he was able to go about his normal duties.[619]

In response to this latest crisis, and with the realistic possibility that some other such problem might arise, Eisenhower wrote a letter for himself and Nixon, regarding the transfer of presidential authority should Ike become incapacitated. If a situation arose that they could plan for, like an operation, the President and Vice President could decide together when and for how long the Vice President would be in charge. If some unexpected, immediate situation arose, Nixon would make the decision alone. The existence of such a document proved unnecessary after the 25th Amendment was ratified in 1967, but it was a wise move by Eisenhower, and it shows that his opinion of Nixon might have been on the rise.[620]

In 1958 FBI Agent G. Gordon Liddy was transferred to Gary, Indiana, which he considered a promotion of sorts because it was away from a "headquarters city." The move conveyed to Liddy that the Bureau trusted him enough to have less oversight of him.[621] Gary, as Liddy described it, was a wild town full of corruption and crime, and for some reason "a target of Soviet bloc espionage."[622] The local authorities tolerated certain types of corruption for the right price, but both the authorities and the local crime figures would deal mercilessly with out of town criminals trying to move in on their turf.[623]

One can see the foreshadowing of the outlook that contributed to the Watergate break-ins when reading about Liddy's time in Gary. When investigating some car thieves, Liddy broke the case by, as he put it, not "hesitating to do whatever was necessary, including intimidating used car dealers so that I could cut through the floorboards of their cars to find secret serial numbers on the frames." He also broke into homes in search of clues for the case.[624] For Liddy, civil rights were overrated—the end justified the means.

One might not be shocked that a man who would go on to work for Richard Nixon would be willing to violate a few civil rights in his zeal to catch bad guys, but Liddy's reaction to Robert Kennedy was genuinely puzzling. Kennedy visited Gary to investigate allegations of corruption, and here was Liddy's response:

> Not long after he finished his work there, the Gary I knew was gone. Half the public officials had been convicted, and the old way of life—in which the victimless crimes of gambling and prostitution were tolerated and controlled and numerous ethnic groups coexisted, each with a piece of the pie—had been destroyed. Whether the current state of affairs in Gary is an improvement, I'll leave it to the judgment of those who live there today.[625]

The view that gambling and prostitution are "victimless" activities is certainly debatable, but even setting that aside, Liddy's preference for the wilder days in Gary is disturbing. It boggles the mind that a law enforcement official preferred a "frontier culture," especially when his own wife was almost gunned down in a shootout in front of a J. C. Penney's.[626] It is clear that Liddy preferred an environment where he could put himself through all sorts of personal tests. But to prefer to live in a world where the weak and innocent were likely to be hurt reflects a great degree of self-absorption, among other things.

As with Liddy, Henry Kissinger's career moved forward in 1958, too. Kissinger took over the Defense Studies Program at Harvard. He used the funding from this program and a couple of other accounts to pay for important men from Washington to come and speak to his students. This served as yet another means of networking for the professor. One of his guests was a Republican member of the House of Representatives named Gerald Ford.[627]

Chuck Colson became the chief aide of Senator Leverett Saltonstall in 1958. It was in this position that Colson first got to know Richard Nixon. Colson came up with the idea of having his boss, Saltonstall, interview important Washington figures. These interviews were taped and sent out to all the TV stations in Saltonstall's home state of Massachusetts. One of the interviewees was the Vice President. Colson later said, "I was awed by Nixon's dazzling ability. He had complete mastery of all the issues, he was quick in mind, and brilliant in his responses." As Jonathon Aitken, who wrote sympathetic biographies of both men, noted, "Not everyone took such a favorable view of Richard Nixon, but Colson was a true believer in him from the beginning."[628]

Nixon got several opportunities as Vice President to practice what he preached regarding getting tough with Communists. This occurred during May 1958 when he and Pat were on a tour of Latin America and when he met with Fidel Castro in the spring of 1959. Also, later in the summer of 1959, Nixon went to the Soviet Union and engaged in the "Kitchen Debate" with Nikita Khrushchev.

The Latin American trip in 1958 was not something Nixon was enthusiastic about when it was initially suggested to him. Nixon was more interested in lobbying the Cabinet into endorsing a tax cut to stimulate the economy. Nixon felt this was especially important with congressional elections coming later in the year. But Eisenhower intervened, stressing the importance of the trip, so Nixon relented. Once he agreed to go, government officials sought to expand the scope of the itinerary. Nixon ended up being scheduled to go to every country in South America except Brazil and Chile. Nixon had already visited with the Brazilian President in 1956 on behalf of Eisenhower, and the Chilean President had his own trip planned and was scheduled to be in Washington while Nixon was down in South America.[629] The goodwill tour in Latin America was a trying time for Richard and Pat Nixon, and it demonstrated both the best and worst traits in the Vice President almost simultaneously.

The first leg of the journey took the Nixons to Montevideo, Uruguay. Nixon visited the university there and met with students and faculty members. Some Communist students tried to disrupt the Vice President's appearance, but the majority of the crowd was favorable to Nixon and cheered him when he left. While in Uruguay, U.S. Ambassador Robert Woodward[630] told Nixon that South Americans respected bravery and were disgusted by male weakness.[631] Given Nixon's beliefs on how to handle Communists, this insight from the ambassador only reinforced Nixon's resolve when he encountered the South American variety.

Expecting difficulties in Peru, Nixon instructed his wife to remain at their hotel while he made the rounds. The trouble started for the Vice President at San Marcos University in Lima. A crowd of thousands alternated between chants of *"Fuera* Nixon*"* (Go home Nixon) and *"Muera* Nixon*"* (Kill Nixon). Nixon yelled back at them, saying "I want to talk to you! Why are you afraid of the truth?"[632] Several students began throwing rocks at Nixon's party, hitting some of them. Nixon was grazed along the throat,[633] and one of his Secret Service agents, Jack Sherwood, suffered a broken tooth. Nixon calmly instructed his people to slowly back towards their cars and leave. Nixon's cool headedness saved the day, but it had its limits. As his car sped away, Nixon stood up in the convertible—one of his men held the Vice President's legs so he would not fall out—and yelled at the students, "You are cowards! You are afraid of the truth!" His next stop in Lima went better. The crowd at Catholic University was pro-American and cheered Nixon when he entered the auditorium for a question and answer session.[634]

As Nixon's entourage returned to their hotel, they were again accosted by an angry mob. Nixon believed it was many of the same people who had disrupted things at San Marcos. As Nixon was about to enter the hotel, one of the demonstrators stepped in front of him and spit in his face. Pat Nixon, who watched the mob from her hotel room window, later commented, "It wasn't just hate those people had in their eyes. It was a sort of frenzy that frightened me."[635]

But Richard Nixon's rough reception had multiple silver linings. He had the exhilaration of contending with Communists and acting bravely. He also enjoyed a rebound effect with the Peruvian public. Embarrassed over how some of their countrymen had treated a foreign dignitary, Peruvians came out in large numbers and cheered for Nixon during the rest of his stops in Peru. Perhaps best of all to Nixon's psyche, he received a message from Eisenhower on his plane's radio telephone while traveling from Peru to Quito, Ecuador. The message said, "Dear Dick, Your courage, patience, and calmness in the demonstration directed against you by radical agitators have brought you a new respect and admiration in our country."[636]

The last stop on the Nixons' tour of Latin America was Venezuela. Nixon had been warned by Jacob Esterline, the CIA's station chief, to expect trouble. Esterline wanted Nixon to cancel this leg of the trip since the CIA had obtained information that local Communists were plotting to kill him. When Esterline persisted, he was told by one of Nixon's men to let the matter drop. But Esterline was still arguing his case the day before the Nixons were due in Caracas, the capital of Venezuela. Esterline was told by Allen Dulles, the Director of the CIA and a friend of Nixon's, that the Vice President and his wife were going through with the trip "for [his] own political purposes." Esterline later said, "It soured me on Nixon. I realized that he was driven above all by his ambition, his single-minded ambition to become President."[637]

In fairness to Nixon, though, he contacted the Venezuelans ahead of time and asked if they wanted to cancel the trip. They assured him that things would be okay.[638] Setting that issue aside, Nixon might not have only been thinking in the terms Esterline ascribed to him. For Nixon, it was a fundamental truth that the best way to deal with Communists was to stand up to them. The last thing he would want to do is retreat in the face of opposition. He believed that would send the wrong message and embolden Communists in future aggressions. To understand any politician, one must accept the need to balance principles and pragmatism. Nixon might have been looking for an opportunity to further his political fortunes, but he was also being true to his understanding of international relations.

On the morning of May 13 when Nixon's party landed in Caracas and got off the plane, Nixon wanted to head straight for the terminal, but the Venezuelan Army Band started playing the Star Spangled Banner followed by their own national anthem. The Nixons stood respectfully, but several Venezuelans were not quite as well-comported as their Yankee guests. Richard and Pat Nixon stood their ground as saliva—made brown from chewing tobacco—soaked them. They had been warned to expect trouble, and they stood up to it—it was Nixon at his best. But he did nothing to shield his wife as her new red suit was soiled and people spat in her face—Nixon at his worst. Whatever it means to be presidential, it should not include letting your spouse be treated that way. Politicians' spouses expect to make sacrifices, but with Richard Nixon it was virtually always politics before marital considerations.[639]

When the songs were over, the Americans headed for their waiting cars. A young woman intercepted Pat Nixon and spat in her face. Instead of brushing past her or retaliating, the Vice President's wife put her hand on the shoulder of her attacker and looked into the woman's eyes. After the Vice President's wife made herself seem more human to the young woman, and not just an object of hate, the Venezuelan turned away, embarrassed by her actions.

With the Nixons in different vehicles, their entourage made its way from the airport. They were intercepted by a mob that blocked their path, hurled rocks at their cars, then grabbed hold of the Vice President's car and began to shake it. As the mob hit the car windows with a lead pipe and more rocks, they chanted "*Muera* Nixon." The Secret Service agents traveling with Nixon wanted to start shooting the rioters, but Nixon insisted that they refrain from doing so. The men did not have enough bullets for the entire mob, and Nixon did not want to provoke the demonstrators any further. Even if the had been broken up in the face of American gunfire, Nixon's decision was still laudable—he saved lives.[640]

Several cars behind Nixon, the ever faithful Rose Mary Woods was cut by broken glass. In the car right behind the Vice President, Pat Nixon was uninjured, despite the efforts of the mob. After twelve minutes of uncertainty, the police escort that had been swallowed up by the crowd reappeared and began to create a path for Nixon's party to follow.[641] As the cars began to move forward again, the Secret Service man in Nixon's car said, "I hope Mrs. Nixon gets through." Nixon allegedly replied, "If she doesn't, it can't be helped."[642] Of course, quotations cannot always convey tone and meaning, so even if the Vice President made this remark, it is unclear whether he was trying to convey stoic bravery or if he was just afraid and was refusing to go back.

Rather than just assume the worst about Nixon, there are a couple of things worth noting. The Vice President had demanded that Pat's car be right behind his, even though it was protocol for the car behind him to just contain Secret Service men. Thus, Nixon was lessening the proximity of the maximum number of defenders, and he was putting his wife more safely within a cocoon of protection.[643] Also, when the path was cleared for Nixon's entourage to proceed, he decided to scuttle his schedule in the face of such hostility. When the entourage had gotten away from the mobs, Nixon had his driver pull over, so he could check on his wife.[644]

Nixon decided at that point to head for the American embassy. When some of Venezuela's leading officials were on their way to see Nixon, it was suggested that Nixon's car with its dents and broken windows be removed from view in front of the embassy. The diplomats did not want the Venezuelans embarrassed. But Nixon said he wanted the Venezuelans "to understand what they were facing from Communist agitators."[645]

Later that day Nixon spoke to Venezuelan officials and American businessmen operating in Venezuela. Nixon said he did not believe that the rioters were Communists. He believed that because they were so poor and desperate that they had become tools of the Communists. The Communists could build on the frustrations of oppressed people to foment Marxist revolution. Thus, Nixon said, "It is essential to adopt practices which are above the suspicion of any charges of exploitation of the workers."[646] Saying that most individual rioters were not themselves Communists was a subtle distinction, and it was noteworthy from someone who had just faced a life threatening situation and was known for always seeing Red. Despite Nixon's conservative credentials, liberal politicians could have uttered such words without raising any eyebrows.

Back in the United States, Nixon's troubles, and his handling of them, were being closely followed. Eisenhower responded to the physical threats against Nixon and his party by sending a fleet to the Venezuelan coast, but the crisis was over. When Nixon returned to the U.S., his popularity had surged upward, as had the favorability of his press coverage. When Nixon landed at Andrews Air Force Base, he was greeted with a hug by a recent critic of his, Senate Majority Leader Lyndon Johnson.[647] Eisenhower was also there to greet the Vice President and welcome him home, though no hugging took place between the two of them. A supportive crowd held signs saying things like "Don't let those Commies get you down, Dick" and "Communist cowardice loses—Nixon courage wins."[648]

Despite the positive boost for Nixon's popularity, the Republican Party was headed for trouble. It is worth noting that Eisenhower and Nixon were both in agreement in a lot of areas regarding how the Republican Party should deal with its state of affairs in 1958. They both had similar ideas on the organization of campaigns, the raising and spending of money, and the necessity of analyzing past campaigns and learning from their mistakes.[649] One key area where they differed, however, was in how they dealt with the campaign season. Eisenhower adopted his usual, aloof approach to the elections, whereas Nixon campaigned heavily for his fellow Republicans. Thus, when the Republicans fared poorly, Nixon was tied to that failure. In fact, fellow Republican Tom Dewey warned Nixon not to go down with the sinking ship. Said Dewey, "You're toying with your chance to be President. Don't do it, Dick. You've already done enough, and 1960 is what counts now." Dewey was concerned that the problems the country faced, a soft economy, a lame duck President whose popularity was on the decline, etc., would be too much for even a seasoned campaigner like Nixon to overcome.[650]

Nixon the Battler decided to do what he could for the Republican Party anyway. His decision to campaign led to yet another uncomfortable situation with Eisenhower. Nixon attacked the Democratic Advisory Council, which had made a foreign policy statement that was at odds with the Eisenhower administration's policy. Nixon accused the DAC's members of having "the same defensive, defeatist, fuzzy-headed thinking which contributed to the loss of China and led to the Korean War." When the media asked Ike about Nixon's speech, Ike distanced himself from his VP, saying, "Foreign policy ought to be kept out of partisan debate."[651]

Eisenhower followed this up with a telegram to Nixon claiming the President had been misunderstood, but Nixon refused to let Eisenhower have his cake and eat it too. The Vice President called Secretary of State Dulles and told him that unless Ike came out and publicly supported Nixon, the Vice President would make it known that Eisenhower and Dulles had told him to fight for the Administration's foreign policy. Nixon got the public statement from Eisenhower. Nevertheless, Ike's dislike of campaigning, and the mixed messages coming from on high only made a bad situation worse for Republicans in 1958. They fared even more poorly in the congressional elections than they had anticipated.[652]

Though his party had taken a beating from the Democrats, Nixon was not done fighting. Nixon's next showdown was once again with Latin American communism, but this time it took place in Washington. Fidel Castro had taken over Cuba in January 1959. In April of that year he was invited to Washington to speak to the American Society of Newspaper Editors. Eisenhower refused to meet with the dictator, but Nixon did at the urging of the new Secretary of State, Chris Herter. Whatever Herter hoped would be accomplished, he was disappointed. Nixon, not exactly renowned for his tact, wanted to know why Castro would not hold free elections, and Castro replied that, "The people did not want elections because elections in the past had produced bad government." After three hours of dialogue characterized by blunt, undiplomatic questions and propagandistic answers, Nixon walked away with an impression of Castro as a born leader, but Nixon also saw him as "incredibly naive about communism" and possessing an "obvious lack of understanding of even the most elementary economic principles."[653]

Fresh off his meeting with Castro, Nixon prepared to go to Moscow in July 1959 for the American National Exhibition. This was going to be one of the biggest events in Nixon's life up to this point because it would give him the opportunity to talk to Eisenhower's counterpart, the leader of the communist world—Nikita Khrushchev. Not only did Nixon get briefings from the CIA and the State Department, he also talked with everybody else he knew who had met Khrushchev. Nixon looked over the writings of the Communists' giants, Marx, Lenin, and Stalin, and both the Vice President and Pat Nixon learned a few Russian phrases.[654] Harvard Professor William Y. Elliot recommended that Nixon read a 1957 bestseller, *Nuclear Weapons and Foreign Policy,*[655] and meet with its author. Nixon did not set up that meeting, but Nixon would eventually make the author, Henry Kissinger, a key figure in his administration.[656] In general, as Nixon prepared for his meeting with Khrushchev, he thought of one of Eisenhower's favorite maxims, "In preparing for battle I have always found that plans are useless, but planning is indispensable."[657]

Nixon's perception of Khrushchev was not just based on ideology and American research. In 1956 the Vice President had traveled to Austria to get an idea of what was going on in neighboring Hungary. The Hungarian people had tried to rise up against Soviet domination, but were crushed ruthlessly. It was after seeing the miserable and frightened refugees streaming across the border and hearing their stories that Nixon called Khrushchev "the Butcher of Budapest."[658]

During their first meeting, which took place at the Kremlin, Khrushchev was upset that the U.S. Congress had just passed its annual Captive Nations resolution, which was a statement of support of those Eastern Europeans that suffered under Soviet oppression. Khrushchev, who sometimes engaged in crude language and bullying behavior, blustered on about U.S. foreign policy and the need for the Soviet Union to be ready for war. Nixon tried to change the subject to something more pleasant, but Khrushchev persisted as the conversation went downhill to salty references pertaining to barnyard excrement. Nixon's willingness to match crudities with Khrushchev seemed to earn the respect of the Premier.[659]

Nixon's next encounter with Premier Khrushchev took place at the American Exhibition, which displayed items and things from America like household rooms. The exhibit was designed to promote trade between the two countries.[660] The exchange between Nixon and Khrushchev culminated in the famous Kitchen Debate. This debate was orchestrated by a young American public relations man named William Safire who went on to become one of Nixon's main speech writers years later.[661] As the two argued about the merits of their countries, several Americans there were quite impressed by Nixon. Safire said, "Nixon was superb…cornball though it sounds, he made me feel proud of my country." Don Kendall, the President of Pepsi Cola International, was there because Pepsi had a stand in the exhibit, and he said of Nixon, "He stood toe to toe with Khrushchev and really dished it out to him."[662]

Not every American present was impressed, however. Milton Eisenhower, who was the President's brother and no friend of Nixon, felt that Nixon's responses were extremely undiplomatic. But Nixon was allowed to go on Soviet radio and TV and give an uncensored speech, so he had not alienated his hosts too much. Nixon praised the Russian people then complained about Soviet censorship. It was typical of Nixon—his belief that Communists respected confrontation more than diplomatic congeniality drove him to use his time on Soviet airwaves to challenge his hosts.

During one of their lunches, Milton Eisenhower tried a softer approach. He responded to Khrushchev's almost unrelenting militarism by talking about Dwight Eisnehower's fifty years of service to America. Milton said he prayed for a miracle to occur before Ike's term ended—a miracle that would ensure world peace. Nixon watched Khrushchev as Milton spoke, and noted that despite the fact that the American delegation was moved, Khrushchev seemed unimpressed. The message was driven home for Nixon once again: Communists respected strength, not sensitivity, which they saw as weakness.[663]

As Richard Nixon was worn down by his travels and the general grind of the vice presidency and political life, his friendship with Bebe Rebozo deepened. Rebozo was comfortable sitting quietly through one of Nixon's rambling monologues or just sitting in silence. Historian Herbert S. Parmet noted the reciprocity of the relationship. "Bebe was clearly happy to be at the edge of power, and Nixon for his own part, could unburden himself without guilt. His friend was a refuge, a source of complete trust."[664]

For the 1960 presidential campaign, Bob Haldeman, who once again went on leave from the advertising firm of J. Walter Thompson,[665] was made Nixon's chief advance man. Haldeman picked a friend from his UCLA days, John Ehrlichman, to also work as an advance man for Nixon. Haldeman caught his old friend at just the right time. Ehrlichman seemed to have a lot going for him. He was a husband and father with a successful legal career. He was a devout member of the Christian Science faith, even teaching Sunday school. But Ehrlichman was bored. Civilian life was not as stimulating as flying combat missions over Europe during World War Two. Ehrlichman wanted a challenge. Ehrlichman later wrote that he basically signed on to the Nixon campaign because he wanted excitement. Regarding the Vice President, Ehrlichman wrote, "I was neither his strong supporter nor even an active Republican."[666] In other words both Haldeman and Ehrlichman, men who were destined to become Nixon's most trusted advisors, were not really interested in the issues or drawn to Nixon as a person. It was all about the thrill of the political competition. There were no political causes larger than themselves that they sought to serve. There was no great love for the man who was Richard Nixon, and thus no concern about what was best for him personally. At least, that was how Haldeman and Ehrlichman described it years later, after the pains of Watergate and what it did to their careers.

As with Haldeman, Nixon did not make a stellar first impression on Ehrlichman. As Ehrlichman later described it, he and the VP met in an elevator in Milwaukee. Nixon stared at the floor until Haldeman introduced Ehrlichman. Nixon looked up, said, "Oh, yes. Fine. How are you?" Then Nixon looked away and was again lost in thought. Though Erhlichman saw Nixon several more times during the campaign, the two men never had a substantive conversation until 1962.[667]

Ehrlichman's first big assignment, and one that gave him the kind of excitement he was craving, was to infiltrate the organization of New York Governor Nelson Rockefeller, a moderate Republican who was interested in the Republican nomination for the presidency in 1960. The high point for Ehrlichman occurred in North Dakota where he became a driver in Rockefeller's motorcade. As Ehrlichman described it, "Oh, it was wonderful. The Rockefeller people thought I was from North Dakota, and the North Dakota people thought I was with Rockefeller."[668] Later, Ehrlichman went to the Democratic National Convention, again in an effort to spy on Nixon's competition and give first hand accounts to Haldeman. Ehrlichman contended that overall, though, "The Kennedy fellows were really much better at the dirty stuff than we were."[669] This type of spying was common in American politics in the 1960s, and it is interesting that this was Ehrlichman's introduction to working for Richard Nixon.

Another prominent Watergate figure who joined Nixon in the 1960 campaign was Jeb Stuart Magruder. He was like a younger version of Ehrlichman in a lot of ways. Magruder had served in the military, and he was a churchgoing man who was successful at his job. Magruder's business, though, was selling paper products to wholesalers for the Crown Zellerbach Corporation. Like Ehrlichman, Magruder was bored with the working world and turned in the fall of 1960 to the Nixon presidential campaign, looking for action. Again like Ehrlichman, Magruder was not overly enamored with Richard Nixon. Wrote Magruder, "I had no strong feelings for Nixon at that point, but he seemed well qualified to be President...Certainly I preferred him to Kennedy."[670]

Magruder became the chairman for a ward in Kansas City, taking charge in one precinct and directing the volunteers in neighboring precincts. He enjoyed his responsibilities—doing things like passing out pamphlets, door to door campaigning, and driving people to the polls on Election Day. Though this kind of work was not for everybody, Magruder found it stimulating. At the very least, he thought it was more interesting than pushing paper products, thus leaving himself ripe for the plucking for future campaigns.[671]

In a way, G. Gordon Liddy began working for Nixon in the election of 1960. One of the dirty tricks that Nixon got burned by in 1960 was a flyer regarding the deed on the house the Nixons owned in Washington

DC. The deed included language that basically said the house and property could not be re-sold to African Americans. Previously, the Supreme Court had issued a ruling saying that such language was unenforceable and therefore meaningless. Because the prejudiced language did not matter, there was essentially nothing racist about Nixon owning the house. Nevertheless, a flyer of the deed was circulated in African American communities with the words "FOR SHAME" written in red. In addition to being a dirty trick, the flyers violated a campaign law that said that the producers of political flyers had to identify themselves on their flyers. FBI Agent Liddy was put on the case, but he could not prove that the Kennedys, the obvious beneficiaries of the flyers, were involved.[672] Thus, Liddy saw how some people played the game, and he could not say that it violated his own system of end-justifies-the-means ethics.

To some, Chuck Colson seemed to be working against Nixon in 1960, but that was not really the case. Colson described Nixon as "a man of uncommon intellect and capacity with visions for his country and party, which I enthusiastically shared."[673] In the late 1950s, Colson had worked so well for Senator[674] Leverett Saltonstall that by the 1960 campaign, Colson was managing the Senator's re-election bid. In an effort to get votes for his candidate, Colson was guilty of the kind of political campaign crime that Liddy had investigated. In Colson's autobiography he openly admitted being guilty of "several bogus mailings."[675] For example, he got six leading Irish Democrats to write a letter supporting Kennedy in the presidential race but also supporting Saltonstall for the Senate race, and these letters were mailed to 300,000 Irish families. Though Kennedy and Saltonstall were members of different parties, their names had been linked frequently because of their cooperation in the passing of pork barrel legislation, or as Colson put it, "federal goodies" for the people of Massachusetts. Colson figured he could take advantage of Kennedy's popularity to help Saltonstall in a state that Nixon was sure to lose anyway.[676]

Saltonstall did not even know his campaign manager was behind this project since Colson never told him, and Colson failed to identify on the letters who had produced them. A last minute problem occurred when one of Colson's workers told him that a young female volunteer was threatening to blow the whistle because she thought his scheme was disloyal to Nixon. Colson had informed Nixon's people of his little project, but he did not want his ploy exposed to the public, so he gave the man who told him about the young woman $100—an impressive sum in 1960—to take the woman out and get her drunk. Colson felt it was a worthwhile investment when his candidate won the election.[677]

John Connally was not working with Richard Nixon in 1960, but Connally was working against John Kennedy, at least for awhile. Connally, who had spent the better part of the 1950s primarily concerned with being successful in business, became the campaign manager for Lyndon Johnson during the Democratic primaries. After Johnson conceded defeat and joined Kennedy's ticket, Connally stuck with his patron. Thanks in part to Connally's efforts the Kennedy-Johnson team won Texas in the 1960 presidential race by 50,000 votes.[678]

Another future Nixon insider who had little to do with Republican politics in the 1950s was John Mitchell. One of Mitchell's more significant achievements of the decade was helping Wisconsin improve its borrowing system through the creation of new legislation.[679]

It comes as a surprise to many 21st century young people that the presidential election of 1960 was extremely close. Contemporary students see a race between "that Watergate guy" and the young, handsome, charismatic Kennedy, and they cannot understand why it was not a landslide for the Democrat. But Nixon had a lot going for him. He was the Vice President of the beloved Eisenhower, and Nixon had gained valuable experience as the *de facto* campaigner-in-chief of his party for the last several national elections. The Nixon campaign also had some star power, primarily through the Celebrities for Nixon Committee, which included movie stars like Helen Hayes, John Wayne, Mary Pickford, and Gordon MacRae. There was another celebrity who opted not to join the group because he had been a committed Democrat, but his intense dislike of communism attracted him to Nixon, and he ended up giving some speeches for the Republican candidate. The celebrity's name was Ronald Reagan.[680] Jackie Robinson, the first African American Major League Baseball player, was yet another famous Nixon supporter.

The Kennedy family had a tremendous amount of money to invest in the campaign, but Nixon was not at a complete disadvantage here. The Republicans had generally gotten more support from Big Business than the Democrats since the days of the Grant administration, and the perception of John Kennedy as being anti-business did nothing to counteract that trend.[681]

Despite his advantages, though, Nixon lost in a squeaker. Jonathan Aitken, a member of the British Parliament who wrote a biography of Nixon, cleverly described Nixon's problems. Aitken wrote, "The old saying that victory has a hundred fathers but defeat is an orphan was reversed in the Republican postmortems. At least a hundred excuses and 'if onlys' could be attached to Nixon's defeat, while Kennedy's victory had the one big question mark of electoral fraud hanging over it." Aitken went on to list six factors that did not work out in Nixon's favor: the candidate's health, the TV debates, the Catholic vote, the African American vote, the vice presidential race, and Eisenhower's role.[682] There were other factors that plagued Nixon as well. The Vice President suffered from an ill-considered promise that he would have been better off breaking about how extensively he would campaign. Nixon had a personality that worked against him. It has also been suggested that Howard Hughes' loan to the Vice President's brother, Don, was a factor in Nixon's loss. Some have argued that press bias was yet another obstacle for Richard Nixon in 1960. Finally, there was the well-documented voter fraud that aided Kennedy.

While campaigning in North Carolina in August, Nixon bumped his knee getting into a car. He thought little of it at the time, but within two weeks he was hospitalized at Walter Reed with a serious knee infection. Two weeks in bed put him behind in his campaigning, and Kennedy regained the lead in their seesaw struggle. The first week out of the hospital Nixon visited 14 states, even though he was running a fever of 103 degrees. The next week he hit 11 more states. It was at the end of this grueling two week period that the sweaty, undernourished Nixon had his first TV debate with the tanned, well-rested Kennedy.[683]

The Democrats had proposed that the finalists from the two major parties' conventions should engage in the first ever televised presidential debates. Even though this would benefit the Democrats by raising the visibility of their more obscure candidate to an equal position with the two-term Vice President, Nixon favored the idea. Nixon, the lifelong debater, thought he could get the better of John Kennedy after the Vice President watched Kennedy's acceptance speech at the Democratic National Convention on July 16. Senator Kennedy looked fatigued, and Nixon thought Kennedy's Massachusetts-and-Harvard accent, and his penchant for big words, would be off putting to Middle America.[684]

NIXON AND HIS MEN

Obviously, Nixon miscalculated, but it seemed like a smart move to him at the time.

The contrast between the two men during their first debate was made even greater by the fact that Kennedy wore makeup, and Nixon refused at first before permitting some powder. The powder was intended to cover his five o'clock shadow but ultimately just made the feverish Nixon look even more pale. One might be surprised at Nixon's reluctance to wear makeup since he was a former community theater actor, but Nixon was once almost blinded by a clumsy makeup artist with a powder puff. Perhaps Nixon's biggest mistake regarding his makeup that night was asking Robert Kennedy if the powder job looked good. The brother of Nixon's challenger said with a smile, "Dick, you look great! Don't change a thing!" But Nixon did not look great. His mother called Nixon's secretary, Rose Mary Woods, the next day and asked if the Vice President was ill. Nixon's running mate, Henry Cabot Lodge cursed Nixon after watching the debate and said Nixon "has just cost us the election."[685]

Despite the big deal that is made of the Kennedy-Nixon debates, in the end their importance on the election is overstated. Before the first debate, Kennedy was already ahead in the polls, 51% to 49%,[686] and the vote on Election Day was closer than that. Any damage Kennedy was able to inflict on Nixon was offset by other factors in the end.

One would think that Kennedy's Catholicism would have hurt him against the Protestant Nixon since the United States had never elected a Catholic President. Besides the unfocused religious bigotry against anyone who was not Protestant, there was a specific theme that anti-Catholics could hammer away at in a presidential election. Would a good Catholic President have to subordinate American policies to the will of his Pope? Conversely, if a Catholic President would not listen to the head of his Church, he could be categorized as insincere in his Christian beliefs. It was a perfect Catch-22 for anti-Catholics to stick Kennedy with.

There was anti-Catholic propaganda floating around, but the Vice President himself once again defied contemporary and subsequent stereotypes by taking the high road on the Catholic issue. On a "Meet the Press" broadcast on September 11, 1960, Nixon said, "I have no doubt whatever about Senator Kennedy's loyalty or his ability to put the Constitution of the United States above any consideration." He said he had told his supporters "not to discuss religion, not to raise it, not to allow anybody to participate in the campaign who does so."[687] These were hardly the words of someone who wanted to capitalize on religious bigotry.

Unfortunately for the Vice President, after Nixon took the issue off the table, Kennedy put it back on. The Kennedy campaign asked Catholics to demonstrate their religious loyalty by voting for JFK, and Protestants were asked to vote for the Senator to demonstrate their lack of prejudice. Nixon never responded to Kennedy's use of the religion card, and it hurt the Vice President. In 1956, Ike had won 60% of the Catholic vote; in 1960 Nixon won just 22%. In the hotly contested state of Illinois, Kennedy beat Nixon by about 8000 votes out of 4.7 million, and Chicago had a significant Catholic population.[688]

Nixon also did more poorly than he anticipated with another demographic group: African Americans. Despite the facts that Ike had won 40% of the African American vote in 1956, and Nixon fought for the Civil Rights Act of 1957, Nixon only won 20 to 25% of the African American vote in 1960.[689] This poor showing by Nixon would have been a surprise after Nixon's statement at the Republican National Convention. The Vice President said, "I believe," he told reporters, "it is essential that the Republican Convention adopt a strong Civil Rights platform, an honest one, which deals specifically and not in generalities with the problems and goals that we desire to reach in these fields."[690] Despite Nixon's words, the African American community turned away from him by and large for two other reasons besides the flyer incident that Gordon Liddy investigated. One was that Nixon lost at vote buying. Frequently, both of the major political parties would send money to black churches in an effort to get the support of African American ministers. It could be explained as less crass than it sounds. Such funds could be used for worthwhile ministries, and it would make sense that the churches' ministers would want to inform their parishioners of the support they had received. As a result, the parishioners would be charitably inclined to certain politicians on Election Day. When Republican Party chairman Len Hall made payments to churches, John Kennedy's rich father, Joe, would come behind him and give the churches more money. According to Hall, "I've never seen anything like it. I've paid these fellows more than they ever got before and Joe Kennedy's…raised me every time. We didn't get one of 'em."[691]

The other reason Nixon did so poorly among African Americans was due to how he and John Kennedy responded when Martin Luther King,

Jr. was arrested for his involvement in a sit-in at an Atlanta department store. On October 26 the judge in the case sentenced King to serve four months in prison for violating his parole (King had been cited earlier for driving without a license). John Kennedy called King's wife, Coretta, and assured her of his support. Kennedy's brother Robert called the judge and asked for leniency. Kennedy told the judge that his family was concerned for King's safety while he was in prison. Nixon publicly did nothing, he said, because he wanted to respect the American Bar Association's rules of conduct. Of course he also might have been reluctant to alienate southern whites. Instead Nixon quietly asked the Attorney General, William Rogers to have the Justice Department get involved. Rogers agreed to this, but the White House dragged its feet authorizing it. When the judge decided to release King, the Kennedys looked like heroes, and Nixon looked indifferent. Though the white media virtually ignored this story, African American newspapers gave it a lot of attention. Feelings were passionate enough that Martin Luther King, Sr. retracted his endorsement of Nixon and gave it to John Kennedy instead, saying, "I've got a suitcase of votes and I'm going to take them to Mr. Kennedy and dump them in his lap."[692] Another key supporter lost by Nixon at this point was Jackie Robinson, the baseball player and heretofore a Republican.[693]

Generally, media figures make more out of vice presidential choices and races than voters do. Few vice presidential candidates if any created more of an uproar than Dan Quayle—George Bush's Vice President—yet many of the people who complained the loudest about Quayle would not have voted for Bush anyway. The point is that the vice presidential candidates did not turn the election of 1960 by themselves. But the two men, Republican Henry Cabot Lodge and Democrat Lyndon B. Johnson, did have an impact.

Actually, one of the men Nixon considered for the VP role was a friend from Nixon's days in the House of Representatives, Nixon's future Vice President Gerald Ford, but Ford did not make the short list in 1960.[694] Eisenhower had strongly advocated the choice of Lodge because of their shared moderate outlook and because of Lodge's foreign affairs background. The choice also looked good because Lodge was from Massachusetts, which provided good regional balance with Nixon the Californian. But Lodge was a terrible campaigner. During a speech in Harlem on September 12, Lodge said, "There should be a Negro in the

Cabinet…it is offered as a pledge." But this pledge was not cleared with Nixon who was quite angry when he heard about it. Nixon responded that "the best men possible" would be picked for the Cabinet. Nixon promised that "a man's race or religion would not be a factor either for or against him."[695]

Given mistakes such as this one by Lodge, it was perhaps best that he shared another characteristic with Ike: a disdain for campaigning. Instead of pouring his energy into the race, Lodge frequently took weekends off. He also used to nap in the afternoon. In contrast, Lyndon Johnson campaigned hard and smart throughout the South. Johnson added energy to his party's ticket in a way that Lodge never did.[696]

One thing Nixon struggled with was a question that has haunted several Vice Presidents seeking the highest American office—what kind of relationship is their boss supposed to have to the campaign effort? For example, in 1988 did George Bush want to try to sell the American public on a George Bush administration, or did he want to cast himself in the leading role in what would essentially be Ronald Reagan's third term? Bush opted to be closely associated with Reagan, and Bush became President. But that left the Republican Party expecting conservative leadership, and Bush's moderate policies left them feeling betrayed, which was a feeling they reciprocated at the polls in 1992. In 2000, Al Gore was worried that the public was tired of the Clinton scandals, so Gore distanced himself from the man who was very popular in Democratic circles, and the Vice President ended up losing a close election. Nixon's efforts to define himself in regard to Eisenhower were complicated both by Ike's health and the lukewarm relationship between the two men.

Nixon believed Ike's popularity was an important ingredient to winning the 1960 election, but the two men had never gotten close personally or politically. The initial response from Eisenhower's people to Nixon's staff when help was requested was that Nixon should "campaign as a man in his own right, not as Eisenhower's little boy."[697] Ike had planned to make some token appearances and remarks, but nothing more than that. The eight years together did not do enough to close the gap between Eisenhower and Nixon. Eisenhower had tried to relate to Nixon through fishing, but that had been a disaster, and Ike just never really pursued a genuine friendship after that, either because of the difference in their ages, Nixon's personality, or some combination of the two. As Theodore White noted about Nixon, "In eight years as

Eisenhower's roughneck partner, he was never once invited upstairs to the parlor floor where Presidents entertain their friends. That galled." Eisenhower once hosted a political rally at his farm in Gettysburg. Afterwards, when he invited some friends inside, he left out his Vice President, who was quite upset at the snub.[698]

When the election seemed to be turning in the Democrats' favor, though, Eisenhower changed his mind about campaigning. Ike did not want to see Kennedy win, especially after Kennedy began to attack the policies of the Eisenhower administration. The most galling charge was Kennedy's falsehood that there was a missile gap between the Soviet Union and the United States that favored the Soviets. However, the night before Eisenhower and Nixon were scheduled to meet to discuss an expanded campaign schedule for Ike, Mamie Eisenhower called Pat Nixon, and said that physically Ike could not handle campaigning. Mrs. Eisenhower wanted the Nixons to stop her husband, but she told the Vice President's wife, "He must never know I called you." The Vice President received virtually the same message from Ike's White House physician the next morning.[699]

At the meeting, which took place on October 31, 1960, Nixon shocked both Ike and Len Hall by saying, "Mr. President, I think you've done enough already."[700] Nixon could tell that Ike was surprised and upset, especially since the President had gotten so worked up about joining the fight, but the best that the Vice President could follow up with were, as Nixon himself acknowledged, "some lame excuses."[701] The meeting ended quickly, and Eisenhower was livid. He expected to save the day, not get dismissed. He confronted Len Hall, who had set up the meeting, and wanted an explanation. The President's embarrassment brought out the worst in him as he imitated the Vice President's hunched posture and asked, "Did you see that? When I had a frontline officer like that in World War Two, I relieved him."[702] Mamie Eisenhower finally told her husband that Nixon was just looking out for Ike's health, but it was not until years later.[703]

There was one thing that hurt Nixon's campaign that only Nixon himself was responsible for. While giving his acceptance speech at the Republican National Convention, Nixon said, "I pledge to you that I personally will carry this campaign into every one of the fifty states of this nation between now and November 8." Nixon made good on his promise to visit all 50 states, traveling over 65,000 miles. He delivered 180 scheduled speeches and dozens of unscheduled speeches and press conferences.[704]

Nixon felt it would be such a close election that every state was important, and he wanted to create a contrast between the older Eisenhower with whom he was associated and his own youthful vigor.[705] But it was a mistake. There were certain states that everyone knew were locked in to one candidate or the other. The more logical course of action would have been to concentrate on the states where the outcome was still in doubt. While Kennedy was campaigning in key states in the Midwest and Northeast and drawing big crowds, Nixon was taking a trip to Alaska, which had three electoral votes.[706] The promise became an even bigger problem when Nixon's health turned sour because of his knee infection.

All of the difficulties of the campaign—fatigue, illness, the poor showing in a debate that Nixon had been confident in winning, etc.—made sleep hard to come by for the man who struggled with insomnia. Nixon also struggled with delegating his work. For example, the old debater was proud of the fact that he put in so much time working on his speeches, but it led one of his frustrated speech writers to remark, "He reduced us all to clerks." As Nixon's planning director, Jim Basset, cleverly put it, Nixon "wanted to be horse and jockey."

A result of Nixon's stress (some of which was self-induced) and his workload (most of which was self-induced) was that the candidate's temper would erupt frightfully,[707] which disturbed and demoralized his staff. Perhaps the worst display of Nixon's temper took place in Iowa. It had little to no impact on the election, but it provides a fascinating look at how Nixon handled being pushed past the constraints of his self-discipline. John Ehrlichman had planned a series of appearances in Iowa. They went well, but there were too many of them, so the Vice President was wasting a lot of time driving from location to location. Sitting in the back of a convertible during the trip, Nixon suddenly began kicking the seat in front of him with both feet. This action violently jolted the seat's occupant, Nixon's military aide, Air Force Major Don Hughes, over and over again. When the car finally stopped in the next small town on the itinerary, Hughes got out and walked away in silence. Bob Haldeman was convinced that Hughes would not have come back if not for Haldeman's apology and persuasive words.[708] For all of Nixon's gifts, it was disturbing that he could have behaved so irrationally and been so indifferent to the well being of others.

Don Nixon, the Vice President's brother, was a part of yet another situation that effected the election. This situation actually began to unfold in December 1956.[709] Don Nixon was a man whose entrepreneurial ambition greatly exceeded his entrepreneurial talent. The Vice President's brother had taken control of the family's gas station and general store and expanded the empire to include a coffee shop and two drive-in restaurants (featuring the "Nixonburger"). But he was having trouble funding these operations. He applied for a bank loan of $100,000, but before it was processed, representatives from the quite rich Howard Hughes offered him $205,000. Technically, the money would be a loan from the Hughes Tool Company, which had no history of loaning money to restaurateurs, and it equaled over a million dollars at today's rates. This story broke just a few weeks before the 1960 election, and it looked pretty fishy.[710]

Some writers have suggested that this episode was nothing more than a shakedown by a powerful politician who was willing to sell political favors for money. And Hughes, who had business pending with the Federal Aviation Agency and problems with the Internal Revenue Service and the Justice Department, was certainly in a position to need some favors.[711] But there is another, more likely explanation. Hughes might have been trying to buy influence without Don Nixon realizing it. Don had serious money problems, and the Hughes men who approached him were friends of the Nixon family. Don's widow, Clara Jane Nixon, said, "Don was one of those people who float along with the tide, just accepted it."[712] It is possible that Don Nixon was simply too desperate and gullible to realize he was being used as a pawn by Hughes to gain influence.[713]

It seems reasonable that someone with Don's temperament and circumstances would not be unduly suspicious. Why assume Hughes was trying to get the Vice President to intercede for him with the Executive Branch when the problems were too big for Richard Nixon to control? One of the quite valid criticisms of Nixon as President was that he *tried* to influence the IRS as President, but even then he was frustrated when the IRS would not do his bidding. To assume that he could control not only that office but two others as well when he was just the VP is a stretch, especially given the shaky position he held in the eyes of the Eisenhower administration. Besides which, if Hughes wanted to influence Richard Nixon by providing what turned out to be insufficient funding to a brother Nixon was not particularly close to,[714] then Hughes was not so smart with his money.

Despite the little merit the story deserved, the attention to it and timing of its release were more strikes against the Vice President. Robert Kennedy believed it was one of the main reasons why Nixon lost the election,[715] though it is possible that Kennedy said this to deflect attention from some of the Kennedys' more unsavory deeds in 1960. Whether or not the story received more attention because there was a press bias against Nixon is perhaps subject to debate in some minds, but the press did seem much more enamored with Senator Kennedy than they were with the Vice President. In addition to being more in tune politically with Kennedy, the majority of the national media figures were also quite taken with the charisma and good looks of both Kennedy and his wife Jacqueline. The media was not quite as smitten with the Vice President. Harrison Salisbury of the *New York Times* described Nixon as having "a terrible sleazy quality that crept into many of his appearances." Mary McGrory of the *Washington Post* rather not so poetically described Nixon as "just so icky, so yucky."[716] Attitudes such as these sometimes crept into the reporting of the contest, which helped prompt Willard Edwards of the *Chicago Tribune* to write that the "staggering extent of...slanted reporting" was "one of the most, if not the most, shameful chapters of the American press in history."[717] While this is an exaggeration, it does convey the point.

Both parties looked for dirt on the opposition candidate. However, when the Democrats tried to see if there was a link between Nixon, his friend Bebe Rebozo, and some Miami hookers, John Kennedy's name came up, so they dropped it. The Republicans found quite a bit more material in their search of Kennedy's background. FBI Director J. Edgar Hoover, who liked Nixon, had a wealth of information that he passed on to the Republican campaign. Hoover alleged that in addition to flings with several other women, including prostitutes, Kennedy had a romantic relationship with a Nazi spy during World War Two, and he was probably even married briefly before his marriage to Jackie. Kennedy found out that the Republicans had this information, and he implored a friend who had been in Ike's Cabinet, Maxwell Raab, to get them not to use the dirt. Though these bombshells could have tipped the balance in such a close election, Nixon finally opted to keep them quiet.[718]

Perhaps none of the problems Nixon faced would have mattered in the end had it not been for the voter fraud that took place. As Pat Nixon so bluntly put it, "We won in 1960, but the election was stolen from us."[719] Tom Wicker, a columnist for the *New York Times*, wrote several years after the election that "Nobody knows to this day, or ever will, whom the American people really elected President in 1960. Under the prevailing system, John F. Kennedy was inaugurated, but it is not at all clear that this was really the will of the people, or if so, by what means and margin that will was expressed."[720] The attitudes of Pat Nixon and Tom Wicker were not out on the fringe. There was substantial evidence of voter fraud. In Texas, where Kennedy narrowly won, 100,000 votes cast in the bigger cities were disqualified.[721] In one polling station in Texas 6,138 votes were counted, but there were only 4,895 voters registered. In Illinois, another state narrowly won by Kennedy, there were also irregularities. Some people there had voted up to six times and one voting machine had recorded 121 votes after only 43 people had been through the line.[722]

Eisenhower and other Republicans urged Nixon to contest the election. Ike even offered to help raise money for recount efforts in Texas and Illinois,[723] but the Vice President had to consider the arguments against such a move. One argument was noble; the other was practical. At best, a challenge to the election results would take months, and Nixon was concerned that such instability at the top would undermine American foreign policy. Besides that, Nixon knew that even the recounts might leave Kennedy the winner. Such a development would have made Nixon look like "a sore loser" as he put it, and that image would have haunted him for the rest of his political life.[724] For the good of the country, and for the good of his career, Nixon conceded the 1960 presidential election.

Years later, Nixon would look back and write, "If we had known then as much about how to campaign, etc., as we know now we would have probably won in 1960. Whether that would have been a good thing or a bad thing I am not sure." Nixon was writing about good and bad in regard to the issues the country faced in the 1960s.[725] There is, however, a double meaning that can be read into the quotation. Nixon already knew how to run successful and brutal campaigns, but his operatives would cross the line (or cross it further) by 1972. If Nixon was implying that he should have "out-corrupted" Kennedy in 1960 it would have been a bad thing. Political corruption is a slippery slope downward, and the

Vietnam War provided ample excuse to justify rule breaking. The methods Kennedy used to win the election were bad; if Nixon had used harsher methods in 1960—as he did later—that would have been worse for the institution of the presidency and for the country.

Though Nixon actually got more votes in 1960 than he would in 1968, he lost the 1960 election anyway. Nixon lost by between 112,000 and 118,000 votes, or less than two-tenths of a percent.[726] Because of Nixon's competitive and analytical nature, it was not surprising that he would run again or that he was willing to broaden his perspective on what was acceptable behavior to get elected. The relaxed ethical attitude was unfortunate, both for Nixon and the country. Nixon gained more insights in his eight years as Vice President than just how to be a dirty politician, though. He came to believe that Communists respected strength, not sensitivity, and this perception was reinforced multiple times. He also saw a President who was able to be quite popular with the country, even though he was not that supportive of his own political party. Of course this popularity was established to a great degree by what Ike had done before he entered politics, but Nixon would not take this into account as President, much to his detriment. The vice presidential years were also important to Nixon insofar as they brought key figures in his future presidential administration, such as Haldeman and Ehrlichman, into his professional life.

CHAPTER NINE

The Political Wilderness—1961-1968

After his devastating loss to John Kennedy, Nixon had to figure out what to do with his life. With politics out of the question—at least for the time being—Nixon decided he needed to make some money. An obvious vocation was the law since that was what Nixon was doing before politics entered the picture. Nixon went home to California to practice. Nixon could have made more money in New York, and he had contacts there and in Washington, but California was where his wife wanted to go, and it was where his political base was.[727]

Nixon's defeat at the hands of Kennedy was devastating to the Vice President, but it was good news for two of Nixon's future insiders, foreign policy genius Henry Kissinger and Treasury Secretary John Connally. Because of Kissinger's extensive personal networks in academia and the Democratic Party, he was able to obtain a part time position within the Kennedy administration as a foreign policy consultant.[728] Connally was able to parlay his long time service with Kennedy's new VP Lyndon Johnson, and connections with Speaker of the House Sam Rayburn, into a position as Secretary of the Navy.[729]

Just as 1961 was a year of transition for Nixon, Kissinger, and Connally, so it was for Bud Krogh. Krogh graduated from Principia College in Elsah, Illinois that year and joined the Navy where he served for four years before going to law school.[730]

Though beaten by Kennedy, Nixon still had considerable clout. Thus, it was no great surprise that the new President asked him to the White House only three days after the Cuban exiles failed to oust Castro after their defeat at the Bay of Pigs, which occurred on April 17, 1961. Kennedy wanted to know what Nixon would do to salvage the situation that ended so tragically for the exiles and embarrassingly for the U.S. after Kennedy decided at the last minute not to provide U.S. military support. Nixon replied, "I would find a proper legal cover, and I would go in."

Nixon felt there were at least three excuses for an American invasion. One, the Soviet bloc was aiding the Cuban government, so it would only be fair for Americans to assist the "Freedom Forces." Two, the American base at Guantanamo was vulnerable to Cuban attack. Three, there were still thousands of U.S. citizens in Cuba who needed to be protected. In the end, Kennedy was not persuaded,[731] even with Nixon's promise that "I will support you to the hilt if you make such a decision in regard to…Cuba."[732]

Kennedy was not comfortable with such a solution, believing an American invasion of Cuba would lead to a Soviet invasion of West Berlin. Nixon disagreed, arguing that the Soviets might put pressure on Berlin, but if resolve was shown the Soviets would back off. Kennedy was unmoved by Nixon's argument, even though the new President had advocated full support for the Cuban exiles just six months earlier.[733]

But Kennedy had played to Nixon's vanity by inviting him in for the talk. Kennedy also appealed to Nixon's sensibilities by saying "It really is true that foreign affairs is the only important issue for a President to handle, isn't it? I mean, who gives a [expletive] if the minimum wage is $1.15 of $1.25, in comparison to something like this?" Kennedy was trying to win Nixon over, so Nixon would not rail against the Cuban failure in the press, and it worked.[734] One is left to wonder how Kennedy's comments resonated with Nixon during his own presidency. He was so obsessed with the Kennedy magic that JFK's comments no doubt reinforced Nixon's preference for foreign policy over domestic policy as President. Kennedy also scored points with Nixon when the former Vice President said he was thinking about working on a book. With Kennedy's encouragement, Nixon went on to write *Six Crises*.[735]

The allure of politics was still strong with Nixon, but he was slow to warm up to the idea that he should try to be the next governor of California in 1962. As Californian Republican Caspar Weinberger put it, "Nixon was a reluctant candidate in this race because his greatest interest was foreign policy, and he did not know state issues well." Another problem for Nixon was that his Democratic foe, Edmund "Pat" Brown, had all the advantages of incumbency, so it was going to be a difficult contest. Ultimately, Nixon was sold on the idea as a way to climb back into contention for the presidency down the road.[736] It could keep Nixon viable, but it would also give him an excuse to not run against the incumbent John Kennedy in 1964. If Nixon could not defeat the inexperienced Kennedy in 1960, Nixon's prospects against Kennedy would be truly bleak in 1964.[737] The governor's office in California was a good place to hide. And it looked like a safe bet despite Brown's advantage as the sitting governor. Multiple polls predicted a Nixon victory with one showing Nixon's support in the race at over 60%.[738]

As Nixon was running for governor, he tried to nationalize the campaign at least to a limited degree. Nixon accused the Kennedy administration of "injecting politics in the allocation of defense contracts." But the Defense Department actually awarded more contracts to California under Kennedy that it had under the Eisenhower-Nixon administration, so Nixon gained little traction with this attack.[739]

Some of the people Nixon had working for him during the 1962 campaign would later serve him in the White House. Among them, Bob Haldeman took yet another leave of absence as an advertising executive for the J. Walter Thompson Company to join the fight as Nixon's campaign manager. John Ehrlichman once again worked as an advance man, Rose Mary Woods was still serving as Nixon's faithful secretary, and Ron Ziegler was a twenty-two-year-old press aide.[740] Ziegler outlasted Haldeman and Ehrlichman in the White House, serving as Nixon's Press Secretary even after the others were gone.

Another future Nixon man was involved in a different political campaign in 1962. Donald Rumsfeld from Illinois won in seat in the House of Representatives.[741] Rumsfeld considered, as he put it, "one of the most effective workers on his staff" to be Jeb Stuart Magruder.[742]

One of the surprises about Nixon's bid for the Republican nomination for the governors race was that Nixon had to defend himself from those on the right who were concerned that he was not conservative enough. But he managed to appeal to the extreme right without going so far over that it destroyed his chances in the general election.[743]

Despite Nixon's reluctance to take part in this campaign, once the decision was made, he went all out. He even persuaded his wife Pat to make some speeches, something she had not done for 16 years. As the campaign season unfolded, Nixon dropped in the polls, but he hoped he could make a surge in the final weeks and snatch the victory away from Brown.[744]

On October 22 President Kennedy announced that the Soviets had set up nuclear missiles in Cuba, ninety miles from the Florida shoreline. Kennedy demanded their removal and announced steps to force the issue.

When Nixon heard the TV report, he said to Rose Mary Woods, "Well, I just lost the election." Nixon had been facing an uphill battle, and now the attention of Californians would be on this international drama. It was not a good time for Nixon to persuade voters who were rallying around their President that Kennedy's chief rival in the last election should be the next governor of California. Nixon was proved right on November 6 when Brown beat him.[745]

The next morning Nixon gave the press a tongue-lashing. Nixon had not initially planned to appear before the media. Herb Klein, later a Nixon staffer in the White House, told the media that Nixon was not coming down from his suite to address them; Klein would make the concession speech. There are several versions of what happened next. According to one story, Haldeman, who was watching the press conference on TV, heard some of the reporters snickering about Nixon's no-show. Haldeman began complaining about "the liberal press" and said someone should tell them off. The idea resonated with Nixon, who went down and did just that.[746] According to another version of the story, Klein went back upstairs when the press made it clear that they did not want just a press secretary reading the concession speech. When Klein returned alone, Bill Stout of CBS said, "What's the matter, Herb, is he afraid to come down here?" Of course, Nixon the Battler was not going to tolerate that sort of challenge.[747]

However Nixon got down there, one of the first phrases the defeated candidate threw at those assembled was a reference to "all the members of the press [who] are so delighted that I lost." Nixon went on to say, "I have no complaints about the press coverage." He then turned on his opposing candidate. "I believe Governor Brown has a heart, even though he believes I do not." He complained that the media did not record that Nixon defended Brown's patriotism, but the media actually did publish Nixon's assertion that Brown was an anti-Communist. Nixon had trouble wrapping up his speech, saying he had "one last thing," then offering at least four more things. Contained in this portion of Nixon's speech was his line to the media that "You won't have Nixon to kick around anymore."[748]

The reaction to the speech was passionate. Despite its controversial nature, Pat Nixon, who had been watching on TV at home, yelled "Bravo!"[749] Nixon's meltdown was seen in the Kennedy White House as "entertainment."[750] The media generally reported that Nixon had accused the press of costing him the election, which was not entirely accurate. Nixon thought the press was biased against him, but he thought the Cuban Missile Crisis cost him the election. The Democrats thought the speech was going to be Nixon's silver bullet. If he ever dared to run again, they believed, clips from his last press conference could be used against him. But they had nothing but fool's gold. As historian Stephen Ambrose wrote, "When they studied those clips carefully, they found there was nothing on the tape that was usable. Nixon had eluded them again."[751]

Although Nixon was defeated again, Bob Haldeman did not view the outcome as entirely negative. At least it had kept Nixon in the public eye.[752]

While Nixon was losing his race in California, John Connally was winning the governor's seat in Texas. Serving as governor for three consecutive two-year terms, Connally helped the Democratic Party stay in power despite, according to an author on Connally, "aggressive raids on the Democratic machine by a sophisticated and well-financed Republican organization."[753] Connally's efforts on behalf of the Democrats are all the more noteworthy given his alleged assistance to one Republican President (Eisenhower) and his open assistance to another (Nixon).

Shortly before Nixon was rebuffed in his latest attempt to be a public servant, G. Gordon Liddy decided to leave government work on his own accord. Liddy had greatly enjoyed his time in the FBI, but he believed his opportunities for career advancement were limited, and as he described his feelings, "I felt keenly an obligation to achieve my maximum genetic potential." He decided that he could provide better for his growing family if he worked for his father's law firm in Manhattan, so he left the Bureau in September 1962.[754]

After the 1962 campaign was over for Nixon, he decided to get away for awhile, so he went to the Bahamas without his family. He did not travel alone, though; Bebe Rebozo met Nixon and another friend in Miami. Rebozo had solidified his relationship with Nixon over the years by sharing the Californian's love of swimming, and by being comfortable with Nixon's desire for long periods of contemplative silence. A mutual acquaintance once said of Nixon and Rebozo, "I've seen him and Bebe sit in a room for three hours and neither ever say a word."[755] That was the kind of company Nixon wanted as he plotted his future course.

Though Nixon was still out of office, he was nevertheless considered newsworthy. Less than a week after Nixon's loss in California, ABC ran a special called "The Political Obituary of Richard Nixon." It was obviously premature, and certainly no other politician before or since has had his political misfortune proclaimed and dissected in such a fashion. Maybe Nixon was right—maybe the media really did hate him. Of course, the fact that Nixon was singled out reflects not only on the media but on the one man they chose to target. If one concedes a liberal bias in the media, one is still left with the question of why, among all the conservative politicians of the mid to late 20th century, was Richard Nixon the only one to get such a TV special?

The panel was made up of a host, Howard K. Smith, two Nixon supporters and two Nixon detractors. The supporters included Murray Chotiner, who had worked for Nixon, and a colleague from the House of Representatives, Gerald Ford. On the other side sat Jerry Voorhis, the man Nixon had defeated in a race for a seat in the House in 1946. Alger Hiss was the other anti-Nixon man on the panel.

Given that Nixon had helped send Hiss to prison for perjury regarding his Communist connections, Hiss' place on the panel was a rather peculiar decision by ABC. Certainly the American public seemed to think so since 80,000 people sent in telegrams and letters complaining about it.[756] Regarding the public backlash, Smith later said, "It bothered ABC a great deal, and it didn't leave me unshaken." Nixon responded to the broadcast by issuing a statement that read, "What does an attack by one convicted perjurer mean when weighed on the scales against the thousands of wires and letters from patriotic Americans?"[757] If anything, the ABC special generated public sympathy for the maligned ex-VP.

Ben Bradlee, who was an executive editor for the *Washington Post* when Bob Woodward and Carl Bernstein were writing stories about Watergate, was well acquainted with the practices of the Kennedy administration. Bradlee was at a dinner party with John Kennedy and his brother Robert, who was also his Attorney General. The Kennedys talked openly about wiretapping and using the IRS to harass people they wanted to manipulate, like steel industry executives.[758] Of course, just because one President got away with breaking the law does not mean that every other President can do so with impunity. The Nixon White House needed to be cleaned up, but at least this helps one understand the moral climate of its environment leading up to Nixon's time in office.

When John Kennedy was assassinated in Dallas on November 22, 1963, John Connally was driving the car, and he was wounded during the incident. Apparently, the event caused Connally to take his mortality a little more seriously. He liked to smoke cigars, but after getting shot, he developed the habit of just letting the cigars sit in his mouth unlit.[759]

Nixon was in Dallas the same day Kennedy was killed. The former VP had been in town to deal with one of his law firm's client companies, Pepsi Cola. Nixon was flying out the day of the assassination and did not hear about it until he was in New York.[760] While some conspiracy theorists might want to read something into Nixon's presence in Dallas, it is worth noting that Nixon was doing nothing at this point to secure the Republican nomination in 1964. To the argument that Nixon's inaction just demonstrates how subtle and crafty he was, if he was truly subtle and crafty he would not have been anywhere near Dallas on November 22.

Actually, Nixon learned something rather startling from FBI Director J. Edgar Hoover months after the assassination. Kennedy's killer, Lee Harvey Oswald, had planned on killing Nixon when the former VP had visited Dallas, but Oswald's wife had kept him from leaving the house in time.[761]

After Kennedy's assassination, Kissinger continued his consultancy with the new administration, even working out of the State Department. Ever the master of intrigue, though, Kissinger began playing both sides of the fence. Kissinger served on the staff of Republican Nelson Rockefeller, and he worked as a foreign policy consultant for the Republican Platform Committee in 1964.[762] Kissinger had assured that he would be close to power regardless of which party held the White House.

Near the end of 1963 to early 1964 Gordon Liddy began to re-examine his Catholic faith. He decided that he really could not accept Christianity as being any more valid than Judaism or Islam, so the man who worked so hard to overcome his childhood fears finally overcame his last one—his fear of God. Liddy expressed some regret about this development, acknowledging that "my agnosticism is a poor substitute for the faith I no longer have to give my children." But he also felt a sense of freedom.[763] One is left to wonder if Liddy would have made different choices years later with some kind of Church-imposed moral guidelines still at work in his life. Perhaps it would not have mattered, but it might not have hurt.

Nixon was based predominantly in New York from 1963-1967, and it was at this time that he grew close to John and Martha Mitchell. The Nixons spent many occasions in the Mitchells' home where Richard Nixon would sing and play the piano, and Martha Mitchell would play the southern belle.[764] As journalist and author Tom Wicker described him, John Mitchell was "a forceful man, relentless in his advocacy, blunt to associates and in his public statements." He was the kind of tough-minded man Nixon always admired.[765] Nixon also admired Mitchell for the latter's command of his surroundings in New York; a place Nixon had never been comfortable. Mitchell taught Nixon how to fit in, and the New Yorker served as a sounding board for the future President in much the same way that Haldeman later would.[766]

Chuck Colson sent Nixon a memo early in 1964, urging the former Vice President to run for the presidency. Colson liked Barry Goldwater's politics, but Colson did not think Goldwater could beat Lyndon Johnson. Nixon was intrigued enough by Colson's memo to invite the younger man to New York to meet with him. The relationship between Colson and Nixon grew that day. As they talked, their common economic and political backgrounds became evident to one another. Colson's admiration for Nixon grew even more after Nixon invited him home for dinner and an incident occurred along the way. Traffic got backed up when two drivers got out of their cars and started fighting. Nixon jumped out of his car, broke up the fight, and got traffic moving again.[767]

By the end of the day, Colson had sufficiently stroked Nixon's ego and stoked his competitive fire for Nixon to authorize Colson to go on a fact-finding mission. If the Republican Party would follow in 1964, Richard Nixon was willing to lead them. There was also talk of having Colson manage the campaign. But it was not to be. Many leading Republicans were convinced that Nixon's window of opportunity had closed.[768]

Besides, Nixon had another problem in 1964. Two years after his California defeat, a court ruled that Nixon, Haldeman, and Ziegler were complicit in the mail out of postcards that attacked Pat Brown. The problem with these postcards was that they were not identified as being financed by the Nixon campaign. They were intended to create the impression that Democrats were concerned about the direction in which Brown was leading the party.[769] Such dirty tricks were not unique to

Nixon or the Republican Party, but this trick was illegal, and would leader to bigger crimes.

One of Nixon's forays out of New York occurred in 1964 when he served as one of the speakers at the Republican National Convention, which was held in San Francisco that year. Nixon sought to unify the party with his speech to the Convention, but his efforts were undone by Goldwater. The Republican nominee for President said in his acceptance speech that "Anyone who joins us in all sincerity we welcome. Those who do not care for our cause we do not expect to enter our ranks in any case."[770] Moderate and liberal Republicans were underwhelmed, Lyndon Johnson cruised to victory, and the door was opened for a Nixon run in 1968.

Nixon's work for the Republican Party, and Barry Goldwater as the Republican presidential candidate, was noticed by many. In January 1965 the Republican National Committee met in Chicago, and Goldwater said that Nixon "worked harder than any one person for the ticket. Dick, I will never forget it!" One would think that Nixon was simply playing to his conservative instincts, but reporter and author Tom Wicker observed something else at work. According to Wicker, Nixon was determined "to go anywhere and do anything to support Republicans—whether liberal, conservative or in-between—in order…to rebuild his…party for 1968." Nixon supported Goldwater in part because both men were conservative Republicans, and in part because Goldwater was the choice of the Republican Party that year. Nixon wanted the same kind of support when and if he made his next bid for the White House.[771] Nixon described one way that he openly reached out to both liberals and conservatives at the same time. "In a number of speeches during 1965, I urged my audiences to be Lincoln Republicans: liberal in their concern for people and conservative in their respect for the rule of law." Nixon went on to say in his speeches, "If being a liberal means federalizing everything, then I'm no liberal. If being a conservative means turning back the clock, denying problems that exist, then I'm no conservative."[772]

John Dean capped a successful academic experience with a doctorate of jurisprudence from the Georgetown University Law Center in 1965. He had earned undergraduate majors in English Literature and Political Science with stints at Colgate University and the College of Wooster.[773] Upon getting his law degree, Dean took a job with a firm in Washington D.C. that did not last very long. According to John Ehrlichman, Dean was fired after a law partner accused Dean of improprieties in a radio station licensing case. Dean later said it was just a misunderstanding between him and his employers. But he did lose his job. Dean's first wife was the daughter of a Missouri Congressman,[774] and Dean used this contact to get a job as the chief minority counsel for the House of Representative's Judiciary Committee. Next, he got a position as the associate director of a law reform commission.[775] While Dean's marriage was good for his career, the opposite was not true. Dean admitted that he had put his job first, and it had contributed to end of his marriage.[776]

Interestingly, there was a perception by some Watergate authors, like Dan Rather and Gary Gates, that the leaders in the Nixon White House were rather puritanical and intolerant of those who did not live up to their standards.[777] Yet John Dean, John Mitchell, and Chuck Colson all rose to high levels of authority and they all went through divorces and re-married[778] when such activities were generally frowned upon, especially by the more conservative crowd.

G. Gordon Liddy made another career move in 1965. His and his father's law firm was doing very well, but the relationship between father and son was suffering. Neither man believed in compromise when convinced of his own position. Gordon Liddy decided that for the sake of family harmony, it was time to find something else. He took a job in the District Attorney's office in January 1966 both because he wanted work that was meaningful and because he craved excitement.[779]

By 1966 Nixon had a better attitude about the significance of his defeat in the campaign for governor. As Nixon saw it, "California served a purpose. The press had a guilt complex about their inaccuracy. Since then they've been generally accurate, and far more respectful." Nixon also thought he had learned something—he had to stop letting the press get under his skin.[780]

On the first day of 1967, John Mitchell's name was added to the New York law firm of Nixon, Mudge, Rose, Guthrie, and Alexander. Mitchell solidified his relationship with the future President on trips together to Washington where the two men dealt with regulatory agencies as a part of their legal work.[781]

The death of Hannah Nixon in 1967 hit the family hard. Billy Graham presided over the funeral. As Julie Nixon Eisenhower later remembered:

My father, up until the moment we all had to file past the coffin to leave the church, had been composed and strong for Tricia, me, and the other members of the family. But as he prepared to thank Dr. Graham for being with us, he broke down momentarily. Sobs racked his body and he buried his face in Dr. Graham's shoulder. This lasted for perhaps only five to ten seconds. Because we all loved Nana so much I feel that the true cementing of the Nixon-Graham friendship came at that moment.[782]

The influence of Graham was probably a factor in Nixon's idea of having interdenominational, Sunday worship services in the White House, if he was ever elected President. No previous President had done this,[783] but it made sense. It had been common for Presidents to go to regular worship services, but after the assassination of John Kennedy in 1963 experts believed regular appearances like that would present security risks. And providing adequate security would create disruptions in the worship of other parishioners. The idea of bringing preachers to the President had a lot of merit to it.

While one Nixon relationship was being solidified, another was further fractured. Nixon's relations with the press, which had gone through such storms as the ill-named "Final Press Conference" in 1962, took an even darker turn at Hannah Nixon's funeral. Nixon biographer Jonathan Aitken explained, "He [Nixon] was incensed by the intrusive nature of reporters, some of whom were crass enough to ask him how he was feeling." Nixon was also upset that members of the media took up so much room in the church that many locals were unable to get into the funeral. Wrote Aitken, "There are some family intimates who believe that the time when he began to view journalists as enemies rather than adversaries can be pinpointed to Hannah's funeral."[784]

As of 1967 Maryland Governor Spiro Agnew was committed to Nelson Rockefeller's candidacy—more so than Rockefeller himself as it turned out. When Rockefeller said he would not pursue the presidency, Agnew announced that he would try to get Rockefeller to change his mind. Eventually, Agnew gave in to reality and looked elsewhere, finally settling on Nixon. Agnew's appeal to Nixon was contradictory. Agnew had established a reputation, deserved or not, as a liberal, a perception that was reinforced by his strong flirtation with Rockefeller. Thus,

Nixon's base might be broadened by putting Agnew on the ticket. At the same time, however, Agnew demonstrated his shared outlook with Nixon on law and order by dealing harshly with African American unrest in Maryland,[785] so Agnew's perceived conservatism simply duplicated Nixon's appeal, or his negatives depending on one's politics. Inarguably, though, Agnew's Maryland background would provide nice regional balance for Nixon the Californian.

1967 was also the year when Nixon met with Charles de Gaulle, the Prime Minister of France. One of the matters they discussed was China. One would expect that the two men would not see eye to eye on the subject. Nixon was a firmly committed anti-Communist while de Gaulle had recognized the Communist Chinese government, much to the outrage of his anti-Communist supporters. De Gaulle had rationalized that his course of action was correct "because China is so big, so old, and has been so much abused." He stressed that the United States should not "leave them [the Chinese] isolated in their rage" at the mistreatment China had received from the West in the past. Surprisingly (at the time), Nixon was open to the idea of reaching out to China. The Chinese had split from the Soviets, and Nixon thought this was an opening that had to be exploited. Besides, as China's nuclear capabilities increased, there would be more pressure on the United States to have some kind of relationship with them.[786] In an article in *Foreign Affairs*, Nixon said, "We simply cannot afford to leave China forever outside the family of nations, there to nurture its fantasies, cherish its hates and threaten its neighbors."[787] Nixon was showing that he would not be a one-dimensional thinker when it came to communism.

John Connally decided not to run again for governor in 1968. His personal popularity was probably high enough, and his ability to raise money—always a considerable asset of his—was still there. But, as he announced, he was not sure he would be able to "bring to the office for another two years the enthusiasm, the resilience, the patience that my conscience would demand, and that the state would deserve."[788] In other words, he was getting bored with his job.

Another man weighing the decision to try for office was Richard Nixon. Around Christmas 1967, Nixon struggled over what to do. His daughters encouraged him to run for the presidency; his wife was mortified at the thought.[789] One person Nixon greatly respected outside his family, Billy Graham, encouraged him to make another run. As one

Graham biographer noted, "Graham believed Nixon to possess great moral character and personal integrity, and to be blessed with an ideal family life. Graham also knew...Eisenhower's view that Richard Nixon was better qualified for the presidency than any other individual.[790] While Nixon certainly had the credentials to be President, Graham's great faith in Nixon's character was misplaced. Graham's belief in his friend was perhaps more a reflection on Graham than Nixon. The famous preacher tried hard to be a good person and perhaps had a tendency to believe that his friends had the same commitment to integrity.

When Nixon decided to run in 1968, Jeb Magruder was not at all surprised. Magruder wrote, "I used to see him at many Republican events, and if ever there was a man driven by a hunger to be President, he was one."[791]

Nixon was a little reluctant to make John Mitchell his campaign manager because of Mitchell's lack of experience running campaigns. But Nixon was won over after seeing how Mitchell was able to pull together Republican support for Nixon in Wisconsin. Nixon liked Mitchell's interpersonal leadership abilities,[792] and, as presidential historian Theodore White described it, "like Nixon, Mitchell had made it on his own, and possessed the compass-true conservative instincts of a self-made man." All of these things led Nixon to hand over the reins of the campaign to Mitchell.[793]

Nixon's campaign team had a unique division of labor. Mitchell was the unquestioned manager of the campaign itself. As TV newsman Dan Rather understood it, Mitchell focused on the political aspects of the campaign like which issues his candidate should focus on. It was Mitchell who developed the Southern Strategy, which was the name given to Nixon's efforts to woo voters away from George Wallace of Alabama. Bob Haldeman became the Nixon campaign's Chief of Staff. Haldeman made decisions regarding Nixon's day to day affairs. It was Haldeman's decision to keep the candidate away from the press while flying on Nixon's plane. Minor politicians and low level staff members were also pushed away by the protective Chief of Staff. As Haldeman put it, "The key to an effective Richard Nixon is to keep him relaxed." Haldeman did not want 1960 to repeat itself.[794] Victory was attainable, but Nixon had made some bad choices and had lost his temper in embarrassing fashion. This could be avoided if Nixon was not overtaxed. And being around people too much was something that overtaxed Richard Nixon. Despite

Rather's perception that Mitchell handled the politics, Theodore White believed that in this campaign "Nixon would supply the politics, Mitchell the management."[795] Perhaps the best way to understand Nixon's power structure is by using this formula: Nixon provided the vision, Mitchell, oversaw the strategy for communicating that vision, and Haldeman handled logistical control of the campaign.

Mitchell and Haldeman got along because neither man had much desire to shoulder the other's responsibilities, and they respected each other's abilities. Mostly, they got along because they agreed on how to handle Richard Nixon.[796] Their mutual respect carried over into Nixon's first term, though that respect never extended down through each other's staffs.[797] Ultimately the relationship between Haldeman and Mitchell deteriorated due to Watergate.

Nixon sought to recruit John Ehrlichman to work for him in 1968, but Ehrlichman was candid with the former Vice President about one big concern: Nixon's drinking. Ehrlichman said it was hardly his place to suggest that Nixon stop drinking, but Ehrlichman did not want to invest his energies in a presidential campaign, if the candidate was not in control of himself. Instead of brushing Ehrlichman off or becoming angry, Nixon asked if Ehrlichman thought that was why the campaigns of 1960 and 1962 had failed. Ehrlichman did not think so, but he was still concerned. Nixon said that it was reasonable to expect that he would be in top shape to attempt another bid for the presidency.[798] Ehrlichman's respectful candor was something Nixon did not forget when he staffed his White House, leading to Ehrlichman becoming a major figure and bringing in some of his own people, like Bud Krogh.

Nixon's drinking might not have been the problem Ehrlichman thought it was. Nixon had been taking Dilantin, a stress-relieving drug, for some time, and he would continue to take it. A side effect of the drug is that when mixed with even a little bit of alcohol it can lead to slurred speech, though it does not impair the mind. This side effect might have been the reason Ehrlichman and others thought that Nixon drank too much. A number of other people who knew Nixon well took exception to the view that Nixon had a problem with alcohol.[799]

Once on the job, Ehrlichman found one aspect of it particularly unpleasant: dealing with Helene Drown. She was a friend of Pat Nixon's who had been with her, for example, when Pat found out that Eisenhower had picked Richard Nixon as his running mate. During the

1968 campaign, Mrs. Drown traveled with Pat Nixon and essentially served as a companion and gofer for her. Helene Drown became the conduit for complaints from Pat Nixon to the Republican campaign's staff. Ehrlichman and his crew of advance men felt that Drown frequently turned requests and suggestions into demands. Ehrlichman's men retaliated by assigning Drown to the most unpleasant hotel rooms they could find. Over the next several years the Drown family would visit the Nixons, and Helene Drown seemed to draw out and fan the flames of all Pat Nixon's negativity. In 1971 Nixon had a meeting with John Ehrlichman, Bebe Rebozo, and Rose Mary Woods about this. Nixon wanted the Drowns to stop visiting. Woods suggested tactful ways of making that happen. Rebozo said that tact was not the answer; he suggested dynamite. Nixon decided to have Ehrlichman tell Mrs. Drown's husband, Jack Drowns, that they could not visit. At one point, Nixon said, "Tell Jack that it is for the good of the country that Helene Drown gets out of my house!"[800] This episode is worth noting not only because it once again highlights Nixon's difficulties with personal interactions, but also for something else. Halfway in jest, perhaps, Nixon equated something that was good for him personally with what was good for the country. Perhaps Nixon was sincerely convinced that he could not afford to be distracted from important policy concerns by negativity on the home front, nevertheless, it is easy to read some cynicism and even megalomania into the President's attitude.

Unlike Ehrlichman, who joined the team with some reluctance, Chuck Colson made an effort to be part of the Nixon campaign in 1968, but Mitchell and Haldeman initially shut Colson out. He was, however, able to contribute through the Key Issues Committee. Colson became the staff co-director of this committee, which had the job of helping the candidate form his positions. Colson contributed so many ideas and position papers that his work was eventually turned into a campaign manual, *Nixon on the Issues*.[801]

The matter of who Nixon's opponent would be in 1968 took awhile to resolve. The sitting President, Lyndon Johnson, saw his hopes for another four years evaporate. Johnson's major problem was the country had grown disenchanted with his handling of the Vietnam War, but another trouble spot Johnson had was domestic. In a meeting with Democratic governors in 1968, Roger Branigin of Indiana complained that Johnson had not worked with the governors well enough during the planning for his Great Society legislation. According to Branigin, they had not had input on the legislation, but they received the brunt of the criticism when things were not working out. When Johnson's old friend, Governor John Connally, agreed with Branigin, it opened the floodgates for the other governors.[802] Faced with these two problems specifically, and dwindling support among Democrats in general, Johnson dropped out of the race.

As Robert Kennedy emerged as the frontrunner for the Democrats, it looked like Nixon's presidential dream might once again be frustrated by this powerful family. When Robert Kennedy was assassinated, it opened the door for the eventual Democratic candidate, Johnson's VP Hubert Humphrey, and for Nixon, too.

Connally was a major player in Democratic circles that year. Despite their earlier disagreement, Connally worked on behalf of Johnson to keep Humphrey from straying too far from Johnson's policies in Vietnam. This hurt Humphrey with antiwar activists in the party and contributed to their divisions in the election. Connally thought he had a chance to run as Humphrey's vice presidential candidate, but he was passed over. Though Connally had struck out as a potential VP, he was still a big name in national politics. After the riotous Democratic National Convention burned itself out in Chicago, Connally went home to Texas. Republican agents of Nixon tracked Connally down and made it clear that if he helped Nixon win Texas, there would be a reward in the Nixon administration. Connally was intrigued, and it was not simply a case of a power hunger; his conservative foreign policy outlook had more common with Nixon than with the left of center elements in the Democratic Party. But Connally grew conflicted over his role in the upcoming election. He had not helped Humphrey in Texas until Connally made an appearance at a massive rally late in the campaign at the Astrodome. This open support for Humphrey, and the lack of such support for Nixon might have made the difference in Texas since Humphrey only won by 39,000 votes out of 3,100,000. A Nixon staffer said this about Connally's defection from Nixon's camp, "If the fellow had had more guts, he'd be Secretary of Defense today."[803] As it was, Connally had to wait longer and settle for less from Nixon, who still wanted a leading Democrat associated with his administration.

True to form, Kissinger was in touch with both the Nixon and Humphrey camps during the 1968 campaign. Kissinger contacted the

Nixon people and offered them inside information on the secret Paris peace talks going on between negotiators for the Johnson administration and the North Vietnamese. At the same time, Kissinger had contacted Zbigniew Brzezinski, who was the foreign policy coordinator for Humphrey. Kissinger allegedly promised to produce damaging files on Nixon compiled by Rockefeller's operatives, saying, "Look, I've hated Nixon for years." When Nixon buried Humphrey in the polls, Kissinger changed his mind about helping the Democrats.[804]

At the Republican National Convention, Nixon was harassed by Democratic dirty trickster Dick Tuck, who had plenty of experience making life difficult for Republican candidates. At least some of Tuck's activities at the 1968 RNC seemed harmless enough. For example, he paid pregnant African American women to picket outside of Nixon's hotel. The women carried Republican campaign signs which read, "Nixon's the One."[805]

By the middle of September, Nixon was beating Hubert Humphrey soundly in the Harris and Gallup polls, but the Nixon camp was worried that Vietnam might shake things up.[806] Other than Vietnam, Nixon's main worry was that third party candidate George Wallace might take away potential Nixon votes in the South. Nixon approached Wallace's "let's send a message" rhetoric head on, saying, "Do you want to make a point, or do you want to make a change?…Do you want to get a moment's satisfaction by your vote of protest, or do you want to get four years of action?"[807]

Also in September Nixon discussed the campaign with a couple of his speech writers, pointing out that the press was making Spiro Agnew look bad. Nixon believed the press had turned vicious against Agnew "because he's hitting where it hurts." Nixon was convinced that the press was having its true colors spotlighted by Agnew, and they did not like it. But Nixon could not blame all of Agnew's media problems on the press. The VP candidate said several things during the campaign that proved embarrassing to the Republican Party. He referred to a reporter as a "fat Jap," he also said, "if you've seen one ghetto, you've seen them all," and he used the word "Polack." When Agnew explained that he was only engaging in locker room humor, Homer Bigart replied in the *New York Times*, "locker room humor should never be equated with running for Vice President of the United States."[808] While picking such a running mate might have made Nixon look more presidential be comparison, it also made the future Vice President someone Nixon would not turn to for advice. A worthier candidate might have provided a positive influence on the Nixon White House, but Nixon made his choice and had to live with the consequences. For as much as Colson admired Nixon, Colson did not agree with his hero's choice for VP. Colson said of Agnew, "He was an in-your-face polarizer, which was the last thing we needed when the country was already polarized." Colson had lobbied for Governor John Volpe, but he was unsuccessful.[809]

Nixon had an interesting comment to a question about whether or not he was enjoying the campaign. Nixon replied, "Never do. Campaigns are something to get over with."[810] Nixon was always the battler, never the hedonist. He did not pursue politics for the warm fuzzies. Campaigns were wars to be fought.

Generally, though, Nixon employed a low-key (for a presidential campaign) strategy. Nixon had a comfortable lead in the polls, so he was not going to over do the campaigning as he had in 1960. He now understood that there was no need to try and win all 50 states, he just needed an electoral majority. His slower pace kept him from the kinds of mistakes that plagued him when he was overly tired. Humphrey on the other hand was following a much more active schedule and going to states that were solidly Republican. Humphrey also began to distance himself from Lyndon Johnson's war policy, first calling for an end to the bombing of North Vietnam with conditions then offering a bombing halt with "no periods, no commas, no semicolons." This separated the candidate from Johnson and from Nixon too, whose plan to end the war was fairly vague. In his speeches, Humphrey also hung the rather unstatesmanlike label "Richard the Chickenhearted" on Nixon.[811] Such a name would have been particularly grating to a man like Nixon, who prided himself on his toughness and willingness to do battle.

The margin between the two men began to close as Election Day approached. Between August and October, Nixon's 15% lead in the polls dipped to 3%. Colson openly blamed John Mitchell's poor leadership of the campaign,[812] which did little to help them work together once Nixon was President. Another Nixon man who was unimpressed with Mitchell's leadership was Elliot Richardson, who later became Attorney General. Richardson believed that Nixon only chose the inexperienced Mitchell because Mitchell was trustworthy, and he would not have the political acumen to second guess Nixon, who would be the de facto campaign manager. Richardson considered Mitchell "a political ignoramus."[813] John Dean would later come to a similar conclusion, though Dean phrased his feelings more diplomatically. "Few people who worked for Mitchell did not like him, for he was a very pleasant man to work for," wrote Dean. However, "I quickly realized that in some areas he was over his head and was baptized by fire in learning the ways of Washington."[814]

Perhaps it was not (or not solely) Mitchell's fault. Journalist and author Tom Wicker wrote, "No Republican, as has often been said, unites the Democrats the way Nixon does."[815] And so it went. By the last couple of weeks before the election it looked like a toss up. Kissinger once again contacted the Humphrey camp and expressed his dislike for Nixon. Ted Van Dyke, a close aide to Humphrey, remembered, "We get this letter—when the gap begins to close in the last month—from Kissinger indicating his distaste for Nixon and his willingness to serve. It was grotesque." But Van Dyke maintained, "I wasn't angry at him. I remember Henry being a both-sides-of-the-street kind of guy."[816]

By the day of the election, multiple polls showed the two candidates running neck and neck. Lou Harris' Poll had Humphrey ahead by three points.[817] For some in the Nixon camp, it looked like an ugly repeat of the Election of 1960. In fact, Leon Jaworski, the future Watergate Special Prosecutor, believed that the way the election ended in 1968 was a factor in Watergate. After seeing a big lead evaporate in the end, which stirred up the disaster (from Nixon's point of view) of 1960, Nixon and his men were determined to do whatever it took to hold on to their advantages in 1972.[818]

That night, Nixon forbade his people from turning on the TV in his suite. Nothing would be determined early on, so Nixon did not want to sit around fretting over the significance of early returns. Pat Nixon, their daughters, and Bebe Rebozo got their own updates from aides coming in and out of the suite.[819]

It was probably best that they did not have direct access to what members of the media were saying since some commentators were predicting a Humphrey victory. At midnight Humphrey was still ahead in the popular vote. Early the next morning, TV newsmen were reporting that Chicago Mayor Richard Daley was holding back the results of Cook County. Again, the Nixon team was reminded of 1960 and the voter fraud in Illinois. A short while later John Mitchell was on the phone with a Democrat from Illinois, demanding that the results be released. A half hour later, Daley had complied, and shortly thereafter, TV reports declared Nixon the winner.[820] Nixon won less than 44% of the popular vote, beating Humphrey by less than one percentage point, but Nixon had won a majority in the Electoral College.[821] He was finally going to be President of the United States.

When Jeb Magruder heard that Nixon was elected President, Magruder thought, *Well, he's got everything he wants now, so he must be happy.* But Magruder observed, "He had climbed as high as a man could go, and still he was unsatisfied. He was still driven; he still saw enemies under every bush. I think his occasional outbursts of vindictiveness were expressions of his unhappiness.[822]

One other man who was keenly interested in Nixon's feelings, and concerned about the President-Elect's possible vindictiveness, was FBI Director J. Edgar Hoover. According to Bob Haldeman, Hoover met with him and Nixon and told the pair that President Johnson had ordered Nixon's campaign plane to be bugged by the FBI. Johnson's rationale was that it was a matter of national security. Furthermore, Hoover warned Nixon not to go through the White House switchboard when Nixon first moved in because Johnson had the phones monitored. Haldeman said that he verified the truth of Hoover's accusations after Nixon's team moved into the White House, but they did not have any proof, nor could they find any FBI documentation for the surveillance after Watergate occurred and the White House was looking for cover.[823]

After Nixon won the election, he set to work composing his team for the Executive Branch. The media praised John Mitchell for managing Nixon to victory. Mitchell received far too much credit as far as Elliot Richardson[824] and Chuck Colson were concerned. But it makes sense that the media treated Mitchell this way. There was already enough animosity between the press and Nixon that it is only natural that the men and women who disliked him would grasp for some clever explanation for why he won. The "Mitchell is a genius" argument seemed reasonable enough. Unfortunately, Mitchell's media reputation and friendship with the President-elect gave a lot of authority to a man who did not always take charge of situations and do what needed to be done, despite Nixon's respect for Mitchell's supposed leadership ability.

Perhaps if Mitchell had been more of a take-charge, focused force in the Nixon administration, he would have done something about John Ehrlichman. Ehrlichman developed a dislike for Mitchell during the 1968 campaign[825] and tried several times over the next six years to gain power at Mitchell's expense. This rivalry did not serve the President well.

Bud Krogh had graduated from the University of Washington School of Law earlier in 1968, and he went to work fulltime for old family friend Ehrlichman.[826] Krogh had already worked for him during school breaks,[827] so Krogh's abilities had been established in Ehrlichman's eyes. Ehrlichman and Krogh were not long for Seattle in 1968. As Krogh later described it, "When John Ehrlichman asked me a few days after the election in 1968 whether I would like to come to the White House and serve as Staff Assistant to the Counsel to the President, it took me a full nanosecond to say "Yes.""[828]

The Deputy Attorney General designate, Richard Kleindienst, contacted John Dean, and invited him to New York to meet with John Mitchell, the future Attorney General. The meeting went well, and Dean accepted a position as Associate Deputy Attorney General for Legislation.[829]

Another man ushered into power was a New Yorker. He was told that if he could help Nixon win a plurality in the mid-Hudson Valley region of New York then he would be taken care of, if Nixon won the presidency. With the intervention of a few key men, including House Minority Leader Gerald Ford, the New Yorker became Special Assistant to the Secretary of the Treasury, for Organized Crime. The New Yorker went to Washington D.C. and was concerned about people like William Rudd, a leader of the Weatherman. Rudd gave a speech in 1969 where he talked about tearing down the country and "offing some pigs" and "blowing up pig stations" among other things. The New Yorker wrote, "That, to me, is war. I was ready. And willing [to do something about it]."[830] The New Yorker was G. Gordon Liddy, and he was sitting in the Nixon administration's Treasury Department like a time bomb waiting to go off.

CHAPTER TEN

Damage Control (1972)

When the burglars were caught in the Watergate Building, multiple investigations began in Congress, the Justice department, and the media. It was around this time that the *Washington Post* duo of Bob Woodward and Carl Bernstein was formed. Damage control began even more immediately. While the official White House reaction was that they did not know anything about this espionage against the Democrats, Bernstein remembered something the President had said a year and a half earlier. After the Republicans' performance in the 1970 congressional elections, Nixon had said, "When I am the candidate, I run the campaign." While that was hardly a smoking gun, it was certainly a quotation to note. Who else would want to burglarize the DNC besides someone connected with the opposition campaign? Also it would make sense that Nixon would be actively involved since this would be the last campaign he had a personal stake in. Still, Woodward and Bernstein did not immediately take it for granted that the White House was involved because it struck the reporters as so absurd with Nixon being 19% ahead of McGovern in the polls.[831] What the reporters failed to take into account was that the operation had been planned several months ahead of time when the election was not so close. As recently as May, a Harris Poll had Nixon only 5% in front of McGovern.[832]

John Ehrlichman was informed of the Watergate arrests on Saturday afternoon June 17 by the Secret Service. When Ehrlichman found out that Howard Hunt was involved, the Domestic Affairs Chief assumed Colson was responsible since Hunt had worked for him. A phone call to Colson did little to dissuade Ehrlichman, despite Colson's protests of his innocence. The next day, Ehrlichman and Haldeman touched base and decided to have John Dean determine Colson's role.[833]

During the weekend of June 17-18, John Mitchell, Jeb Stuart Magruder, and other key officials of the CRP were in California to meet with local Republican leaders. Magruder's breakfast was interrupted by a phone call from Liddy who told Magruder to get to a secure telephone because they had a big problem: Jim McCord had been arrested. Magruder did not know McCord well, but the security chief was a good friend of the Mitchells and his connection to the CRP was undeniable. Instead of using a secure phone at a nearby military base, Magruder decided he could not wait, so he called Liddy from a nearby pay phone. Magruder demanded to know why Liddy would use a CRP employee in such an operation. Liddy responded, "I had to have somebody on the inside to handle the electronics. McCord was the only one I could get. You didn't give me enough time."[834]

Liddy had called Magruder, so the latter could warn John Mitchell that questions about the break-in might be at that day's scheduled press conference. Mitchell and Magruder later decided that Liddy should contact the new Attorney General, Richard Kleindienst, and have him use his influence to get McCord out of jail. If McCord, who had used an alias when arrested, could be made to disappear, the CRP would be protected. Magruder's final instructions to Liddy were to "Tell him 'John sent you' and it's a 'personal request from John.' He'll understand."[835]

When Bob Haldeman tracked down Magruder in California, per the President's instructions, and asked him over the phone what was going on. Haldeman realized there was trouble right away because of how nervous Magruder sounded. But Magruder claimed, "Those guys were operating on their own, Bob. They just got carried away." Haldeman wanted to know exactly who had gotten carried away, and Magruder told him, "McCord. He's our security man at CRP. He works for Gordon Liddy." When asked if Liddy was involved in the break-in, Magruder stammered, "Well, I told you…uh…he was working with McCord."[836]

Haldeman had never met either McCord or Liddy, but Haldeman had approved Liddy's transfer to the CRP at the suggestion of John Dean. Even as Haldeman reflected on the Watergate issue, he was struck by his disappointment that the CRP had not provided the White House with more intelligence about the Democrats' activities. As Haldeman described it, Nixon kept waiting for the CRP's intelligence arm to provide them with something useful, Haldeman would pass on the demands to one of his aides, Gordon Strachan, and Strachan would pressure the CRP.[837] So, paradoxically, the White House wanted to distance itself from the overzealous efforts of Liddy et al, while belittling the CRP for not working hard enough to get them the information they wanted. It is hard to escape the conclusion that the White House staff got what it deserved.

Magruder left out any reference to his and Mitchell's culpability, and shared with Haldeman a press release the pair had written that described McCord as being involved in a free lance operation, and left the other CRP employees out of it. Haldeman was temporarily placated, but he wanted to know how big a problem this was. He contacted Ehrlichman, who told him, "We're in a bit of a bind on this one, Bob. One of those Cubans had a check on his person signed by Howard Hunt." Haldeman was alarmed by such a careless mistake by Hunt and the operative. Haldeman asked if Ehrlichman thought Colson was connected to Watergate. Ehrlichman replied, "I'm afraid to speculate. If Brother Colson is involved in this little jamboree, we're in for a lot of problems."[838]

Next, Haldeman got Colson on the phone, who said the same things he had said to Ehrlichman. Colson was not involved, the accusation was unfair, he had not seen Hunt in months, Hunt was off his payroll, the break-in was "idiotic," and more of the same.[839]

Finally, it was time to check in with the President. Haldeman felt comforted after talking with Nixon because the President seemed so unconcerned on the phone. Regarding any White House involvement, Nixon said, "It has to be some crazies over at CRP, Bob. That's what it was. And what does it matter? The American people will see it for what it was: a political prank." At the time, Haldeman had no idea that Nixon had lost his temper during a conversation with Colson;[840] the President's reaction had seemed mild to the Chief of Staff.

Colson genuinely believed Nixon had no inside knowledge about this matter. As Colson recalled, "I was one of those who talked to him the day after the break-in, and he was as shocked as I was."[841] Of course, if this was true then Magruder's account that Nixon had given the final go ahead must be in error. The President's first impression, according to his memoirs, was that Colson was not as shocked as Nixon was. Regarding Colson, Nixon wrote, "I had always valued his hardball instincts. Now I wondered if he might have gone too far."[842] Colson sensed Nixon's concern, noting, "I was clearly suspect number one with the President."[843]

DNC Chairman Lawrence O'Brien agreed with the President, a definite rarity, and suspected Nixon's hatchet man. O'Brien believed that the facts were "developing a clear line to the White House," and directly to the office of one Charles W. Colson. O'Brien also observed that while this burglary had been interrupted, his political enemies might have engaged in other such activities.[844]

Colson was not suspect number one, however, with the staff at the *Washington Post*, which was still not entirely convinced that the break-in was the result of Republican operatives. City editor Barry Sussman believed, "It could be crazy Cubans" who were responsible for trying to spy on the party that was seen as soft on Castro.[845] But reporters Woodward and Bernstein continued to investigate with Woodward in particular cultivating a number of informants, the most famous of whom was known as Deep Throat. Deep Throat, who turned out to be FBI official Mark Felt, fed Woodward many leads over the next couple of years. As Watergate researchers Colodny and Gettlin pointed out, some of Deep Throat's information was wrong.[846] But it did not matter; the sheer bulk of material he gave Woodward provided enough stories for the *Washington Post* to keep Watergate in the news, which helped frustrate Nixon's efforts to move the nation past it.

After the regular Monday morning senior staff meeting at the White House, John Ehrlichman invited Colson into Ehrlichmnan's office. They talked about the break-in and then, while Colson was standing there, Ehrlichman called Attorney General Richard Kleindienst and said, "Dick, this break-in business. I had a report Saturday that one of the men assigned to Colson's unit here, a fellow by the name of Howard Hunt, may have been involved. Can you check it out? The President will need a full report." Colson was shaken by Ehrlichman's effort to push Colson into the line of fire. Colson did have ties to Hunt, but the unit Ehrlichman referred to was the Plumbers, which had actually operated under Ehrlichman's authority,[847] directed by Ehrlichman's man, Bud Krogh.

When John Dean found out about the arrests at the Watergate Building, he, like Ehrlichman, blamed Chuck Colson. Dean's assistant, Fred Fielding, told him that one of the Cubans had a check from Howard Hunt. Dean replied, "Leave it to Colson to blow the election."[848] But even if Watergate had been Colson's fault, and it was not, Colson could not be the only scapegoat. Dean had done little to derail Liddy's plans.

On the same Monday morning when Ehrlichman was trying to connect Colson to Watergate, June 19, Jeb Magruder called Dean. An agitated Magruder had plenty to say to the White House Counsel, including, "We've got a real problem, John....Listen, John, this is all that dumb [expletive] Liddy's fault....He never should have used McCord....It was stupid....I think you should talk to Liddy, John. I can't talk to him because he hates my guts....You can find out what else went wrong."[849]

Magruder was nervous as he talked to Dean—Magruder spoke too fast and his voice occasionally cracked—which was not comportment that was respected in the Nixon White House. But Magruder's characterization of the issue was one that was widely shared by Nixon's team. Magruder said, "Basically this thing is going to be a tough PR problem. But I think we can handle it."[850]

Dean was not even off the phone with Magruder when Ehrlichman called. Ehrlichman's suspicions about Colson's connection to the burglars matched Dean's own. Ehrlichman said to Dean, "I called Chuck over the weekend to ask about Hunt's well-being, and Chuck sounded like he hardly knew the man. Said he hadn't seen him in months. Said he couldn't imagine how a thing like this could have occurred. Now, I'm not totally satisfied our Mr. Colson is telling all. Why don't you have a little chat with him and find out what you can, and find out what happened to his friendship with Hunt?"[851]

Dean made the call and dropped Ehrlichman's name, but he had not even started asking questions when an angry Colson cut him off with a profanity. "I talked to Ehrlichman about it over the weekend! I told him I had no idea where Hunt was, or what he was doing! I haven't seen Hunt in months! He's off my payroll."[852]

Colson slowly began to wind down, so Dean interrupted him. "What's the story of Hunt's relationship to you?"[853]

Colson replied, "I hired him as a consultant for *Ehrlichman*." Colson had sent Hunt to work on the Pentagon Papers for Ehrlichman. Colson had also used Hunt to interview Dita Beard over the ITT case, he admitted, but that was months before Watergate.[854]

Later that morning G. Gordon Liddy came to see Dean and the two men took a walk. Dean began to question Liddy, but once again the Counsel was interrupted by someone who could not wait to talk. Liddy said, "This whole [expletive] thing is because Magruder pushed me. I didn't want to go in there. But it was Magruder who kept pushing. He kept insisting we go back in there." According to Dean, it was the first he had heard of a previous entry.[855]

Liddy did take the blame for using McCord, saying, "John, I know using McCord was a serious mistake. I accept full responsibility for it. It's my fault, and I don't want to put off responsibility on anybody else. But I do want you to know why I did it. And that's because Magruder cut my budget so much and was pushing me so hard I had to use McCord. I didn't have time to do anything else. Jim's a professional, and I trusted him. He was the only guy I could turn to."[856] Liddy had already been using McCord for technical advice on proposed operations, and that, plus McCord's background with the CIA, convinced Liddy that McCord was worth the risk.[857]

There was more. Dean asked Liddy if anyone in the White House knew about the operation ahead of time. Liddy replied, "I don't think so. The only person who might have known about it is Gordon Strachan." This was a disturbing possibility for Dean because Strachan was one of Haldeman's aides. Dean reasoned that if Strachan knew, then Haldeman and Nixon must have known, too. Dean made it clear that he wanted to end the conversation at this point, but Liddy said, "I understand that perfectly, John. I'll walk on the other side of the street. That's probably best. But before I go over there, I want you to know one thing, John. This is my fault. I'm prepared to accept responsibility for it. And if somebody wants to shoot me…" Liddy paused for a moment then pushed forward. "…on a street corner, I'm prepared to have that done. You just let me know when and where, and I'll *be* there."[858] The conversation got much less dramatic after that with Liddy promising that his people would not cooperate with the investigation and coaching Dean on how to proceed with his work.[859]

Liddy had also told Dean that the people involved in the case would need financial help. They would have lawyers to pay, and they needed to provide for their families. Dean agreed to take care of it.[860]

During the afternoon, a meeting took place between Ehrlichman, Colson, Dean, and a White House staffer named Bruce Kehrli. Dean has alleged that Ehrlichman ordered him to have Howard Hunt flee the country, which Dean did by placing a call to Liddy and telling him to pass along the message. Dean claims he had second thoughts. After pondering them for awhile he said that getting Hunt out of the country was a mistake. Colson agreed with him, so Ehrlichman changed his mind and had the Counsel call Liddy back to rescind the order. Liddy said he would try his best to catch Hunt, Dean hung up the phone, and the meeting resumed.[861]

Ehrlichman and Colson both deny Dean's version of events, contending that it was Dean who came up with the order on his own.[862] Ehrlichman might have lied to protect himself, but Colson certainly had no incentive to protect Ehrlichman, so once again Dean's version of the story is called into question. According to Colson, he found out what was happening with Hunt when Colson asked Haldeman where Hunt was, and Haldeman told him to check with John Dean. Dean said, "Hunt has been ordered out of the country," smoothly deflecting the origin of the order. Colson pointed out—with a healthy dose of obscenities—that such an order "could make the White House a party in a fugitive-from-justice charge." This was what allegedly prompted Dean to get on the phone and rescind his order.[863]

On June 20 a meeting was arranged to discuss Watergate. Haldeman and Ehrlichman were joined by John Mitchell, John Dean, and the new Attorney General Richard Kleindienst. According to Haldeman, Mitchell seemed lighthearted, which helped convince the others that the Watergate problem was going to be easy to contain. The Chairman of the CRP said, "I don't know anything about the foolishness at the DNC. I do know *I* didn't approve the stupid thing." After hearing that, Haldeman and Ehrlichman felt much better.[864] Dean had been the second to last to arrive at the meeting, showing up just before Kleindienst, and one thing the young Counsel noted was that he had never seen Haldeman, Ehrlichman, and Mitchell together like that before. When Dean arrived, Ehrlichman said, "We thought we should have our lawyer here when the Attorney General of the United States, who is cooling his heels in the west reception room, pays his visit." Dean thought this was said to somehow needle the former Attorney General, which Ehrlichman liked to do. Dean was surprised by the joviality of the attendees and saw it as an attempt to stonewall each other.[865] The White House staffers were further comforted by AG Kleindienst's comments that he saw no connection between the White House and anyone involved with the break-in. This gave Ehrlichman some peace of mind about Colson. It was agreed that the CRP would handle press inquiries, and it seemed like this big mistake would be easily contained.[866]

After the meeting, Dean rode with Kleindienst back to the Justice Department, and Kleindienst was seething. He was appalled at the stupidity that led to the break-in. He was amazed at G. Gordon Liddy's audacity. Liddy had tracked Kleindienst down on a golf course over the weekend and told him, "John Mitchell wants you to get the men arrested at the DNC out of jail." Kleindienst had told Liddy to go away. Kleindienst told Dean, "If John Mitchell is in trouble, I'll resign before I'd ever prosecute him," Kleindienst said. But the same such consideration would not be extended to John Ehrlichman; Kleindienst would do nothing for him. "He's managed to make everyone hate him, and someday he may regret that." Kleindienst reacted with alarm to Dean's comment that the President might somehow be involved.[867]

Dean's outlook was not quite the same as that of Kleindienst. Dean agreed with Kleindienst's characterization of the break-in, which decades later Dean still referred to as "utterly stupid." But Dean knew that the White House had some pretty big skeletons in the closest. If Watergate did have any tendrils leading into the White House, then other things might be exposed, like wiretappings and the break-in at Fielding's office.[868]

Ehrlichman met with the President after the Watergate meeting was over to discuss some domestic issues. During this meeting the President interrupted their discussion to talk about wiretaps. Nixon commented that wiretapping had been done by every President since World War Two. According to Nixon, "We've reduced the number of wiretaps by fifty percent in this administration. Robert Kennedy tapped the most when he was Attorney General. It's been a steady downtrend since then." Ehrlichman believed the President was thinking about how to spin Watergate to the press, and Ehrlichman wondered how Nixon was going to make the leap from national security wiretaps to illegal eavesdropping on political opponents, but Nixon moved on to something else.[869]

According to Haldeman's diary, the Chief of Staff's impression of the President's response was the same as Ehrlichman's. Nixon did not see the Watergate break-ins as a legal or moral issue, but a PR problem.[870] Nixon was recorded on the White House taping system blaspheming and saying, "The [Democratic National] Committee isn't worth bugging in my opinion. That's my public line."[871] The President would have been much better off if the second sentence had gone unsaid.

In Nixon's memoirs, he wrote that Colson and Haldeman had both mentioned the Bay of Pigs, and that made Nixon think that the Watergate break-in could actually be used to his advantage. Nixon believed that if the Cuban involvement in the break-in could be played up in the media and some sympathy was generated among the public, then Nixon could get Bebe Rebozo to start a bail fund for the burglars. And it could serve to remind the public of the Democrats' handling of the Bay of Pigs fiasco and parallels could be drawn to McGovern's foreign policy.[872] Things did not unfold this way, but it is interesting that Nixon was thinking Watergate could be turned into a plus for his campaign.

That afternoon, Magruder came to visit Dean and as the two of them walked over to the CRP's headquarters for a meeting, Magruder had some new information for the White House Counsel. Dean recorded the conversation in his autobiography. Magruder said, "You know, John, Mitchell approved this thing down in Florida." Dean replied that he did not know that, and Magruder continued. "Well, yeah, after that second meeting, I felt I had to bring it up with Mitchell again because Colson was just pushing me like mad. He kept calling me and asking what's going on. So I went to Mitchell and I told him. I said, 'Listen, if we don't take care of this, Colson's going to take it over!'" Dean thought that Mitchell's antipathy towards Colson pushed the ex-Attorney General over the edge and got him to OK Liddy's reckless plan.

Magruder had more. "So what happened, John, is we were afraid Colson would take it over. And do you believe *this?*" Magruder laughed and tugged Dean's arm—the kind of gesture that almost prompted Liddy to kill him—and said, "We were afraid *Colson* would screw it up! Can you believe that?"[873]

A tape from June 23 reveals the following from a conversation between Nixon and Haldeman about Watergate. Nixon asked, "Did Mitchell know about this thing to any much of a degree?" Haldeman replied, "I think so. I don't think he knew the details, but I think he knew."[874] This would seem to contradict Magruder's recollection that Mitchell got approval over the phone from Nixon for the Liddy plan with Haldeman sitting in the room with the President.[875] But it is possible that Nixon was talking about the details of the plan, such a distinction might allow for a legal testimony of ignorance. Thus, Magruder could have been telling the truth, and Nixon did give his approval through Mitchell for Liddy's plan.

Earlier that day Dean had told Haldeman that Mitchell and Dean had cooked up the idea of having the CIA tell the FBI to not investigate past the Watergate Seven (the five burglars and Hunt and Liddy who had also been arrested by this point). Haldeman ran this plan past Nixon who agreed to it. Nixon biographer Jonathon Aitken believed that Nixon was motivated by a desire to help his friend John Mitchell, but Aitken also believed that there were a lot of other forces at work in Nixon's mind. According to Aitken, Nixon was displaying characteristics of both his parents—the kindness of his mother for a friend in need, and the combative nature of his father against the hated Democrats and media figures who smelled blood. Also, Nixon was stopped by his disdain for interpersonal conflict from telling Mitchell to fall on his sword for his commander-in-chief.[876]

In Haldeman's account of this conversation with Nixon, Haldeman wrote that he was not sure how to sell the CIA on the idea of discouraging the FBI. Nixon suggested that Haldeman warn the CIA that an investigation of Hunt and the Cubans would "open up the whole Bay of Pigs thing again." Haldeman did not know what that meant, it obviously had different ramifications to the CIA than it would have to the Democrats and their foreign policy, but Nixon was confident it would do the trick. Haldeman and Ehrlichman met with the appropriate CIA officials and tried to sway them, but the CIA had already told the FBI that there was no Agency involvement.[877]

Chuck Colson was either a very good actor or genuinely outraged by the stupidity of the Watergate break-ins. The Democratic National Committee headquarters at the Watergate Building would not be the place to go for good information about what the Democrats were planning. At one point, Colson ranted, "Idiots! Anybody who did that should be sent to Siberia! Whoever heard about it should have fired them!"[878]

Several theories developed as to motives behind the Watergate break-ins. One theory has it that since Hunt and McCord both had strong ties to the CIA they were operating under orders to get caught on purpose. The possible motives cited for this theory are that the CIA wanted to get Nixon off its back since he was trying to both reorganize the Executive Branch, and utilize his own intelligence gathering apparatus, and/or that the CIA wanted a monopoly on spying on the Democrats.[879]

Dean wanted to play up the CIA connection as an excuse for getting the CIA to provide money for the burglars, but CIA Director Vernon Walters vetoed that idea, forcing Dean to try other avenues.[880] After Dean struck out with Walters, Mitchell, Haldeman, and Ehrlichman all thought that money for the defendants should be raised by Herb Kalmbach, the President's personal lawyer.[881]

In July the White House staff was still trying to act as if it was business as usual, but over at the CRP Magruder was growing concerned. Haldeman assistant Larry Higby called Magruder and told him that Haldeman wanted McGovern's campaign schedule. Magruder said this would not be a problem because the press would publish McGovern's appearances a few days in advance. "Not good enough," Higby said, "We need it further in advance." When Magruder said he could not accommodate him, Higby pointed out, "You can put a guy in his headquarters." Magruder objected, saying, "We're in the middle of a criminal case already. I'm not going to put anyone in McGovern's headquarters." Higby let the matter drop, but Haldeman did not. He personally called Magruder, and when Magruder continued to demur, Haldeman was furious.[882] It would not have been illegal to have a Nixon loyalist volunteer to serve in McGovern's campaign and share whatever he learned with Magruder, but it would have certainly left the CRP looking bad, given the illegal spying that had already taken place. If this was some kind of test from the White House to see if Magruder had maintained his resolve, Magruder failed.

Not everyone was worried about Watergate. John Connally was still focused primarily on getting Nixon re-elected. Larry O'Brien claimed that Connally was using federal aid as a carrot and a stick to get support for the President. More aid was promised where support for Nixon was forthcoming. When that support was not so clear, there was the threat of reduced aid. O'Brien agreed when an interviewer asked if Connally was guilty of "political blackmail." A more benign project Connally was involved in was setting up a group designed to appeal to independent voters for Nixon.[883]

Chuck Colson called Magruder to ask for his help for the "Democrats for Nixon" organization, yet another Connally initiative. At the time Magruder feared that this project would bring Colson into Magruder's sphere, but Magruder soon realized his fears were misplaced. As Magruder got to know Connally better, the CRP man described the Texan as "the most impressive political figure" he had ever known. Connally's personality and clout were too strong for Colson to dominate, and with Connally in the way, there was no chance that Colson would find an opening to get involved with the CRP.[884]

On August 9, more than two months after the initial break-in, Nixon told Haldeman that the IRS had evidence of payments from one of Howard Hughes' businesses to DNC Chairman Larry O'Brien. Nixon had been informed of this by Connally. Nixon wanted the IRS to publicize this information and bring O'Brien in for questioning. Nixon felt the IRS had not been diligent enough in this matter, so he wanted Haldeman and/or Ehrlichman to pressure the agency.[885]

Actually, the IRS had investigated Larry O'Brien at the behest of Ehrlichman, who suspected that O'Brien would not want his expenses, which greatly outweighed his salary, to become public knowledge. This information was used to pressure O'Brien into lightening up on the Watergate break-in. It was effective, as far as O'Brien was concerned, but there were too many people invested in the investigations to turn them all off.[886] It is worth pointing out that getting the IRS to investigate someone under these circumstances was arguably an abuse of power.

Colson was not so afraid of Watergate investigators that he got out of the dirty tricks business. Colson had handbills sent out that falsely claimed to be from the "Gays for McGovern Fund-Raising Party." Colson was so proud of his work that he sent a handbill to Bebe Rebozo down in Key Biscayne, Florida.[887]

As the Watergate scandal refused to die, Kissinger brought it up to Haldeman, asking what the story was really about. Haldeman replied, "I wish I knew" and started talking about something else.[888] Actually, Haldeman did know, though perhaps he did not understand the legal ramifications of everything he knew.

Magruder perjured himself before the grand jury on August 16. He had been prepped for this engagement by John Mitchell and John Dean. Mitchell coached Magruder while Dean pretended to cross examine him. Their efforts to obstruct justice paid off. Assistant Attorney General Henry Peterson, who was reporting regularly to Dean, told him that Magruder had survived the Grand Jury appearance "by the skin of his teeth."[889] Magruder had told the prosecutor, Earl Siburt, that Liddy and Hunt had acted on their own initiative. Magruder did not think that Siburt fully believed him, but Siburt was focused on nailing Liddy and Hunt, and Magruder's testimony, such as it was, made Siburt's job easier.[890]

Magruder was growing uncomfortable with his role in the crimes and the coverup and by the attitude of his White House contact. John Dean kept telling him, "Don't worry Jeb, everything'll be all right. We'll protect you." Magruder wondered why Dean kept giving him assurances Magruder was not asking for, and Magruder wondered what to make of the consistently vague nature of the promises.[891]

The supposed need for the Watergate break-ins seemed increasingly difficult to understand as McGovern's candidacy became weaker. In August McGovern cut loose his running mate, Thomas Eagleton after the negative publicity that followed the disclosure of Eagleton's battle with mental health. Eagleton had been hospitalized for depression three times in the 1960s, and he had twice received shock treatment. Such revelations made the public uncomfortable with the thought of Eagleton being a heartbeat away from the presidency. Prominent Democrats including Senator Ted Kennedy, former Vice President Hubert Humphrey, DNC Chair Larry O'Brien, and others turned down McGovern's requests to replace Eagleton on the ticket.[892]

On August 29, Nixon was asked at a press conference if it would be good to assign a special prosecutor to investigate Watergate. Nixon said such a prosecutor was actually unnecessary because there were multiple investigations already under way. Among those the President listed was the one being conducted in the CRP, first by Mitchell before he stepped down as the CRP head, then by his successor, Clark MacGregor. "In addition to that," said the President, "within our own staff, under my direction, the Counsel to the President, Mr. Dean, has conducted a complete investigation of all leads which might involve any present members of the White House staff or anybody in the government." According to Nixon, Dean had found no one in Nixon's administration involved in what the President termed "this very bizarre incident." Actually, the first Dean had heard of a "Dean Investigation" was when he watched the President's news conference. The Dean Investigation was a lie. The Counsel was not trying to find the truth; he was trying to cover it up. The lie was closely held—Dean was badgered by Press Secretary Ron Ziegler for information about the Dean Investigation because Ziegler had to face the White House reporters who wanted details. For Ziegler, thinking he had not been informed about it was almost as frustrating as finding out there was nothing to be informed of.[893]

Dean's coverup was easier after being identified by Nixon as the man in charge of the investigation. It helped Dean find out things from people who were investigating the case. He was already getting briefings from the

FBI. Dean used such information to coach witnesses who faced questioning.[894]

Part of the coverup strategy was to portray Gordon Liddy as a man crazy enough to cook up the Watergate break-ins on his own.[895] It was a logical move, and to a degree the media went in that direction on its own, because of Liddy's over the top personality, but in the long run, the strategy had a potential flaw. Painting Liddy as too much of an extremist might alienate him, which would not be good because he was keeping silent so far, and the White House did not want to jeopardize that.

Interestingly, Nixon was the target of some political spying himself. The office of Dr. John Lungren, who was Nixon's physician, was broken into during the campaign season. Though cash was available, the burglars ignored it and instead went through Nixon's medical records.[896] Apparently nothing useful was found because Nixon's health never became a campaign issue.

Gordon Liddy and the White House staff were pleased with the arraignment hearing of the Watergate Seven presided over by Judge John Sirica. The judge ruled that the trial would not start until November 15, so the White House would stay in the clear until at least after the election. Even better, the trial was later delayed and did not actually begin until January 1973. Liddy was also happy that Sirica was to be the presiding judge. Liddy wrote, "The combination of Sirica's ill temper, little education, and carelessness increased the chances for a reversible error considerably, and that was the only chance we had."[897] Liddy was willing to sacrifice himself for the team, but he was not anxious to do so.

Nixon was talking to John Ehrlichman about George McGovern on September 8, and the President referred to his opponent as "a Communist SOB."[898] Given the state of the Cold War, and Nixon's perception of his rival, it was easy for the President to rationalize the illegal activities of his people as being in the interests of national security.

A week later, Nixon had a meeting with some of his top aides regarding the reorganization of the Executive Branch after the anticipated Nixon victory. As the plan was discussed, Nixon launched into a tirade against IRS agents who would not comply with his agenda. It was a matter of great frustration for Nixon since, constitutionally speaking, he was supposed to be the Chief Executive. But Nixon was only the second Republican President since January 1933, so there were several generations of Democrats throughout the Executive Branch, which was pointed out by John Dean. The practical side of the problem was that Nixon's people felt that prominent Americans who supported the President would find themselves audited, but when Nixon and Dean tried to target prominent Democrats, the IRS resisted. A frustrated Nixon wanted access to the tax files of Democratic enemies and said, "There are ways to do it. [Expletive] sneak in in the middle of the night." Haldeman replied, "We sure shouldn't take the risk of getting us blown out of the water before the election." Haldeman later characterized his reply as an example of deflecting Nixon's dark impulses in the hopes that they would later subside, rather than directly confronting Nixon and risk alienating the President.[899] Be that as it may, it is disturbing that Nixon was still contemplating such activities two months after the Watergate burglars were caught.

As Haldeman was (allegedly) keeping the President restrained, the Chief of Staff was at the same time encouraging Dean to do more to keep things under control. Dean was concerned about Congressman Wright Patman's committee.[900] Patman wanted to hold hearings to follow the money trail of the Watergate defendants.[901] Haldeman suggested that Dean call John Connally for a way to deal with Patman. Connally told Dean that Patman had some contributions from an oil lobbyist that he would not want publicized, but Connally would provide no more help than that.[902] Here lies one more situation that historians and commentators can spin either way. Nixon critics can argue that it shows how ruthless and dirty the Nixon people were—they would engage in political blackmail to protect their President. Nixon supporters can look at the same evidence and argue that this shows the hypocrisy of Nixon's enemies. One of the men leading the attack against the coverup was himself hiding a dirty little secret, thus strengthening Nixon's claim that Watergate was just about politics. It is also worth noting that John Connally made decisions that kept him out of prison—White House corruption was not a blackhole that pulled innocent staffers in with irresistible force. As far as Patman was concerned, his own committee voted against giving him subpoena power. Due to political forces both seen[903] and unseen, Patman was successfully defanged.

As part of Jeb Stuart Magruder's efforts at Watergate damage control, he spoke with Theodore H. White, who had written books covering the last several presidential elections. According to White, Magruder's first line of defense was that the equipment used by the Plumbers on the

Watergate break-in was second rate, and if the higher ups at the CRP had really been involved, they would have used the best equipment. Another line of defense was Magruder's quite accurate contention that he and Liddy did not get along. Magruder said this resulted in Liddy reporting to someone else, so Magruder did not know what Liddy was doing. Magruder went on to illustrate how he could be responsible for approving expenditures, yet not know about the break-in. Magruder showed White the authorization for sending $1,625,000 to Peter Dailey for television and radio campaigning. Magruder asked, "Do you think...I will ever know what stations he's going to be running programs on? Or what every one of these messages or programs will say?"[904] White asked Magruder about the incredible amounts of cash that were flowing in and out of campaign headquarters. Magruder repeated Mitchell's dictum that the campaign would rely on cash for everything since there had been such a high credit card debt run up in 1968. Magruder pointed out that with credit cards, people tended to spend more. Using cash as much as possible was supposed to create more fiscal responsibility.[905]

John Dean got married in October on Friday the thirteenth. The day of the wedding, his important new friends, Haldeman, and Ehrlichman, and Press Secretary Ziegler, all called him to say there was a crisis at the White House and he needed to drop everything and get over there. They were kidding, but they might hot have felt like joking around if they had known how Dean had financed his upcoming honeymoon. He took $4,850 out of a White House campaign fund, and left a check in its place. He was obviously not trying to steal the money since he did leave his name there,[906] but most employees would not borrow thousands of dollars from their employers without permission.

The Deans left on their honeymoon the next day, but the trip was interrupted by a call to return Washington from Larry Higby. Dean's wife, Maureen, and many others referred to Higby as "Haldeman's Haldeman"—tthe man who was to Haldeman what Haldeman was to Nixon. A call from Higby would only come at the behest of Haldeman or Nixon himself. So, the honeymoon was over.[907]

The need for Dean's return was caused by the *Washington Post*, which had exposed the dirty tricks of a young lawyer named Donald Segretti, who was working for Nixon's re-election. The White House wanted Dean to serve a dual purpose—he was to coordinate with Ron Ziegler on how the White House should respond to the stories in the *Post*, and

Ehrlichman wanted Dean to be the one to tell Segretti to disappear for awhile. As far as Nixon supporters were concerned, the *Post* was making a mountain out of a molehill in the last few weeks of the campaign. The newspaper was trying to smear Nixon when everyone knew that dirty tricks were standard operating procedure in a big election.[908] To Nixon critics the handling of this matter was another example of the grubbiness of the Nixon people—they were trying to hide their true nature yet again.

On October 26, Henry Kissinger declared at a press conference that "peace is at hand" in Vietnam, only the South Vietnamese government under Thieu refused to accept the agreement Kissinger had worked out with North Vietnam's Le Duc Tho. Among other things, Thieu objected to any agreement that allowed a large number of North Vietnamese soldiers to remain in South Vietnam, which was certainly an understandable position for him to take. In November, the North refused to agree to Thieu's terms, and Kissinger's imminent peace was falling apart.[909]

Nixon dealt with this crisis by putting enormous pressure on both sides. He told Thieu the U.S. would rescue South Vietnam if the North violated the treaty, but Nixon also told Thieu that if he did not sign the agreement, the U.S. would make its own treaty with the North. With North Vietnam, Nixon gave them 72 hours to resume discussions. When North Vietnam held out, Nixon ordered that bombing be resumed. The "Christmas Bombing," as it was called, saw more tons of bombs dropped on North Vietnam for a 12 day period starting on December 18, than were dropped from 1969 to 1971.[910] The bombing campaign caused a great deal of outrage from those who believed that either Nixon was jeopardizing the peace agreement, or he had overstated the peace prospects to seal the election. But it worked—both the North and South quickly agreed to a deal.

A month before the election, Senator Ted Kennedy's subcommittee on administrative practices and procedures began to look into Watergate. Among other things, this could be seen as quid pro quo since in 1971 the White House had sent Howard Hunt to dig around for information on Ted Kennedy's Chappaquiddick tragedy. Kennedy had kept a low profile in response to Watergate until polls indicated that this scandal was not opening up comment on previous scandals.[911]

McGovern also weighed in on Watergate, saying shortly before the election, "If Americans vote for Richard Nixon next week, they will be voting for Watergate corruption, Nixon recession, Connally oil, and Republican reaction."[912]

Though Billy Graham's comments in some earlier elections left little doubt as to which way he leaned, the 1972 presidential election was the only one where Graham made public who he would vote for when he came out for Nixon.[913] Graham was just one contributor to the Nixon landslide in 1972. As presidential historian Theodore White put it, "The facts remain—and the after-myth of a contrived or rigged election cannot change them. Americans were given an open choice of ideas, a free choice of directions, and they chose Richard Nixon."[914] This was hardly unexpected. According to a *Time*/Yankelovich Poll, two-thirds of all Americans felt that Richard Nixon was more "open and trustworthy" than George McGovern,[915] who was generally perceived as someone who pandered to extremes.

Nixon certainly did not win the election through cultivation of the press. While he might have made some overtures to the media early in his administration, he had long since given up on them, circumventing the press as much as possible so he could try to control his public image. From Franklin Roosevelt through Lyndon Johnson, the Presidents averaged between 24 and 36 press conferences a year. Nixon averaged seven a year from 1969 to 1972.[916] Maybe if he had worked more on his relationship with the media, they would have shown him some mercy on Watergate. But maybe not.

Nixon later wrote, "My first priority after the election was to end the war." Demonstrating the passion of some of the anti-Nixon forces, author Fawn Brodie considered Nixon's words "perhaps the most chilling single line in the entire 1120 pages" of his memoirs.[917] Though Nixon's strong arm approach had its critics, it does seem a little over the top to categorize his desire to stop a long and unpopular war as "chilling."

With the 1972 election behind him, Nixon instructed Bob Haldeman to divert $350,000 from leftover campaign funds into a safe deposit box.[918] Nixon might have wanted to feather his nest or he might have been concerned about Watergate. Either way, this money was convenient for paying off Watergate burglars.

In the first Cabinet meeting after the election, Nixon thanked his Cabinet officials for their efforts then left the room. Haldeman proceeded to tell everyone assembled to send Nixon a letter of resignation ASAP.

Some men were kept in place, some were shuffled to a different department, but in the end eight new men were brought on board.[919]

Nixon's goal was to overhaul the entire Executive Branch, not just the Cabinet. Resignations were demanded from virtually all of the political appointees and their staffs. Nixon's wife, Pat, was dismayed by the handling of the White House personnel. She saw a big part of the problem to be the President's reliance on Bob Haldeman. Pat Nixon and her daughters saw their father as being more sensitive than he was perceived by the public. They believed part of the negative perception was due to the heavy handed practices of Haldeman and his retinue of overworked, blindly loyal aides. The Nixon women believed the Haldeman team translated Nixon's wishes into reality without the humanity that Nixon would have displayed if he had handled things himself.[920] Of course, if Nixon had been so humane, he could have made sure that they were handled in a more sensitive fashion.

Meanwhile, Haldeman and Ehrlichman were moving forward with Nixon's plan to reorganize White House operations. Nixon, who had quickly and increasingly begun to isolate himself during his first term, would have been even more tightly isolated if his plan had been carried out. The plan was that six key aides would oversee all areas under his authority with Haldeman and Ehrlichman controlling their access to the President.[921] It was a dream operation for a President as stiffly introverted as Nixon. Furthering his sense of isolation, Nixon, Ehrlichman, Haldeman, and Haldeman's top aide Larry Higby spent most of the next two months at Camp David, not the White House. They spent the bulk of their time focused on the government reorganization and—for Nixon and Haldeman—negotiations over the end of the Vietnam War.[922] When it came to Agnew, Nixon had given his Vice President a short briefing on the reorganization plan then Agnew was passed off to Nixon's staff. Nixon wanted to reorganize Agnew's staff, but the President decided this would be overreaching.[923]

Haldeman and Ehrlichman adopted their President's attitudes that anyone who was not 100% for Nixon was against him, and critics did not have to be catered to because Nixon's landslide victory meant the country was behind him. This not only meant that the Executive Branch was going to be purged of the unfaithful, it also meant that little effort would be made to reach out to critics.[924] When a reporter suggested to Henry Kissinger that maybe it was time for improved relations between the

White House and the media, Kissinger replied that such an improvement "will not come from this House until the press acknowledges it was wrong." Kissinger was not talking about his own feelings; he loved the media.[925] But Kissinger was in a definite minority. For example, Haldeman had an old friend, Franklin Murphy, who convinced the Chief of Staff that he and his trusted ally Ehrlichman should meet with Roger Heyns, the President of the American Council on Education. Murphy thought it would be good if the relationship between the White House and academia could be improved. Certainly with the war coming to an end in Vietnam, the door was open. The meeting took place, but Heyns was put off by the arrogance of Haldeman and Ehrlichman, and certainly as a leader in academia, Heyns was no stranger to arrogant people. Apparently, Haldeman and Ehrlichman were in a class by themselves.[926]

Nixon's reorganization was unpopular with White House staffers and Cabinet officers who worried about being cut off from the President. It was also unpopular with members of Congress who felt that their own special relationships with Executive Branch departments would be less meaningful, if these departments were suddenly less relevant to the President.[927] It was unfortunate for Nixon that he had burned such bridges when his Watergate troubles came to a head. But another White House staffer besides Haldeman and Ehrlichman, saw the positives in the reorganization. John Dean, by his own admission, believed that the reorganization could be good for him. He knew as long as he was keeping a lid on Watergate, he had to be taken care of.[928]

If Nixon had ever created his "super Cabinet" of a handful of key aides, George Shultz would have been one of those aides. Shultz wanted George Bush to be Shultz's number one aide and run the Treasury Department. Nixon told Bush that he could work for Shultz, but Nixon preferred that Bush become the Republican National Committee chairman. Bush was reluctant to head the RNC because he was concerned about the effects of the Watergate scandal. Nixon assured Bush that the President was not involved, so Bush agreed to Nixon's proposal with the condition that Bush would be allowed to sit in on Cabinet meetings.[929] It turned out to be a very good deal for Bush. The plan to funnel everything through Nixon's key aides fell by the wayside after about six months anyway,[930] and Bush had put himself in a position to confront Nixon on Watergate in a Cabinet meeting during Nixon's endgame with the Constitution.[931]

Neither the huge re-election victory, nor the Watergate adversity did anything to draw Colson close to Haldeman and Ehrlichman. On the Monday after the election, Nixon toasted Colson for his election strategy and encouraged him to stay on for another four years. "There'll be increased responsibilities—great things to be done," promised the President. Haldeman and Ehrlichman sat quietly through the toast and were openly relieved when Colson expressed his desire to move on from government work. According to one of Colson's White House sources, Ehrlichman was telling people that the Nixon administration would be able to put its Watergate problems behind it once Colson was gone. Colson was disturbed at the thought of being a scapegoat but not enough to stay and fight.[932]

As it turned out, however, Colson was able to solve a big part of his Watergate problem before he left the White House. On November 13, Colson invited John Dean to come to Colson's office and listen to a taped phone conversation between Colson and Howard Hunt. The bulk of the dialogue pertained to Hunt's demands that he and the others facing charges should be taken care of very soon. But the part Colson was excited about was when Hunt acknowledged that Colson had "absolutely nothing to do with" the planning or implementation of Watergate.[933] Colson thought he was home free, and if the future investigations had just focused on Watergate, he would have been right.

As Haldeman and Ehrlichman seemed to be growing in power, Henry Kissinger was shrinking. Nixon was frustrated with Kissinger's popularity—Nixon and Kissinger had just been picked to share *Time* magazine's Man of the Year award. To Nixon it was like asking Gladys Knight to share an award with one of the Pips. It was frustrating that a subordinate was being given equal credit for progress in the developments in Vietnam. Nixon was also upset at how the press was characterizing those developments. When negotiations were unexpectedly stalled in December—after Kissinger had imprudently said, "peace is at hand" back in October—Nixon ordered a massive bombing campaign. Critics in the media complained that Nixon was taking too hard a line but Kissinger was advocating a softer approach. The reality was that Kissinger and Nixon were in agreement. Kissinger later wrote that he allowed reporters to run with wrong conclusions. He claimed he said nothing to mislead the media, but he allowed that they might have misread him, and he did nothing to correct them. Kissinger wrote, "It is one of the episodes of my public life in which I take no great pride."[934]

Nixon was irate at the way the media had spun what was happening, and he blamed Kissinger. Nixon had Colson investigate Kissinger's phone calls, though Kissinger never learned if Colson was just tracking Kissinger's contacts or the contents of the calls.[935] Either way, Kissinger could hardly complain since he had advocated the monitoring of other people's phone calls.[936]

A couple of weeks after the trial of Liddy and Hunt was supposed to have started, they met with their lawyers at Hunt's house (the two defendants were out on bail). Hunt complained that none of the defendants were being provided for like they had been promised. Hunt was doubly upset because he had recruited the Miami team personally, and he felt responsible for them. They could not pay their legal bills, and their families were having a hard time making ends meet. Furthermore, Hunt thought McCord was acting strange and could not be trusted. Hunt, who was something of an accomplished author, suggested that he and Liddy should write a tell-all book about their escapades on behalf of the White House. When Liddy began to balk, Howard Hunt's wife, Dorothy, interjected that the White House had done nothing for Liddy. The only money for expenses that he had received since his arrest had actually been part of what was given to the Hunts. Rather than join forces with the Hunts, Liddy pointed out that he had not been motivated by money in his efforts for the President, and he was not going to betray the man now just for the sake of financial security. "I just want everyone in this room to understand one thing: *I am not for sale!*" With that Liddy and his lawyer stormed out of the Hunts' house.[937]

December was a trying month for some of those involved in Watergate. Hunt received a devastating blow on December 10 when his wife died in a plane crash at Midway Airport in Chicago.[938] John Dean also had troubles. As Watergate journalist and author George V. Higgins wrote, "Dean's modus operandi was reactive, he did not dream up obstructions, but improvised them from ideas derived from others. When they were neutralized, he was paralyzed." Such a man was not the ideal person for the White House cover up. Higgins went on to write, "What Dean did [to maintain the coverup], didn't work. And as early as December of 1972, he knew it wasn't going to."[939]

CHAPTER ELEVEN

The Breakup—1973

Nixon had grand dreams as his second term began in January 1973. "I was going to build a new Republican Party," he said. "And we were going to move the southern Democrats to us. They were ready to go, and with Connally at the top we could have done it."[940] Nixon seemed to have plenty of reason for optimism. His overtures to China had not only improved relations with the most populous country in the world, but they also improved relations with the Soviet Union, which could not afford to antagonize its two major rivals into an alliance with each other. American diplomacy had helped pry Egypt out of the Soviet sphere of influence, which created new opportunities for peace in the Middle East. The role of the United States was being resolved in Vietnam. And despite the turmoil generated by the antiwar protesters, Nixon had won a tremendous electoral victory in November 1972, so he should have been able to bring a lot of pressure to bear on Congress to carry out his agenda. But the Watergate story just would not go away,[941] and it eventually forced Nixon to break up the team he relied on so heavily.

Around that time, Henry Kissinger happened to bump into Joseph Califano, an old friend who had worked for Lyndon Johnson. Kissinger noted how triumphant Nixon had been in his re-election and wondered aloud how the Democrats would bounce back. Califano said that Watergate would take care of the problem. Kissinger later mentioned this to Ehrlichman who brushed it off. "Wishful thinking!" said Nixon's Chief Domestic Policy Advisor, "If that is what they are counting on, they will be out of office for thirty years."[942] It would turn out that it was not Califano who was the wishful thinker.

Kissinger became concerned as he observed Nixon in early 1973. Nixon's great passion had always been foreign affairs; domestic policy tended to bore him. Up to this point, Nixon used to make extensive written comments on memoranda that Kissinger sent him. Now, though,

Nixon's remarks were much less detailed. Once, Nixon returned an options paper with every option checked off, even though some were contradictory. Kissinger believed at first that it was the typical Nixon lethargy that followed success. Kissinger saw the President as someone energized not by success but by tension. Nixon, the great battler, was deflated by success; it gave the fighter nothing to fight. But Kissinger came to see that there was more to Nixon's lack of focus this time than his old personality quirk.[943]

There seemed to be cause for celebration for Southeast Asia when a peace treaty was signed, but the South Vietnamese were not entirely jovial. The Vice President of South Vietnam, Nguyen Cao Ky, referred to Nixon's use of the term "peace with honor" as "a sanctimonious passage which I could not stomach, so nauseating was its hypocrisy and self-delusion." The reason for South Vietnam's frustration was that North Vietnamese forces still in South Vietnamese territory were not referenced in the treaty; they could stay there, and the United States was no longer protesting it. Leaders of other countries in the region took it for granted that the North Vietnamese would break the treaty. But Nixon felt compelled to make such a bad deal because he was afraid that Congress was about to pull the plug on military operations in Southeast Asia.[944]

Nixon did not want to celebrate over Vietnam, and his attitude towards the press was about as bad as usual. When Nixon announced at a press conference on January 31 that "peace with honor" was achieved in Vietnam, he said to the reporters on hand, "I know it gags some of you to write that phrase, but it is true, and most Americans realize it is true."[945] Actually, Nixon's phrase was not true, and his comment to the media was needlessly provocative. But Nixon just could not seem to get past the bitterness he felt towards his political enemies.

When they continued to criticize him even after he was re-elected with 62% of the popular vote, Nixon wanted to strike back hard, which he clearly expressed in phone calls to Chuck Colson in January 1973. Nixon had also discussed this theme with Haldeman and Dean near the end of 1972. For all the talk about Colson appealing to Nixon's dark side, Colson was not alone. As Nixon complained about his enemies, Dean said he was making notes on people who had been against the President. When Nixon talked about abusing power by using federal offices for personal gain, Dean is heard on White House tapes saying, "That's an exciting prospect."[946]

Nixon and Colson had conversations on January 3 and 4, which were centered both on attacking his political enemies and managing the Watergate situation. As future Special Prosecutor Leon Jaworski later listened to tapes of these conversations, he wrote that the word "sleazy" came to mind. Colson told the President that Colson had gotten word to Hunt to expect a pardon within the year, but no explicit promise had been made. The President believed a pardon could be justified since Hunt's wife had just died,[947] but the White House did not deliver in time to satisfy Hunt.

Meanwhile, Bud Krogh was preparing for confirmation hearings to be the Under Secretary of Commerce. He was being moved away from the center of action that was the White House, so his move could have been interpreted as a demotion, but the White House needed to free itself of a man with close ties to Liddy and Hunt. As the Senate's Commerce Committee prepared for Krogh's confirmation hearing, a staffer contacted Liddy for an interview. Liddy did not want to be interviewed by them because he could not tell the truth about his activities without sinking Krogh. Liddy could not lie because that would be perjury, and if he refused to testify, it would make Krogh look bad. Liddy tried to contact Krogh for guidance but was brushed off. An intermediary arranged for Liddy to be called by Krogh's secretary. She apologized on Krogh's behalf and asked that Liddy just not return the Senate staffer's phone call. That made sense to Liddy, and the problem went away.[948]

Two days later, January 6, Liddy received a phone call at home from a man who did not identify himself, but Liddy recognized his voice. It was John Dean, the man who, according to Richard Nixon's public comments, was supposed to be seeing if the White House was involved in Watergate. Liddy later wrote that Dean promised him that he and the other defendants would be taken care of. Among other things, Liddy was allegedly promised he would receive living expenses, money for his lawyers, and a pardon within two years.[949] If true, Dean must have believed he could deliver on all this, otherwise the defendants would start making a lot of noise.

Also in January, Jeb Stuart Magruder testified as a witness for the prosecutors against the burglars. Magruder committed perjury, saying, among other things, that he had not authorized Liddy to do anything regarding the Democratic National Committee's headquarters, nor had Magruder received any intelligence gathered from the DNC. Magruder looked over at Liddy at the defense table, where, much to Magruder's surprise, Liddy favored his old boss and nemesis with a smile and a wink.[950]

By committing perjury, Magruder was continuing to be a good soldier for the White House. Serving the interests of the Nixon administration had been paramount for Magruder; more important than law or morality, but it did not have to be that way. George Bush, for example, was one prominent Republican who refused to be a tool of Nixon staffers. When he would receive word from Chuck Colson or someone else on the White House staff, asking him on behalf of the President to do something he did not agree with, Bush would simply tell the staffer to have the President call him. Nixon never followed up on such things.[951] Of course, this did not necessarily mean that the staffer had overstepped his bounds; the lack of a call from the President might have just as easily been a manifestation of Nixon's disdain for personal confrontation.

Magruder thought he had positioned himself for some important role over Nixon's next four years. Magruder had tried to ingratiate himself to both Haldeman and Mitchell, and it had seemed to work. But a lunch shared with Mitchell late in January changed Magruder's mind. Mitchell praised Magruder's work in various government jobs then shifted gears and suggested that maybe Magruder should consider a return to the business world or running for office. Not only was Nixon's staff trying to freeze Magruder out, but they were working on something even more sinister. Magruder started getting phone calls from Haldeman, Larry Higby (AKA "Haldeman's Haldeman"), and John Dean. They all wanted to talk about Watergate-related matters. They would ask him questions about what had happened then express ignorance and surprise at what Magruder said. He did not realize he was being tape recorded, but it did occur to him that the men in the White House began to see him as a scapegoat.[952]

On January 30, Liddy and McCord were found guilty after the jury had deliberated for 90 minutes. Judge Sirica announced that the sentences for Liddy and McCord and the five who had already pled guilty would come in February,[953] the judge wanted to give them time to sweat, and those seven were not the only ones feeling the heat.

Despite their desire to scapegoat Magruder if necessary, the Powers That Be did not want to antagonize him needlessly, and he had failed to act on their prompting to leave town. Haldeman and Dean arranged a place for him in the Commerce Department as Director of Policy. It was one of the few Level Four jobs in the Executive Branch that did not require a Senate confirmation hearing, and the White House wanted to avoid those when its Watergate people were involved.[954] They had gotten Krogh through the process unscathed, but they did not want to tempt fate.

Democrat Sam Ervin became the chairman of the Senate's Watergate investigating committee when it was formed on February 9. This gained the attention of Richard Nixon who, Watergate researchers Len Colodny and Robert Gettlin pointed out, understood the importance of such a development better than Haldeman and Ehrlichman. Nixon trusted his top two aides, but they were really still political novices compared to Nixon. The President knew the country would be riveted by Senate hearings, so he definitely could not ignore the Watergate issue any longer, even assuming that he had been ignoring it up to this point.[955]

In addition to worrying over Watergate and questions involving the Fielding break-in—which investigators had stumbled upon[956]—the White House had a new concern in February. *Time* magazine was working on a story on the wire tapping of government employees and media figures, something the White House had engaged in starting in Nixon's first year in office. John Dean checked with John Ehrlichman about it and learned that Ehrlichman still had files on that operation. But Ehrlichman told Dean to have Press Secretary Ron Ziegler deny the story. Dean later told Nixon that the White House was "stonewalling totally" on the story. Nixon replied, "Oh, absolutely!"[957]

By late February, Nixon was quite pleased with John Dean. In diary entries made on February 27 and 28, Nixon described him as "an enormously capable young man" and Nixon wrote that "I am very impressed by him. He has shown enormous strength, great intelligence, and great subtlety." Dean also scored points with the President by reading *Six Crises*, the first book Nixon authored.[958]

Thus Dean had a lot of credibility when he reported to the President on March 17 that Ehrlichman might be vulnerable if Liddy or Hunt decided to talk about the break-in of Dr. Fielding's office. Nixon expressed ignorance of, and outrage regarding, Ehrlichman's involvement, but Nixon seemed to be playing to the tape recorder here since, setting aside the possibility that Nixon ordered it, Ehrlichman had already discussed the matter with him.[959]

Dean could not seem to put the stress of Watergate out of his mind. A night out with his wife Maureen and Richard and Marney Kleindienst did little to lift Dean's spirits. As the Deans left the Kleindiensts' house, Mrs. Kleindienst handed a cloth poster that said, "KEEP ME GOING, LORD." It pictured a red fireball rolling down a mountainside. Outside, Dean asked his wife, "Think this would look nice in my prison cell?" Maureen Dean was not amused.[960]

The next Monday was not so amusing either. On March 19, Dean found Paul O'Brien, a lawyer for the CRP, at his office door. Hunt had not contented himself with just trying to get a message through to Colson; Hunt had a message for Dean, too. Hunt told O'Brien, "You tell John Dean that I need $72 thousand for support and $50 thousand for attorney's fees. You tell Dean I need the money by the close of business Wednesday. And if I don't get it, I'm going to have to reconsider my options. And I'll have some seamy things to say about what I did for John Ehrlichman while I was at the White House." Hunt was going to be sentenced on Friday, so he wanted the money situation squared away before then.[961]

Presidential historian Theodore White pointed out that Hunt really did not have a pressing need for money. Because of the death of his wife, he had just received $260,000 worth of life insurance, and he was receiving royalties for numerous spy novels he had written. He was comfortable enough financially that his stock brokers had just recently invested more than $100,000 for him.[962] Yet he demanded the huge payoff nevertheless.

When Bud Krogh saw Dean that day and asked, "How are things?" Dean replied, "Bud, I'm scared, really scared. I'm so scared I can't even make love to my wife."[963]

Also on March 19, Senator Sam Ervin threatened the White House in an effort to get Nixon's staffers to come and testify before his Watergate committee. Ervin said he would send the Sergeant-at-Arms of the Senate to the White House to arrest staffers who refused to co-operate. It was a bluff, but it was a big news story.[964]

The next day Nixon and Ehrlichman met with George Bush, the current Chairman of the Republican National Convention. Bush admonished Nixon and his aide to get the full story out about Watergate. Bush believed it was the only way to bring the problem to an end and get the media and the Democrats to move on. Nixon said he agreed,[965] but he did not follow through on it sufficiently.

On March 21, Dean told the President that Magruder knew all about the break-ins and that Colson might have been involved in it, too.[966] Actually, Colson had legal deniability. Dean on the other hand had bigger problems. He was guilty of at least six different actions that could have been construed as obstructing justice, which he failed to tell the President about during this meeting.[967] Later, Dean testified that he realized from some of the President's comments that Nixon was involved in the coverup before March 21.[968] Any prior knowledge by Nixon is not clear from the White House transcripts of this meeting. If Nixon was already in the loop, then one is left to wonder why he peppered Dean with over 150 questions concerning the possible criminal involvement of Mitchell, Colson, and Haldeman in the Watergate mess.[969] Of course, one could easily offer a contrary argument. Maybe Nixon asked Dean so many questions because he wanted to know how much information was out there.

It was during this March 21st meeting that Dean described their Watergate problems as a "cancer on the presidency." Dean said that he, Haldeman, Ehrlichman, and Mitchell were all a part of the problem because of their approval of payments to the Watergate defendants. Dean also passed on Hunt's immediate demand for cash. Nixon and Dean discussed pardons for the Watergate Seven, but they agreed that such pardons would make Nixon's involvement in a coverup too obvious.[970] Regarding a payment for Hunt, the transcripts have been interpreted different ways. Nixon talked about raising a million dollars for the men in prison, but there was some concern expressed over whether or not that would ultimately be enough. There was also a concern that if the President okayed payments, and that came out, then Nixon would definitely be linked to the coverup.[971]

R.W. Apple, Jr. believed that Nixon had decided against the payments,[972] but Stanley Kutler argued that Nixon favored them, since the President started talking to Rose Mary Woods about "a need for substantial cash for a personal purpose" right after the meeting with Dean.[973] Nixon later wrote that he had asked Woods about unused campaign funds, and she said they had $100,000. But when Nixon mentioned the matter to Haldeman, the Chief of Staff had said that they should not pay any more money because blackmail would never stop, then Haldeman said to the President, "You should stay out of this."[974] While that all sounds reassuring to Nixon supporters, the reality is that

Hunt received the money that night.[975] And according to Special Prosecutor Leon Jaworski, "Within a short time Haldeman informed Nixon that funds had been paid to Hunt,"[976] so Nixon was not totally out of it.

During a March 22 meeting with Haldeman, Ehrlichman, Mitchell, and Dean; Nixon drew a distinction between his own attitude and that of former President Eisenhower. Ike had wanted to make sure that his people were clean when accusations arose. But Nixon made it clear, "We're going to protect out people, if we can."[977] Despite that sentiment, Nixon primarily wanted to take care of Nixon. There was general support in the meeting for the idea of Dean producing some kind of statement to explain Watergate in such a way as to take heat off the President. The idea was popular within the group except for with Dean. Nixon urged Dean to go off to Camp David and get away from it all, so he could concentrate and put together a first-rate report. But Dean made his lack of enthusiasm clear, saying "I was everywhere—everywhere they look they are going to find Dean." Nevertheless, the others persisted in saying that this was the route to take.[978]

John Mitchell also suggested that Nixon's top men should appear before the Grand Jury and testify without immunity. Mitchell, Haldeman, Ehrlichman, and Dean would be putting themselves at risk, Mitchell reasoned, but they would probably be okay, and such a gesture would certainly undermine the perception that the White House was covering up. There was some talk that Dean might be spared from an appearance because he was the Counsel to the President and could claim attorney-client privilege, but protecting Dean was not the primary concern of those assembled. The problem with this scenario for Dean was that he was chief architect of the coverup, so he would be the most vulnerable of all of those in Nixon's inner circle.[979] As with the idea of a report by Dean, the President's Counsel was made to feel expendable.

Nixon's top men never worked out the logistics of testifying, but that did not trouble the President because he firmly believed his problems could be solved in writing. He wanted a written report from Dean to give to investigators, and he was also willing for his staff and himself to respond to written interrogatories from investigators. This was something he talked about with his staff on multiple occasions in February and March 1973.[980] Not having to face his accusers, or see his closest advisors face them, appealed to the President on multiple levels. It appealed to his introverted nature to avoid having to respond to hostile questions from people he did not trust or like. It appealed to the tactician in him, that he and his men could take their time with questions and lawyer their way through them. On a more statesmanlike level, it appealed to his respect for an independent Executive Branch, that he would get privileged treatment during the investigation. Nixon espoused executive privilege, a belief that since the Executive Branch is not subservient to the other branches, there are limits as to what those branches can demand from the executive. Such a belief was convenient insofar as it provided a good argument to keep the President's key aides from testifying before Congress. Judge Sirica noted in his book on Watergate that while "there is no mention of the idea of executive privilege in the Constitution," it is a "common sense notion that a President must have some privacy...if he is to function effectively." Unfortunately, "the limits of this privilege are vague at best."[981] Few things were uncomplicated when it came to Richard Nixon.

Haldeman and Ehrlichman left the meeting, and Nixon and Mitchell spent some time encouraging young Dean to put his head on the chopping block. Nixon also took that opportunity to say to Mitchell, "I want you all to stonewall it, let them plead the Fifth Amendment, coverup, or anything else, if it will save it."[982] Perhaps those words resonated with Dean as he tried to figure out how to save himself.

Dean went to Camp David as ordered and tried to do as he was told, but he realized it was impossible to present even a whitewashed version of the facts without implicating himself. Dean decided not to write the report, but to instead cooperate with investigators in an effort to minimize his punishment.[983]

On March 23, Judge Sirica dropped a couple of bombshells on the White House and its coverup efforts. He handed out maximum penalties to the four of the Watergate burglars and Howard Hunt. The four were sentenced to 40 years in prison, and Hunt got 35. Sirica suggested, but did not promise, that leniency was possible, if they decided to cooperate with the continuing investigations.[984] It has been argued that Sirica was overstepping his bounds here. The sentences he handed out were not even close to typical sentences for first time offenders. Instead of basing their punishment on the crimes with which they were charged, the judge was using the sentences to force information regarding other matters out of the criminals.[985] Still, it is difficult to feel sorry for these men who had broken the law and were obstructing justice. As writer George V. Higgins put it, Judge Sirica was "a nice guy if you like martinets, a useful man if you dislike perjurers in power."[986]

The other bombshell came courtesy of James McCord. He was different from the other men involved in the Watergate break-in. He was not motivated by anti-Communist ideology like Liddy, the men from Miami, and to a lesser extent Hunt. McCord was also not captivated by the idea of living a life of intrigue like Liddy and Hunt. McCord was simply a man on a job. The job happened to be illegal, but McCord thought the people who endorsed it were powerful enough to make his problem go away. McCord had been patient, and Dean had strung him along with promises, but McCord had his limits, and the Watergate judge found them. Judge Sirica read a letter from James McCord, who had decided to take matters into his own hands and provide information in exchange for leniency.[987] McCord alleged that the defendants had been pressured to keep quiet, and they had been pressured into committing perjury.[988]

A few days after the McCord letter became public knowledge, John Connally was talking to John Ehrlichman about a problem involving some oil companies. Connally switched topics. "The President has got to start saying more about Watergate," the Texan said. "He's got to speak out." The President would have spoken out if he had gotten the Dean Report, but Nixon was quickly losing confidence in Dean's ability to be a good soldier.[989] The Counsel to the President had already decided to cooperate with authorities, and the McCord letter pushed Dean further down that road, despite his assurance to the President that the letter would generate "lots of heat, little legal effect."[990] Apparently the heat it did generate was too much for Dean.

At about the same time, Jeb Magruder well understood the danger that James McCord posed to him. And Magruder was not blind to the implications when the White House denied Dean knew anything about the break-in before hand but had no comment on Magruder's innocence.[991] These troubling developments helped Magruder admit to himself that what he had done in authorizing the break-ins and helping with the coverup was wrong. He contemplated fleeing the country but decided that was impractical. He also thought about suicide but decided that things were not *that* bad. He knew that legal trouble was brewing and asked John Mitchell for advice. Mitchell gave him a name to call, "but don't tell your lawyer the truth," Mitchell said. "Tell him the coverup story." Magruder took Mitchell's advice, but his lawyer saw through his story and urged him to open up. Magruder did the next day, which led his lawyer to contact the prosecutors' office. Magruder worked out a deal where he agreed to give his full cooperation in exchange for only being charged with one count of obstruction of justice.[992]

On March 26 Liddy continued to invoke the Fifth Amendment and accepted the process rather stoically, but Howard Hunt had a different way of dealing with things. He was pretending to cooperate, but he was not saying anything to hurt the White House, he was laying it all on Liddy. Since this was where the White House wanted the blame to fall, and Liddy had accepted that, Hunt was really not doing anything to make it worse. When the two men began to speak to each other about pardons, Liddy said he was hoping for one in two years. The thought of two years in prison disturbed Hunt, so Liddy tried to reassure him. Liddy said that as the leader of the operation, he would probably have to stay in prison longer, but Hunt and the others might have a Merry Christmas. Hunt replied that he would rather have a happy Fourth of July.[993]

Hunt then began to complain that he had not received as much money as he thought he should have gotten. He said he assumed that Liddy had helped himself to the remaining GEMSTONE budget, to which Liddy replied, "Howard, I do not steal from my clients." The now irritated Liddy walked away to cool off and was surprised by what Hunt was doing when Liddy returned. "I saw him sitting like an Indian fakir on his cot, mumbling. He called it 'transcendental meditation.' I called it starting to crack. If Hunt went bad, the President had a serious problem. I began thinking about a way to solve it."[994]

Colson wrote in his autobiography that Hunt had not actually spoken to him in March; Hunt had spoken to Colson's lawyer, David Shapiro. John Dean had wanted Colson to make contact with Hunt to see how well Hunt was holding up. Shapiro had vetoed the contact and went in Colson's stead. Shapiro said nothing to Colson about a pardon, but Colson's lawyer did say that Hunt wanted more money to keep his mouth shut about the White House. Shapiro said, "Chuck, you stay away from this or I'll break your neck. If you pass that message on, you are involved in an obstruction of justice." Mystifyingly, Colson had not considered the fact that arranging payments for felons to keep quiet about their crimes was an obstruction of justice. He had been so caught up in the White

House mentality of protecting the President, and safeguarding national security interests, and fighting tough against political rivals; that he allegedly did not realize the territory the White House had gotten into. Thus, Hunt was—from his point of view—left hanging.[995] This is one of the gray areas of Watergate. Nixon later called Colson and asked if the two of them had ever discussed clemency for Hunt. Colson assured the President that they had not, but a White House tape later revealed that the President and his hatchet man had discussed such a deal.[996] Perhaps Colson's memory was lacking, or maybe his thinking was wishful, but if Colson had talked to Nixon, maybe some sort of promise had been offered to Hunt in the heat of the moment that was vague enough for all parties to walk away believing what they wanted to believe.

Haldeman called Colson in late March with an invitation to come visit him in the White House. Colson was surprised when he arrived in Haldeman's office, and the Chief of Staff invited him over to sit by the fire. Haldeman asked how Colson's law practice was doing. The congeniality of the stern and busy Haldeman, who had never really liked Colson, made him wonder about the man's agenda. According to Colson's autobiography, the following conversation took place.[997]

"Chuck," Haldeman said, "we have to get rid of this Watergate mess. It is hanging like a dark cloud over the President. He trusts you and needs your best advice. What can we do? What are we doing wrong?"

"Bob, I told the President last week to hire a criminal lawyer, someone who can get all the facts, piece the whole mystery together and give the boss cold-blooded, hard advice. Then get rid of the culprits. It's the only way."

Haldeman thought about it then laughed. "You lawyers are all alike. This is a public relations problem. We've got too many lawyers now."

Haldeman was wrong about how to handle the problem, but then he was wrong about the nature of the problem. In a meeting with the President and Ehrlichman on March 27, Haldeman and the others were concerned that Magruder was going to lie and say that Haldeman was involved in planning Watergate.[998] They were oblivious to the fact that their real danger was from John Dean.

Judge Sirica was outraged by Liddy's lack of cooperation. While all American citizens have the right not to testify against themselves and their spouses, such a right is not extended towards covering up a government conspiracy. On April 3, Sirica sentenced Liddy to serve a year and a half for contempt of court. Sirica suspended the twenty years Liddy was sentenced to, pending completion of the contempt time, which meant Liddy was facing 21.5 years in a federal prison.[999]

John Ehrlichman could not sleep on the night of April 13. He knew that men were testifying about the money that had been given to the Watergate Seven. He had heard from Chuck Colson that John Dean was trying to cut a deal for himself by offering the prosecutors other targets. Colson also told Ehrlichman that Dean was feeding information to the media in an effort to get them to pressure the authorities to make a deal with Dean.[1000]

Investigators found the enemies lists that Dean eventually turned over to be of particular interest as an example of White House heavy handedness and potential abuse of power. Dean produced this information to show what a morally corrupt environment the White House was. Interestingly, these lists were originally created by Dean as his recommendations of targets for White House retribution.[1001] Dean was helping himself to look good by making the White House look bad, but it was Dean who had originally produced the badness that he was now using to make himself look good. That's irony.

Ehrlichman decided that night on April 13th to go ahead and make the report for the President that Dean had failed to do. According to Ehrlichman's report, the White House really was fairly free of culpability regarding Watergate. Dean had taken part in discussions with Mitchell and the CRP about Liddy's proposed operations, but Dean had objected and stopped the program. Haldeman and Colson had wanted "intelligence" on the Democrats, but when the White House used that word, it had a different connotation than when Liddy and Hunt used it. Mitchell had tried to get John Dean to raise money for the defendants, but only to provide them with living expenses and attorney fees, and Dean could not sufficiently provide even that. Alas, as a result of this effort, Haldeman, Colson, Ehrlichman, and others became aware "of some specific aspects of this activity."[1002] On its own the report it was very reassuring, and portions of it were even true.

On April 15 Ehrlichman remarked to Kissinger that "our major problem is to get John Mitchell to own up to his responsibility."[1003] There were others who would have had the same advice for Ehrlichman and Haldeman. Attorney General Kleindienst wanted Nixon to give both staffers a leave of absence or worse. Nixon protested against this course of action, but he later broached the idea with both men. Their initial response was the same as Nixon's had been: they protested.[1004] They did not want to give up their jobs, and it would make them look guilty. Of course, Dean was already making them look guilty, especially Ehrlichman, who Dean had accused of ordering him to destroy some of Hunt's belongings and to tell Hunt to flee the country.[1005] Dean was telling the investigators about crimes and coverups by Haldeman and Ehrlichman because the Counsel was trying to get the best deal possible for himself (according to Haldeman)[1006] and/or because these things were true (according to Dean).

Nixon talked to Bebe Rebozo about taking money out of Nixon's savings account and paying for the legal bills of Haldeman and Ehrlichman. Rebozo said that if money was going to be provided, it needed to be raised by Rebozo and others; it should not come from Nixon himself. When Nixon later offered financial help to them, they declined.[1007]

Mitchell and Haldeman promised Jeb Magrauder they would give him some money for his legal problems, but their promises were vague and Magruder was nervous. Magruder had been given a considerable amount of campaign funds for various expenses, and he had $7000 left over. He decided to hold on to the money, reasoning that any legal fees he incurred as a result of the campaign were campaign expenses. But when the existence of the money was revealed to the Watergate investigators, it was a matter of considerable embarrassment to Magruder, and his lawyers insisted that he return the money.[1008]

On April 17 Nixon told the press that he was allowing his staff to testify before the Senate Watergate Committee, which was a change of policy. He went on to say that his staff members would not be granted immunity from prosecution in exchange for their testimony. While this might have appeared to some as an effort by Nixon to make sure that any guilty parties did not get off easy. Nixon described the move to Henry Kissinger as an attempt to put "the fear of God into any little boys." It was a reference to John Dean, who had enough information to sink the President, and enough guilty conduct to need to make a deal with the authorities. Nixon was hoping to discourage Dean, and at the same time, he was hoping this gambit could spare him from having to get rid of Haldeman and Ehrlichman.[1009]

Over the next few weeks, though, the sharks continued to circle, and Nixon believed that he had no choice but to cut loose two of his most trusted aides. As usual, the President's discomfort with direct confrontation showed itself, as he pressed Kissinger to encourage Haldeman and Ehrlichman to quit. Unfortunately for Nixon, Kissinger had been so far out of the loop in regard to the Watergate coverup that he really did not know how to argue to the two men that quitting was a logical option.[1010]

On the morning of April 29, Nixon invited Haldeman to Camp David for a meeting, but Nixon made it clear over the phone ahead of time that he wanted Haldeman's resignation. Haldeman felt that losing his job would make him look guilty, but, good soldier that he was, he told Nixon that he would comply. Nixon then added, "Uh, I'd like you and John [Ehrlichman] to come up to Camp David together." Knowing how Nixon operated, Haldeman realized that Nixon wanted Haldeman in the room when he forced Ehrlichman to resign. Ehrlichman was more likely to talk back, and Nixon wanted Haldeman's support. Here, Haldeman drew the line, insisting that the President meet with two men separately. Nixon agreed, but added "talk to John on the way up and explain to him what the situation is."[1011] Nixon the Battler still was not good at hand to hand combat.

Later that day, Nixon had an emotional talk with Haldeman in person. Nixon had decided that Haldeman and Ehrlichman had to resign, even though, the President said, what had happened was really his own fault. Nixon had encouraged Colson's dirty politics, approved Mitchell as campaign manager, and ordered Dean's coverup. The President implied that ultimately he might resign, too. Nixon shook Haldeman's hand, which even though they had known each other since the 1950s, had never happened before.[1012] Interestingly, while Haldeman believed Nixon cared about those who worked for him, the Chief of Staff wrote in 1978 that Nixon did not know how many children Haldeman had. "He never asked," wrote Haldeman, "and I was his closest professional associate."[1013]

Nixon said to Haldeman, "Last night before I went to bed, I knelt down and...prayed that I wouldn't wake up in the morning. I just couldn't face going on." Despite the fact that Haldeman was being forced out of his job, and the whole world would know about it, he was touched by this confession from Nixon. Haldeman felt a rare connection with the man he had known for so long but who had been so guarded. Haldeman wrote that he was hurt when he learned that Nixon had said the same thing to Ehrlichman. Haldeman wrote that he considered Nixon's words "just a conversational ploy—a debater's way of slipping into a difficult subject."[1014] Haldeman would have been surprised to learn that while it was more than a debater's ploy, it was even less personal than he thought. Right before Nixon had spoken to Haldeman, the President had delivered this line to Len Garment, who was helping with Nixon's Watergate defense.[1015]

Ehrlichman believed, "In retrospect, it seems that most...of the President's problems would have evaporated had he stepped in" and told the American people what he knew. "During my last 90 days with Nixon my great crime was not forcing him to make a full disclosure."[1016] A couple of trials would determine that Ehrlichman was guilty of other crimes as well.

The departure of Haldeman, Ehrlichman, and Dean coupled with the earlier loss of Colson would greatly change the personal dynamic of Richard Nixon's White House, and it was a change that was needed. It might not have transformed it for the better, but it is hard to imagine that it could have been worse. Certainly Colson did not remember it fondly. He later said, "The White House is a place where everybody competes with everyone else for power and access, so there's constant fighting, maneuvering, petty bureaucratic, territorial warfare. Nobody really did like anybody else. That's one of the things that I found quite distasteful about politics."[1017] Of course, Colson's perceptions were colored by the fact that a lot of his colleagues did not find him to be a very likable person at the time, but his views seem consistent with others.

Nixon's perspective, however, was different. He had apparently enjoyed it for awhile, but he remarked to one of his sons-in-law, David Eisenhower, that after Haldeman and Ehrlichman were gone, it was not fun to be President.[1018] It was an interesting observation since neither Haldeman nor Ehrlichman were ever made to feel like anything other than employees by Nixon. Maybe the presidency ceased to be fun because Nixon felt guilty about encouraging illegal behavior then forcing his men to resign when they got caught at it. And maybe the President was troubled because he knew the bloodletting was not over.

CHAPTER TWELVE

The Beginning of the End—1973

The day Nixon had Haldeman and Ehrlichman resign, the President called Kissinger to inform him of what was happening. Losing Haldeman and Ehrlichman had the President very upset, but he was also firing John Dean, which did not have the President upset at all. Nixon said to Kissinger, "I hope you will help me protect the national security matters now that Ehrlichman is leaving." It was a reference to the wiretap records, though Kissinger did not realize that was what the President was talking about until Ehrlichman told him the next morning. Kissinger wanted no part of such records at this point, and suggested someone else worry about them.[1019]

On the morning of the day Haldeman and the others left office, April 30, Haldeman said to George Bush, "I'm all right George. Jo[1020] and I were sitting around the breakfast table this morning, reading our lesson from the Bible, and we came across the passage where it says 'If you know you have not sinned then nothing else matters.'"[1021]

Later that morning, Haldeman convened the senior staff to announce his and Ehrlichman's resignations. Loyal to the boss to the bitter end, Haldeman encouraged the survivors of the purge to work even harder to help the President achieve his goals.[1022] Decades later, Nixon said, "One of the biggest mistakes related to Watergate—and I know I've said this before—was letting Haldeman go. He was loyal and tough. Haig [Haldeman's replacement] was good, but he was nothing like Haldeman."[1023]

Nixon appeared on TV that night to announce the shake up. The nation was informed that Haldeman, Ehrlichman, Dean, and Attorney General Richard Kleindienst were all leaving office. Nixon referred to Haldeman and Erhlichman as "the finest public servants it has been my privilege to know." But then the President did something rather dishonorable to the finest public servants he had known. Nixon said, "I will not place the blame on subordinates—on people whose zeal exceeds their judgment, and who may have done wrong in a cause they deeply believed to be right." As Judge John Sirica wrote, "In a characteristic Nixon touch, he blamed those who worked for him while denying that he was doing so."[1024] Kleindienst was disappointed at the guilt by association with the other three that he was sure would be affixed to him, but he refrained from criticizing Nixon.[1025]

The TV appearance could have re-established the President, but he was too distraught.[1026] When Nixon was done filming, he mumbled to his gathered family, "I hope I don't wake up in the morning."[1027] When Kissinger called afterwards to offer words of solace to the President, Kissinger saw one immediate manifestation of Haldeman's departure. Rose Mary Woods answered the phone in the First Family's private residence. Her long time loyalty and patience were rewarded by her renewed proximity to Nixon. Haldeman had isolated the President from his personal secretary, so the Chief of Staff could better control access to him, but now Haldeman was as good as gone and Woods was back on the inside.[1028]

It did not take Haldeman long to feel his loss of status. He went to his office the morning after Nixon's TV announcement. The now ex-Chief of Staff wanted to tie up loose ends but found a FBI agent at his door. Haldeman was allowed to go in, but he had to leave his briefcase outside, and he could not take any material from his office with him. Haldeman found some solace in the fact that Nixon was not behind these measures. The President was on his way to a Cabinet meeting when he saw the guard at Haldeman's door. Nixon angrily shoved the man against the wall and went on to his meeting. Afterwards, Haldeman, still in his office, heard Nixon come back by and apologize to the guard.

Though Haldeman was to be swept out by Watergate, he still had an important duty to perform for his boss: he needed to get a replacement to serve the President. Haldeman had the unenviable job of calling his own successor, Alexander Haig, on Nixon's behalf and offering him the job. Haig was a career Army officer who had served temporary duty working for Kissinger, which had brought Haig into the President's orbit. Haig had major misgivings about another political assignment, especially with Watergate hanging like a cloud over the White House. Haldeman had to share Haig's objections with the President before calling back and telling Haig that Nixon still wanted him before Haig agreed to come one board.[1029]

Haldeman maintained contact with Nixon and his new Chief of Staff, but Ehrlichman was cut off. In fact, over time Haldeman began to get frozen out, too, despite his best efforts at maintaining the connection. Ehrlichman later wrote that he was "both bothered and amused" that the wall of protection that Haldeman had erected around the President was now being used against the former Chief of Staff.[1030]

Haig did not relish squeezing Haldeman out. Quite the contrary, Haig admired Haldeman. Though many perceived Nixon's first Chief of Staff as arrogant, Haig saw Haldeman as just the opposite. To Haig, Haldeman was a man who sat unobtrusively against the wall during Cabinet meetings and took the least desirable seat on the President's helicopter. Haig saw Haldeman as a man who was "entirely selfless" and "in no way intoxicated by power."[1031]

During Ehrlichman's last conversation with President Nixon in person, Ehrlichman brought up the fate of Bud Krogh. In Ehrlichman's autobiography, he described the following conversation between himself and the President. Ehrlichman said, "You know, it would be terribly unjust if Krogh were punished for the Fielding thing. Please promise me you won't let him go to jail for it—after all, he was just doing what you wanted him to."

"You mean a pardon?" Nixon asked.

"Yes."

"All right."

Nixon looked at Ehrlichman and asked, "Did I know about it sooner?"

When Ehrlichman nodded, Nixon said, "Well, if I did, it evidently didn't make an impression on me. I didn't remember it." Nixon apparently did not remember his promise, either. Krogh served several months in prison starting in 1974.[1032]

In an effort to get Watergate behind him, the President announced he was going to release the transcripts of 47 taped conversations. Nixon said on TV, 'The documents will once and for all show that what I knew and what I did with regard to the Watergate break-in and coverup were just as I have described them to you from the very beginning." But the tapes did nothing to help the President. Those who believed in him did not need the transcripts. Those who did not believe in him were skeptical that the written transcripts provided the full account of what happened. While transcripts did nothing to help him, they did hurt him in one way. The excessive use of the phrase "expletive deleted" prompted Chuck Colson to say to his lawyer, "He's dead in the Bible Belt." His lawyer replied, "He's dead, period."[1033]

While Colson and Ehrlichman tried to protect themselves and their colleagues by attacking John Dean's veracity, Nixon's current employees were also engaged in discrediting him. It was leaked from the White House that Dean was so afraid of going to prison and being victimized by homosexual rape that he was making up allegations to have something to bargain with.[1034] It was also leaked that Dean had helped himself (without permission) to $4,000 of campaign money to fund his honeymoon.[1035]

The anti-Dean campaign was not without impact on Dean who wrote, "Every base motivation was attributed to me...the stories stung." But Dean told himself that he was not lying, and in his words, hi "loyalty to Richard Nixon had died a long, painful, and justifiable death."[1036]

Rose Mary Woods' renewed access to power was manifested again after Nixon decided to make Alexander Haig his Chief of Staff. Woods called Kissinger on May 2 to break the news about Haig. It was an awkward situation because Kissinger had been Haig's boss, but as Chief of Staff, Haig would now outrank Kissinger. Woods was calling Kissinger to win his support for the idea. Nixon did not officially need Kissinger's blessing, but Nixon could hardly afford a public conflict with one of his few staff members who was popular with the press. Since Nixon disliked personal conflicts, the loyal Rose Mary Woods was helping him avoid one. Kissinger wrote, "I...decided to put the best face on the situation and to make the inevitable easy on everybody."[1037] Whatever his intentions were, though, Kissinger's actions belayed his claims. When talking with Nixon, Kissinger would criticize Haig then Kissinger would talk to Haig speak unkindly about the President.[1038]

Though Alexander Haig did not pay as much attention to public relations as Bob Haldeman, Haig did make strides to improve the outside relations of the White House. Haig pledged to the Cabinet that its status would be raised and that of the White House staff would be lowered. The new Chief of Staff also promised that the White House would do a better job of reaching out to Congress, something that was sorely needed.[1039]

The White House was not the only place where changes were occurring. By May 2, Hunt threw in the towel. He called a meeting with Liddy and their five associates and said, "Gordon, I may as well tell you now. I'm not holding out any longer. There's no point to it. I'm cooperating with the prosecutors." Liddy started to reply, but decided not to waste his breath. He walked out of the room and never spoke to Howard Hunt again.[1040]

A few weeks after Haldeman resigned, he allegedly learned from Kenneth Clawson, a former aide of Chuck Colson, that Colson was blackmailing the President with tapes Colson had made of conversations he had with Nixon regarding Watergate. Haldeman claimed that as he ruminated over this, other things came to mind that seemed to confirm the validity of the story. For example, Haldeman said he was surprised to learn that Nixon's post re-election shake up was supposed to include Colson. According to Haldeman, Nixon wanted Colson out because of Colson's vulnerability on Watergate. Haldeman was surprised because Colson had been such an effective operator for the President.[1041] But Haldeman's account would seem to have a credibility issue. Colson went out of his way to describe how badly Nixon wanted him to stay.[1042] Perhaps, one could argue, Colson was lying in an effort to be self-serving. However, Haldeman wrote about how Colson resisted being cast aside, so Nixon went to considerable lengths to sweeten the deal.[1043] Such sweeteners make sense to Haldeman in light of the blackmail story. But if Colson really did not want to go, and Nixon was being blackmailed by him, then why would Colson go? Besides, of all the men in Nixon's inner circle who wrote about him, Colson's attitude towards Nixon is the most charitable. Colson's fond recollections seem hard to reconcile after their relationship was that of a blackmailer and his victim.

After the Watergate burglaries had been exposed, Bud Krogh originally claimed he did not know anything about either them or the burglary in the Ellsberg case (AKA the break-in at Dr. Fielding's office). In the spring of 1973, however, Krogh admitted that his earlier claim regarding Ellsberg, given under oath, had been incorrect. Krogh's new testimony was that he had actually ordered Liddy and Hunt to break into the office of Ellsberg's psychiatrist. His justification for the break-in and the coverup was that John Dean had told him these things were necessary for reasons of national security.[1044] It had been easy for Krogh to go along with this because he really did see the Ellsberg affair as a national security related issue. Ironically though, it was Dean's information that investigators used to put the heat on Krogh and prompt his confession.

Krogh had asked for and received permission from the President through Ehrlichman to change his statement.[1045] This is not to say that the White House was happy that one of their insiders had confessed to Watergate crimes. According to author Fred Emery, "Krogh's defection was second only to Dean's in the damage it inflicted on Nixon's cause."[1046]

Elliot Richardson became Attorney General after Kleindienst's resignation. When Nixon had announced Kleidienst was out, the President said the new AG would have "absolute authority to make all decisions bearing upon the prosecution of the Watergate case and related matters." Nixon also authorized Richardson to appoint a Special Prosecutor,[1047] and promised full White House cooperation.[1048]

Richardson had already served the Nixon administration first as Secretary of Health, Education, and Welfare then as Secretary of Defense. Richardson decided to bring in Archibald Cox as Special Prosecutor despite some concerns. Cox had worked for President Kennedy as part of Kennedy's Academic Advisory Group and had gotten so close to the Kennedys that he drew guard duty over Robert Kennedy's body as it laid in state in St. Patrick's Cathedral.[1049] There was private speculation that Cox envisioned himself on the Supreme Court if Ted Kennedy won the presidency in 1976.[1050] Cox even gave a speech attacking the Nixon administration shortly before beginning his investigation.[1051] Talking to a reporter for the University of California student newspaper, Cox confessed that he "had such sharp philosophical and ideological differences with the administration's Justice Department operation that he could not consider taking a job with the department." Cox said after he became the Special Prosecutor that he was (according to a writer with the *New York Times*) "renouncing any personal antagonism toward the president [and] saying that no one would be more relieved than he if the tape recordings showed the President to be not guilty." But Henry Kissinger predicted, "Cox will be a disaster. He has been fanatically anti-Nixon all the years I've known him."[1052] And while Cox may have renounced his antagonism toward Nixon, the new Special Prosecutor did not extend the same consideration to the President's number one hatchet man. When Cox saw the paperwork that investigators had submitted failed to link Colson to Watergate, Cox asked, "Where's Colson? Why isn't he in this? We've got to get Colson."[1053]

There was more to be concerned about than just Cox's politics. The men from the Attorney General's office who had been working on the investigation resented the fact that a man who had never prosecuted a case was placed in charge.[1054] Actually, Richardson had been interested in seven other men before Cox, but the others had turned him down. So Richardson decided to make lemonade: If Cox wanted to be the Special Prosecutor, he could hire an experienced prosecutor for the courtroom part of the job; Cox would simply be in overall command.[1055] Besides, if Cox was perceived as a Democrat, then by picking him, it would make Richardson's own confirmation by the Senate a smoother process—an important consideration for a Nixon man during the height of Watergate.

Two significant things happened on May 18. One, James McCord testified before the Senate Watergate committee that he had been promised a pardon if he would keep silent about who ordered the Watergate break-ins. Two, Cox told Richardson that Cox would take the job as Special Prosecutor.[1056] Jeb Magruder felt the original prosecution team was composed of "fair-minded men...there was a certain objectivity in their investigations that prevented them from taking an accusing stance. Not so with the Cox team. They were young, surprisingly inexperienced in the field, and out to wreak vengeance rather than administer justice." Magruder noted, "most of the Cox team had served in the Kennedy and Johnson administrations or were allied with them philosophically." Really, it would hardly be likely that the prosecutors of a Republican scandal would have Republican sympathies, but Magruder observed that in their arrogance and in their mistrust of their political enemies, the new investigators "embodied the very characteristics they so passionately despised."[1057]

John Connally returned to the White House in May as a presidential advisor. Though Nixon had said only recently that Connally would be a great presidential candidate in 1976, Connally did not last long in the Nixon administration this time. The President ceased to be enamored by Connally's blunt style when the former Democrat—he had just recently switched his affiliation to the Republican Party—told Nixon that the public did not believe him on Watergate. Furthermore, Connally told Nixon to fire Haldeman's people, which also did not sit well with the President. After just a few weeks back in the White House, Connally decided he was no longer the apple of Nixon's eye, so the Texan went home again.[1058]

Actually, though, Connally misread the situation. Nixon had wanted Connally as Secretary of State. The problem was that Henry Kissinger also wanted the job. Kissinger was popular enough in an unpopular administration that he could force Nixon's hand on the issue. Kissinger explained his ambition to his aides as a desire to protect American foreign policy. Kissinger was afraid Watergate might leave the President so distracted or desperate that foreign policy would suffer. That might have been part of the truth, but Kissinger was also shrewd enough to know this might be his last chance to come out ahead of his rival, the current Secretary of State William Rogers.[1059] Plus, Kissinger knew that he would not be able to walk over Connally as he had Rogers, so Kissinger wanted the job for himself.

As the stress of Watergate weighed on the President, he sought to get out of the office as much as he could. He only spent thirteen days in the White House in May and ten days there in June. He went to Key Biscayne, Florida and San Clemente, California in his search for a little peace,[1060] but he did not find it.

On Sunday, June 3 stories appeared in major newspapers around the country that John Dean told authorities he had met with Nixon at least 35 times to discuss the coverup of Watergate. In his memoirs, Haig wrote about the conversation he had with Nixon on this latest revelation. "Al," Nixon said to his Chief of Staff, "this Dean testimony is fatal to me."

Haig replied, "Mr. President, I must know in order to serve you. Is Dean telling the truth?"

"No, Al. He's lying. But the damage is done. The question is, should I resign, put an end to things, save the country the agony of what's coming?"

"Mr. President, you don't have the luxury of resigning. It wouldn't serve due process. You just can't do it."[1061]

The next day Nixon talked to his Press Secretary, Ron Ziegler, about the coverup. Nixon stressed that it happened because Dean and Magruder were trying to protect John Mitchell.[1062] Even if it were true that Dean was not operating to protect the White House, Nixon's assessment would still be inaccurate. Dean and Magruder participated in the coverup at least partially to protect themselves.

Later in the month, the White House obtained records from the FBI proving that the Kennedy and Johnson administrations tapped more phones than Nixon ever ordered, and some of the Democrats' taps were even more personally motivated than Nixon's. For example, Attorney General Robert Kennedy ordered a tap on the phone of Frank A. Capell who wrote a book about the alleged affair between the AG and Marilyn Monroe. But Nixon's men did not feel they could release all the details of their findings without making the partisan war they were in take an even worse turn.[1063]

John Dean testified on June 25 before the Senate Watergate Committee. He started with a 245-page statement, which described the moral and legal corruption of the Nixon White House and followed it up by smoothly handling 4 days of questions and answers.[1064] It was devastating to the Nixon camp.

In July, while Nixon was in the hospital with pneumonia, Haldeman aide Alexander Butterfield was being questioned by Senate staffers. Acting on a tip from John Dean, a Republican counsel asked Butterfield about Nixon's behavior during one of his meetings with Dean. Butterfield replied, "I was hoping you fellows wouldn't ask me that," then he described the White House taping system. Nixon was stunned. Rose Woods called Butterfield on the phone and chewed him out. "You dirty bastard," she said. "You have contributed to the downfall of the greatest President this country has ever had." Democrats howled in outrage over secret tapes, saying that their Presidents would never do such a thing, even as workers at the Kennedy Library started erasing some of John Kennedy's more "sensitive" secret tapes.[1065] The library later admitted to the existence of 125 tapes and 68 Dictabelt recordings.[1066]

Nixon had kept the taping system a secret even from many of the staffers who worked closest with him, like John Ehrlichman. The former Domestic Policy Advisor knew that Nixon had taped at least one conversation with John Dean, but Ehrlichman had no idea that *he* was being taped or that everyone else who met with the President was, too. When a reporter on Ehrlichman's front lawn informed him of Butterfield's testimony, Ehrlichman's responded, "That's great. Now all the innuendos and questions will be answered with some hard evidence."[1067]

When the existence of the tapes was made known, Alexander Haig suggested that destroying the tapes might be a wise option. As Haig put it to Nixon, "Mr. President, I've been in a good many meetings with you, and we both know how the conversation goes. You set up straw men; you play the devil's advocate; you say things you don't mean. Others do the same. There is gossip and profanity. Imagine publishing every word Lyndon Johnson ever said in the Oval Office. No President could survive that." Haig thought Nixon was open to this line of reasoning. Curiously, though, Haig recorded in his memoirs that he would resign before accepting an order to burn the tapes himself.[1068]

Nixon decided his lawyers should weigh in on this decision, and they were divided. One advocated destroying the tapes immediately, arguing that they were the President's property to do with as he wished. Another lawyer said such an option was unthinkable because the tapes were obviously evidence in an ongoing investigation.[1069]

Nixon opted to not destroy the tapes because he thought, ironically as it turned out, they would save him. He felt the tapes could be used to prove that John Dean lied, and Nixon saw a related benefit to them. As he said to Alexander Haig, "We don't know what other lies may be told by people who are trying to save themselves. Who knows what Ehrlichman might say, or even Bob Haldeman. The tapes are my best insurance against perjury. I can't destroy them."[1070] It was a fascinating rationale by the President. Haldeman and Ehrlichman were in serious legal trouble because they had tried to protect the President. Now he believed that they might betray him to save themselves. Perhaps Nixon's attitude makes sense. He had made a big deal about protecting his people then he threw Haldeman and Ehrlichman to the wolves. Since he had betrayed them to save himself it is not surprising that it occurred to him that they were capable of the same type of self-serving behavior.

But the President was not the only one interested in what the tapes had to say. The Ervin Committee in the Senate voted unanimously to ask the President for all of his tapes pertaining to Watergate. He refused on the principle of separation of powers. It was wrong, Nixon argued for the Executive Branch to be submissive to the Legislative Branch in this way. Special Prosecutor Archibald Cox was also interested in some of the tapes, and when Nixon refused him, too, Cox went to Judge John Sirica to compel the President to cooperate. Sirica ordered Nixon to turn over the tapes Cox requested by August 7, which set up a dispute the Supreme Court would have to settle.[1071]

Nixon argued that if private conversations with a President could be subpoenaed then in the future, advisors and foreign officials might not be as candid as a President would need them to be. Nixon wanted to be able to send over transcripts made by him or his staff that would contain the relevant material. Nixon argued it was a national security issue. Cox did not see it that way. According to him, "Any blanket claim of privilege to withhold this evidence from a grand jury is without legal foundation."[1072] How could the White House be the arbiter for what information should be released when it was the White House that was under investigation?

It was a good point, though not one the White House was interested in conceding. From the point of view of Nixon and his supporters, Cox was not interested in the truth; he was on a fishing expedition, looking into Watergate and whatever else he could in an effort to persecute, if not prosecute the President. Bebe Rebozo was caught in the line of fire, as his records were subpoenaed going back to 1968. Rebozo was accused of money laundering campaign contributions.[1073]

John Connally was at a gathering of members of the Republican National Convention in September. He told some reporters, "There are times when the President of the United States would be right in not obeying a decision of the Supreme Court." One prominent politician who disagreed was Ted Kennedy who said on the Senate floor that if Nixon refused a Supreme Court order to turn over the tapes then Congress would have to impeach him.[1074]

Another scandal Nixon had to deal with was totally unrelated to Watergate; it involved Spiro Agnew. During Ehrlichman's last meeting with Nixon, the President told him, "I'm going to have to get rid of him [Agnew]. They've got the evidence. Agnew has been on the take all the time he's been here!" This was particularly distressing to Nixon for two reasons. One, he saw, correctly, that any scandal in the Executive Branch at this point hurt his credibility with the public. Two, Nixon saw Agnew's incompetence as being so obvious that the President believed Agnew was an "insurance policy" against Nixon's impeachment.[1075] If Agnew was forced out, it would be one less argument in favor of leaving Nixon in office.

Spiro Agnew resigned from the vice presidency in October after pleading no contest to the charge of receiving bribes while he was governor of Maryland.[1076] Years later he said that it was not his guilt that drove him out of office, but fear that Nixon's new Chief of Staff, Alexander Haig, would have him killed.[1077] This seems a little extreme even for the Nixon administration. If Nixon's men had been willing to go to such lengths, one would think they would have solved their problems by killing John Dean.

The leaks which made Nixon so miserable when they were occurring in the White House were just as frustrating when they sprung up from Cox's office or the Ervin Committee. There was little Nixon could do when Sam Ervin decided to work with the famous Watergate reporters Woodward and Bernstein, but the President could do something about Cox. Besides the leaks, Nixon felt that Cox had exceeded his mandate by investigating all manner of things involving the President. They fact that Cox's non-Watergate related investigations produced nothing but bills for the public justified Nixon's ire (at least to Nixon's loyalists). Between Cox's wanderings and his leaks, the President had finally had enough. Cox was going to have to change his ways or be forced out.[1078]

After the Agnew resignation the President needed his new Vice President to be someone Congress would like. Nixon could certainly not afford to antagonize Congress as they were investigating him, and picking a darling of their's might provide him with a powerful advocate. Thus, Nixon chose Gerald Ford, a man who was in his 14th term as a Representative. As White House staffer Robert C. McFarlane noted, "Ford was liked on the Hill...on both sides of the aisle. Most people in Washington recognized that in the wake of the Watergate trauma, Ford's would be precisely the type of personality needed to make up for the absence of character in the White House."[1079]

Nixon's troubles with the Watergate investigation made it difficult for the American public to give him the benefit of the doubt on other matters, like the controversy over his taxes. According to the tax forms submitted for Nixon in 1969, he had made $328,000 over the previous year and paid $72,700 in taxes. The next year Nixon made $263,000 but paid only $793. Over the next two years his income was about the same, and he still only paid a paltry amount. The IRS audit of the President's finances was leaked to the press,[1080] which to a degree undermined the case that the President was controlling government offices for his own gain.

It looked like Nixon had cheated on his taxes, but the truth was more complicated than that. Nixon had donated his private vice presidential papers to the National Archives. The tax deduction for such a donation was over $300,000. Congress had passed a law disallowing such tax deductions effective after July 29, 1969. Nixon had made the decision before the deadline, but the staff member who was supposed to process the paperwork waited until after the deadline. To protect the President's interests, and perhaps save his own job, the staffer backdated the paperwork, so the President could get his deduction. Since the process had been started before the deadline, there has been some debate since then over whether or not Nixon should have been able to claim the deduction. When Nixon found out about the problem, he professed his ignorance over the staffer's handling of the affair and said he would abide by the ruling of the investigating congressional committee. It was in his response to this matter that Nixon offered his famous "I am not a crook" line. The congressional committee ruled against him, and that, coupled with Nixon's very defensive and awkward handling of the issue only increased the cynicism directed at him.[1081] One of the Special Prosecutors who investigated Nixon wrote, "On an emotional Richter Scale, this shock registered higher with many Americans than the 'Saturday Night Massacre' or the eighteen-minute tape gap."[1082] Both of which will be explained shortly.

Nixon was so busy defending himself from the many fronts he was being attacked on that he neglected the thing which was most precious to him politically—foreign policy. Henry Kissinger was managing Mid East affairs virtually single handedly.[1083] If Kissinger had been responsible for some aspect of domestic affairs, then Nixon's lack of interest would be less surprising, but Arab-Israeli tensions were, as usual, at a boiling point. And, most relevantly to Nixon, the threat of greater Soviet involvement in the Middle East was ever present, too.[1084]

In an effort to regain his focus and expedite the endgame of the Watergate affair, Nixon proposed a compromise for Archibald Cox. Instead of turning over subpoenaed tapes to the Special Prosecutor, Nixon proposed that a Senate Democrat be allowed to listen to them and make transcripts. The Democrat who Nixon had in mind was John Stennis of Mississippi, who was a former judge and the Chairman of the Senate Select Committee on Standards and Conduct. Stennis and Cox both wanted time to think about it, meanwhile word leaked out of Cox's office that the offer was on the table, despite the fact that the White House had stressed how sensitive this matter was. It was precisely leaks of this nature that Nixon used as part of his justification for not turning over tapes with national security issues discussed on them.[1085]

According to Elliot Richardson, Cox had concerns about the "strength of character and sense of justice" of Stennis. Haig took that to mean that Cox, a northeastern liberal Democrat, did not trust Stennis because of his southern conservative Democrat background. After several days, Cox formally rejected Nixon's compromise proposal. But Richardson seemed to indicate to the White House that he thought the Stennis compromise was worthwhile, and Stennis had decided he would do it if everybody agreed. Nixon met with the ranking Senators from both parties who were investigating Watergate, Sam Ervin and Howard Baker. Both Senators agreed, at least partially because Stennis was a colleague of theirs, and they did not want to offend him. The White House had counted on this collegiality in the Senate. Nixon had decided if Cox was the only obstacle to the plan, Cox would be fired. Now, the President felt he had the leverage to do so.[1086]

Attorney General Eliot Richardson had a change of heart, though, after talking with Cox. The AG called Haig and said, "I cannot fire Cox, and if I am asked to do so, I myself will have to resign." Richardson met with Nixon, who made it clear that Cox needed to go but asked Richardson to stick around for a few days. Kissinger was negotiating with the Soviets over a cease fire in the Arab-Israeli War, and Nixon did not want his government to look weak and divided. Richardson refused. The AG resigned on October 20, his Deputy Attorney General, Bill Ruckelhaus, also resigned, but the number three man at the Justice Department, Solicitor General Robert Bork, fired Cox.[1087]

Nixon felt further justified in firing Archibald Cox by a couple of other developments. Robert Bork argued that the Constitution gave the President the "power to control prosecution." The Special Prosecutor served at the President's pleasure—when the President was displeased it was certainly within his authority to fire the Special Prosecutor.[1088] And Cox had given a press conference where he said, "I think there is a question of whether anyone other than the Attorney General can give me instructions that I have any legal obligation to obey."[1089] Cox felt that he had been given a free hand by virtue of the terms of his hiring, but Nixon felt that Cox was being insubordinate to the head of the Executive Branch of the government.

In response to the three men losing their jobs, which the media dubbed "the Saturday Night Massacre," 22 impeachment resolutions were introduced in the House of Representatives. The Speaker of the House decided that the Judiciary Committee under the chairmanship of Peter Rodino would handle the matter.[1090] Newspapers and *Time* magazine called on Nixon to resign. The President's approval rating dropped to 17%, according to a Gallup Poll.[1091]

John Dean considered the President's actions, "a little terrifying."[1092]

The day before "the massacre" John Dean sealed his plea bargain with the prosecutors. He pleaded guilty to obstruction of justice and promised to be a government witness in the other Watergate trials in exchange for immunity in any other Watergate crimes for which he might be culpable.[1093] As they rode down the elevator from Sirica's courtroom, Cox said, "I look forward to talking with you, Mr. Dean. I'll give you a call early next week, and see if we can arrange a meeting." Dean replied, "I'd like that, Mr. Cox."[1094] Little did Cox know that his work on Watergate was almost over.

Leon Jaworski became the Special Prosecutor for Watergate and related cases on November 1. The main reason Nixon was comfortable with the appointment of Jaworski was because of who vouched for the man. John Connally and Alexander Haig were impressed by him. It also helped that both Democrats and Republicans had considered him worthy to be a candidate for the Supreme Court.[1095]

Meanwhile a Court of Appeals had ruled that Nixon needed to turn over the tapes that the Special Prosecutor's office had requested. Nixon complied in this specific matter, but did not concede the general principle, as he subsequently fought against turning over additional tapes.[1096]

Nixon had another problem: one of the tapes he had agreed to turn over was flawed. As Fred Buzhardt, one of Nixon's private lawyers, began listening to the tapes, Buzhardt made an alarming discover. One of the tapes had been partially erased. It was explained to Buzhardt that Rose Mary Woods had accidentally erased about four and a half minutes. She had gotten distracted while trying to find a meeting recorded on the tape she was making a transcript of. Buzhardt heard four and a half minutes of dead air then there was a pitch change and more dead air. In all there was 18 minutes and 15 seconds worth of material erased.[1097]

Buzhardt asked the President if he knew anything about the doctored tape. Buzhardt thought that generally Nixon was a bad liar because the President had the tendency to repeat himself two or three times when he was making something up. Nixon denied knowing anything about what happened, and though Buzhardt was skeptical, Nixon did not give himself away like he normally did when lying. What made the circumstances even more suspicious was that written records showed that Watergate was definitely discussed during the erased section.[1098]

Jaworski had been a prosecutor for the military during the Nuremberg trials of Nazi war criminals, and he reminded Bud Krogh of the lesson of Nuremberg: the defense that one was just following orders did not justify everything. Krogh agreed and stated in court, "I cannot assert 'national security' as a defense" anymore.[1099] Like those who knew Krogh in the White House, Jaworski was impressed by the former White House aide, who Jaworski saw as "a good man who had been thrust down a crooked path."[1100] Krogh decided to take his future into his own hands, and pled without obtaining a plea bargain. He decided to just enter a guilty plea and let the chips fall where they would. His admonition to the public was to "Always ask yourself about every decision—'Is it right?'" Krogh was prompted to pursue his course of action after hours of daily Bible study with his wife, Suzanne. Krogh, like some of the others involved in the Watergate scandals, turned to God for comfort in the midst of the crisis. Later, Krogh was sent off to Allenwood Prison in Pennsylvania,[1101] sentenced to six months.[1102]

Krogh's turnabout, which only became public with his guilty plea on November 30, was a major blow to Nixon's inner circle. Krogh said that Nixon personally ordered Krogh and his Plumbers to find out everything they could about Ellsberg and his associates, and it was a matter of national security.[1103] It was a setback for the Nixon administration to have a White House insider give up on the national security defense, but it was also a blow on a personal level. It was easy for the insiders to say deprecating things about men like Dean and Magruder—sometimes because they were true and sometimes because it felt good—but everybody liked Krogh. It was an impressive achievement of Krogh to be so appreciated by so many people, given the intense rivalries that swirled around the President. Krogh said in an interview more than thirty years after Watergate that people liked him because he liked them. It was not that he lacked the ambition that prompted so many people in the Executive Branch to see everyone else as a rival, but Krogh believed he was in the White House to help people.[1104] It was an attitude that was greatly appreciated. Therefore when he decided to cooperate with the investigators, it was a personal loss to those maintaining the coverup, not just a political loss.

Jaworski's net spread ever wider as his office began to investigate John Connally. The former Secretary of Treasury drew attention because it came to light that price controls on milk had changed quickly after multimillion-dollar contributions by the dairy industry to Nixon's re-election campaign.[1105]

Watergate did not just hurt those involved in the break-ins and the coverup, the fall out obviously hurt friends and families, too. Billy Graham tried to find the right balance when talking about the issue, saying, "I have been dismayed and shocked by the revelations of Watergate," but "while I cannot defend the Nixon administration's wrongdoing, I am disturbed by the 'overkill'." Such measured responses only succeeded in getting Graham attacked from both sides on the issue. He was criticized by those who thought Nixon was guilty. As one letter writer put it, "he was wrong about Nixon, and he might be wrong about God!" And supporters of the President were frustrated that the popular evangelist would not go to bat for his friend.[1106]

Nixon was so weakened by Watergate that his opponents in Congress felt comfortable attacking him on other fronts. In November, the War Powers Act was passed. According to Nixon, this decision "denied to me and my successor, President Ford, the means with which to enforce the Paris agreement at a time when the North Vietnamese were openly and flagrantly violating it."[1107] From the point of view of his adversaries in Congress, Nixon had promised an end to the war in one year, and that was four years ago, so he should not have needed military forces in Southeast Asia. If such forces were needed, then Congress could exercise its constitutional powers to declare war. Such thinking might have comforted the framers of the Constitution, but it was of little solace to the South Vietnamese who were victims of northern aggression.

Nixon, however, was able to take a little solace in a court ruling handed down on December 19. Judge Sirica gave Nixon two of his tapes back, saying they had nothing on them relevant to the Watergate investigation and were therefore protected by executive privilege. The Special Prosecutor's office concurred.[1108]

John Ehrlichman received a Christmas Eve phone call from the President in 1973, but other than that the two men had nothing to do with each other. Despite the high stature Ehrlichman had achieved in the Nixon administration, there was little that bound the men. Haldeman on the other hand was frequently in touch with the President, but these contacts pertained to Watergate and other work-related matters.[1109]

By the end of the year, Julie Nixon Eisenhower had made at least 150 public appearances, and she frequently ended up speaking about Watergate and defending her father. Conservative commentator George Will wrote, "Anyone thinking that Nixon deserved a better fate from Watergate should remember his silence as his brave daughter Julie crisscrossed the country defending him against charges he knew to be true."[1110]

Special Prosecutor Jaworski had reached two conclusions by the end of the year. One, "through tapes which could not be denied, I recognized that Dean had been amazingly accurate" in his testimony of wrongdoing in the White House and among the CRP employees. Two, "I had expected to find all sorts of wrongdoing by [Nixon's] aides…but it had never occurred to me that the President was in the driver's seat."[1111]

Bebe Rebozo was with the First Family as they celebrated New Year's Eve in San Clemente. When Rebozo was alone with the President, Nixon asked if he should give up. Rebozo replied, "No, you have to fight."[1112] Such a sentiment was music to the ears of Nixon the Battler, and the fight continued.

CHAPTER THIRTEEN

The End—1974 and Beyond

Richard Nixon's choice at the beginning of the year was to continue the fight. He was going to in his words "use the full power of the President to fight overwhelming forces arrayed against" his administration. He believed, accurately, that if he resigned he would look guilty.[1113] Nixon also felt he was being hounded for things that Kennedy and Johnson had gotten away with, and the whole Watergate mess was just an example of partisan politics. From Nixon's point of view, the Democrats and the press had changed the rules regarding the White House, and if the Republicans in Congress would just get up and fight for their President the whole matter could be resolved satisfactorily.[1114]

William Saxbe was sworn in as the new Attorney General on January 4. Nixon wanted a Republican, and he needed someone that the increasingly hostile Senate would confirm, so he picked one of their own, a fellow Senator. Though Saxbe was a Republican, John Dean described him as a liberal,[1115] and Saxbe had also demonstrated that he was an independent thinker on Watergate. Saxbe once remarked that the Nixon administration's claims of ignorance on the matter reminded him of "the guy playing piano downstairs in a bawdy house saying he doesn't know what's going on upstairs."[1116] Saxbe later played a pivotal role in Nixon's stormy, last Cabinet meeting.

It was in January when the White House wrapped up what it called "Operation Candor," an effort by Nixon and his staff to demonstrate how forthright Nixon was and how little merit there was in the attacks on him. On January 8, Nixon dealt with some non-Watergate problems by releasing one white paper on his involvement in a situation known as the Milk Scandal and another white paper on the ITT Scandal. While critics conceded that the President went into more detail on these issues than he

246

had before, many people were still unsatisfied. The *Chicago Sun-Times* summed up the feelings of Nixon's critics when it said the President "cannot expect now to have undocumented narratives accepted on faith."[1117] And even if Nixon had satisfied the public with these white papers, neither of them did anything to turn down the heat from Watergate.

The House Judiciary Committee, made up of 21 Democrats and 17 Republicans, was considering impeachment over Watergate. Worse yet for Nixon, six of the Republicans on the committee had either personal or political differences with him that were so great Nixon thought the six might side with his enemies. At this point many White House aides were thinking it was not a matter of if Nixon would be impeached so much as when.[1118]

Democrats booed Nixon in the House chamber during his State of the Union address when he stated his continued desire to not turn over tapes to the Special Prosecutor. As usual, the President based his position on executive privilege. In response to the boos, Nixon said, "I want you to know that I have no intention whatever of walking away from the job that the people elected me to do for the people of the United States."[1119] Nixon also declared, "One year of Watergate is enough." He called on the Special Prosecutor's Grand Jury to wrap up their business quickly. This was rather irksome for the Special Prosecutor, Leon Jaworski, because, as he noted in a letter to one of the President's lawyers, Nixon was the one who was delaying the investigation. Requests for materials and information were sometimes not acted on for months.[1120] What Jaworski did not point out, but could have, was that sometimes when the White House did respond it was not with compliance but with a challenge through the courts, which furthered slowed the process

As bad as things were for the President, they were even worse for John Ehrlichman. In the interim between Bud Krogh's guilty plea and sentencing, Leon Jaworski met with Ehrlichman and his lawyers. At first Ehrlichman betrayed little feeling as Jaworski read off a list of 13 possible charges he was thinking of pressing against the former Chief Domestic Advisor. But near the end of the list when Jaworski said that Ehrlichman might be liable for mutilating a government document, Ehrlichman threw his pencil on the floor and declared, "*That* I did not do!" Jaworski wrote that he had to fight the urge to grin at Ehrlichman,[1121] who seemed to essentially be admitting guilt on the other 12 charges. Ehrlichman's recollection of the meeting was slanted differently. The last charge, which pertained to records of the break-in of Dr. Fielding's office, was so far off the mark that Ehrlichman, who had been obeying his lawyers' admonition to remain silent during the meeting, simply could not stand the unfair accusations any longer.[1122] Perhaps Ehrlichman was telling the truth, but from Jaworski's point of view, it gave the Special Prosecutor confidence that the man was guilty and nervous.[1123]

One crisis Nixon faced that was not related to Watergate or Vietnam was the oil embargo placed on the U.S. by nine Arab nations in response to American support for Israel during the Arab-Israeli war of 1973. The six-month embargo lasted until March 18 when seven of the nine countries promised to resume the oil trade with the United States.[1124] While it lasted, the embargo drove up gas prices, which drove up business expenses all over the U.S. and severely hurt the economy. Bad economies prompt public dissatisfaction the White House, as Herbert Hoover and Jimmy Carter could attest. Thus, Nixon's critics were even more emboldened.

The loss of so many key aides also hurt, particularly for a man like Nixon who only wanted to deal with a select few. The President was by and large only working on presidential business with Chief of Staff Alexander Haig, Press Secretary Ron Ziegler, and personal secretary Rose Woods.[1125] Nixon's most prestigious aide, Henry Kissinger, was ambivalent in his support of his boss. Sometimes Kissinger would say things to his own aides like "That SOB has got to go. He's going to have to resign. It's inevitable." But then Kissinger would soften and say, "No he shouldn't do it."[1126] Other than family members and Bebe Rebozo, Nixon's only other significant human contact was with his Watergate lawyers. Nixon became a benchmark by which isolated Presidents are measured.[1127]

Bob Haldeman, John Ehrlichman, John Mitchell, Chuck Colson and three other men were indicted for their alleged roles in the Watergate cover up on March 1. And Mitchell had other problems. He and another government official, Maurice Stans, went on trial in New York for impeding a federal investigation of Robert Vesco, who made a generous—and secret—contribution to Nixon's re-election campaign in 1972. At least on this last issue, Mitchell caught a break. He and Stans were quickly found not guilty, despite John Dean's testimony against them.[1128]

The House Judiciary Committee voted to subpoena 42 taped conversations on April 11. Just five days after the House vote, Jaworski petitioned for 64 such conversations. It was tough getting blows on both fronts, and Haig noted in his memoirs that the House Judiciary Committee under Peter Rodino had "some of the most outspoken radicals in the House." Yet Nixon's Chief of Staff also conceded that of the 17 Republicans on the Judiciary Committee, only three of them voted against the subpoena.[1129] Nixon had his natural, liberal enemies, but he had alienated a lot of people who were once his allies, and, one hopes, some were simply basing their decisions on legal and moral principles.

Haig met with Special Prosecutor Jaworski on April 28 in the midst of this latest struggle. Haig did not want to offer Jaworski anything new, but the Chief of Staff hoped to sway the Special Prosecutor's thinking. Haig tried to undermine Jaworski's faith in those who had been implicated in crimes and were now cooperating with investigators. A special target of Haig's, and many of those who stayed loyal to the President, was Dean, about whom Haig said, "The tapes after March 21 show Dean to be a subtle but clear liar." Jaworski felt that the tapes he had listened to actually supported Dean's testimony.[1130]

Nixon steadfastly refused to totally yield on the issue of the tapes, but he did try to once again come up with a compromise. The President appeared on TV at the end of April with 1200 pages of transcripts from the subpoenaed tapes. Nixon declared that these transcripts "will, at last, once and for all, show what I knew and what I did in regard to the Watergate break-in and coverup were just as I have described them to you from the beginning."[1131] Nixon said, "I had no knowledge of the coverup until I was informed of it by John Dean on March 21."[1132]

The transcripts Nixon and his staff produced were edited. The official rationale was that they would leave out information not relevant to Watergate. But even at best, there was a little more to it than that. Nixon was, as usual, overly concerned about his public image, and he wanted to show respect for his deceased, pious mother. As a result, he personally wrote in "expletive deleted" to keep his swearing out of the public record. Even mild curse words were omitted by use of a phrase that brought more attention than the words themselves would have.[1133] Nixon's clumsy efforts to look perfect ended up making him look worse than average.

As Watergate historian Keith W. Olson wrote, "As an attempt to win public support, Nixon's release of the transcripts proved an unqualified disaster. The negative impact rivaled that following the Saturday Night Massacre." Republican politicians were highly offended by what was revealed. Their leader in the House said Nixon should think about resigning. Senate Republican leader Hugh Scott called the transcripts "deplorable, disgusting, shabby, [and] immoral."[1134]

When the Watergate transcripts were made public, Billy Graham was shocked by the level of his old friend's vulgarity. Graham's wife Ruth said, "The embarrassment was the hardest thing that Bill has ever gone through personally." On May 28 Graham made a statement to the Associated Press that made the front page of the *New York Times*. Graham's statement read in part:

> While we have no other President's transcripts by which to compare these, I must confess that this has been a profoundly disturbing and disappointing experience... Though we know that other Presidents have used equally objectionable language—it does not make it right. 'Though shalt not take the name of the Lord thy God in vain' is a commandment which has not been suspended, regardless of any need to release tensions."[1135]

Despite Graham's stinging words, he was only rejecting Nixon's behavior, not his friendship.

Another person who read the transcripts with great interest was Jeb Magruder. Because of his continuing loyalty to the President—at least, up to this point—he was devastated by how Nixon and his inner circle had characterized him. Earlier the President had called Magruder a "real stand-up guy" while Magruder was participating in the coverup. But when the pressure got too great on him, and Magruder began to cooperate with the prosecutors, there were comments about Magruder "getting weak" and that he was "not too bright." Magruder had received a series of phone calls from White House people trying to extricate themselves from Watergate. The transcripts recorded Ehrlichman saying after one such conversation, "That phone call I taped will beat the socks off Magruder." Reading the transcripts literally reduced Magruder to tears.[1136]

While many people were offended by the tone of the transcripts, the bigger issue was that many Americans did not believe Nixon's sanitized transcripts could be relied on to get at the truth. An increasing number of people saw executive privilege and national security arguments as excuses by the Nixon White House to not be as forthcoming as possible. People thought the investigators should get the unvarnished account of what had gone on in the White House, but Nixon still held out.

Making matters worse for the President, his staff had mistakenly edited eight transcripts that the Special Prosecutors office had already received from the White House. The Special Prosecutors were highly disturbed by the editing jobs that they could compare with their tapes. Some statements were omitted, others were added, some were attributed to the wrong speaker, and others were listed as unintelligible on the transcripts when the investigators could clearly discern them. In short, the Special Prosecutor's office had lost all faith, if it ever really had any, in the willingness of the White House to help them discover the truth contained in the evidence.[1137]

The President was informed as of May 5 that he was named as an unindicted co-conspirator by the Watergate Grand Jury in a 19-0 vote. They had actually voted on this in March, but Special Prosecutor Jaworski kept it a secret while he tried to work out an agreement with the White House to get the tapes he wanted. By May 5, Jaworski had reached the end of his rope. Nixon was informed that unless he turned over 18 tapes that Jaworski wanted, Nixon's status would be revealed to the nation. Call it blackmail or call it a bargaining chip, the pressure was on the President. Nixon spent a few days listening to the tapes then talked about the issue with his Chief of Staff. Nixon said, "There's no need for me to go on listening to those things. On this business with Jaworski, the answer is no. No more tapes. We've done enough. We're not going any further, not with Jaworski, not with the Judiciary Committee. We're going to protect the presidency. You tell them that." At this point, Haig could only come to the conclusion that it was not really the office of the presidency that Nixon was protecting. Nixon must have heard something on the tapes that he had forgotten; something that clearly linked him to criminal wrongdoing.[1138]

After announcing their intention not to cooperate any further, one of Nixon's lawyers argued in court that Jaworski's subpoena for the tapes should be quashed. Nixon's newest argument was that because Jaworski was a member of the Executive Branch he had no right to sue another member of the Executive Branch.[1139] And the battle continued.

Jeb Magruder got his sentence on May 21—it was ten months to four years. Before Magruder's term actually started, he was very surprised to get a letter from his old nemesis Chuck Colson. The letter discussed the mutual Christian faith both men had embraced in the midst of their Watergate struggles. Colson also offered an apology for the antagonisms in the past.[1140]

Magruder began serving his sentence in Allenwood Federal Prison Camp in Pennsylvania in early June. Bud Krogh was already in Allenwood, but he left on Magruder's second day. The prosecutors wanted to move Krogh to Fort Holabird in Baltimore, so he could be questioned in the Ellsberg case.[1141] Despite the fact that their overlap was brief, Magruder was grateful to see Krogh. Like seemingly everyone else who knew Krogh, Magruder genuinely liked him, and it was nice to see a familiar face on an otherwise dreary occasion. Also, Krogh's tips on how to survive the prison experience were greatly appreciated by Magruder.[1142]

In June Kissinger gave a press conference after his successful diplomatic work in the Middle East. Instead of being asked about foreign affairs, though, the Secretary of State was questioned about his role in White House-sanctioned wiretapping, which was discussed by Nixon and Dean on one of the White House tapes. Kissinger turned angry and defensive. He threatened to quit over the matter but did not follow through on it.[1143]

Nixon hoped to take his mind off Watergate with his own trip to the Middle East, but even on the way there the scandal nipped at him. There was a story in the *Washington Post* about Kissinger and the wiretaps. Kissinger, always sensitive to slights real and imagined, angrily confronted the press, even though Nixon's Chief of Staff pointed out that it would make Watergate the lead story on the President's overseas trip. Kissinger again threatened to resign in protest over his mistreatment. Eventually,

Nixon sent a letter to the Senate Foreign Relations Committee, absolving Kissinger of blame in the matter.[1144]

Kissinger's public attitude toward wiretapping seemed to mellow over time. When he dealt with the subject in his book, *Years of Upheaval*, he pointed out that "on this issue, hypocrisy is rampant." According to Kissinger, the other major Western democracies wiretapped their own citizens far more than Nixon's people did. And, Franklin Roosevelt wiretapped more people, and more types of people, than Nixon did. Finally, Kissinger concluded, warrants were only required for national security wiretaps after the Supreme Court decreed so in 1972, and Nixon had ended his taps by then. Or at least he had ended the ones associated with Kissinger.[1145]

As of late June, Nixon recorded in his diary that Haldeman was "really a tower of strength"[1146] after the two of them had talked. For all his legal and administrative faults, it was remarkable that Haldeman was still focused on helping and encouraging the President after being thrown overboard more than a year earlier. A cynic might say that Haldeman was no fool for reaching out to the man who could pardon him and make his legal troubles vanish, but Haldeman's handling of himself in the midst of his personal crisis is nevertheless remarkable.

Nixon also received encouragement from his daughters and his sons-in-law, who all expressed their love and support for him during this difficult time. Daughter Julie used to leave a copy of the New Testament on the President's nightstand, opened to various passages that she found uplifting.[1147]

In June Chuck Colson pled guilty of trying to malign Daniel Ellsberg in an effort to influence Ellsberg's trial.[1148] When Colson went into the courtroom to make his confession, both John Ehrlichman and G. Gordon Liddy were there. At the sight of Colson, Liddy jumped to his feet and saluted—a show of respect for a fellow warrior who had not betrayed the commander-in-chief.[1149] Colson was sentenced on June 21 to one-to-three years. Though Colson maintained his loyalty to and friendship with Nixon, the former hatchet man did read from his prepared statement that Nixon had wanted Colson to "disseminate damaging information about Daniel Ellsberg." Basically, Colson was accusing Nixon of being guilty of the activity that was sending Colson to prison.[1150]

Leon Jaworski was not sure what to make of Colson's spiritual conversion and subsequent confession. Wrote Jaworski, "I found him difficult to understand, and...even more difficult to accept as fully truthful. However, he testified openly and competently at the Fielding break-in trial."[1151] In fact, Colson was called on to testify 45 times in Watergate and Watergate-related trials, and he was the only one of the inner circle not to be charged with perjury.[1152]

Colson began his prison sentence on July 8. He was sent to Fort Holabird Prison, which had previously served as an army barracks. By the time of Colson's imprisonment, it primarily housed underworld figures who were testifying against former associates.[1153] Colson's life in prison was a total change for a man who had served a President. Colson was stripped and searched and handed a pair of underwear that was labeled to indicate he was the sixth owner. Within the week the man who had written memos for Nixon was now cleaning toilets used by 40 men in the prison dorm.[1154]

Three days after Colson went to prison, John Dean was questioned in front of the House Judiciary Committee by James St. Clair, one of the President's lawyers. St. Clair believed if Dean was discredited, it could save the President. But Dean's superior grasp of the facts left St. Clair looking confused. It was an opportunity lost by the Nixon team.[1155]

Nixon had taken a trip to the Middle East in mid June and went to Europe in early July, making stops in Belgium and the Soviet Union. He wanted to stress the importance of his foreign policy work and take attention away from Watergate. But as Watergate historian Keith W. Olson noted, "With no specific crisis in U.S. relations with any of the countries the President visited, and with the majority of Americans believing the House of Representatives should impeach him, Nixon's trips seemed hollow attempts to...divert attention from Watergate."[1156] In other words, the public recognized an expensive PR stunt when it saw one.

The President could ignore the obvious for only so long. On August 1, Nixon said to Chief of Staff Haig, "Al, it's over." This was Nixon's response to the Supreme Court's decision that executive privilege did not protect his no-longer-secret tapes. Nixon had to turn over 64 more tapes, and two of them would reveal his guilt in the coverup. At Haig's suggestion that the President resign the next night, Nixon the Battler re-emerged. "This is my decision and mine alone," the President replied, "I've resisted political pressure all my life, and if I get it now, I may change my mind."[1157]

Jaworski had a theory for why Nixon had never destroyed the tapes. The Special Prosecutor wrote, "During 1972, and perhaps during the early part of 1973, he thought the tapes possessed extraordinary monetary value. He hoped to realize a fortune for them. And his background showed him to be a man greedy for both money and power."[1158] But the notion that Nixon thought the tapes could bring him money displays a fundamental misunderstanding of who Nixon was. Nixon was so concerned about his image that he wrote in "expletive deleted" for the mildest of curse words. Anybody who was going to fight that hard to protect his image was certainly not going to sell tapes that cast him in such a negative light.

Speech writer and Nixon loyalist Patrick Buchanan recognized that the end was near and tried to explain it to one of Nixon's daughters, Julie Nixon Eisenhower, who continued to believe that her father was a virtuous man who needed to keep fighting. Buchanan said, "It's a straight road downhill—for him, for the conservative cause, and for the country. There comes a time when you have to say, 'It's finished, it's over.' The problem is not Watergate or the coverup; it's that he hasn't been telling the truth to the American people."[1159]

The President received a shock on August 6. At a Cabinet meeting, Nixon had once again changed his mind, saying it would weaken the presidency if he resigned because he had not done anything that was impeachable.[1160] Kissinger referred to the episode as "Vintage Nixon." Kissinger elaborated, "Fearing individual rejection, he had assembled the largest possible forum: hoping for a group vote of confidence, he sought to confront them with a *fait accompli* and thereby triggered their near-rebellion." Gerald Ford started the "near-rebellion" by saying that if he had known earlier what he now knew then he would not have made a number of statements as Minority Leader or as Vice President that favored the President. Henceforth, said Ford, he would not speak on the topic of Watergate at all. Ford tried to soften the blow by praising Nixon's foreign policy and his work on the inflation issue, which caused Nixon to take the discussion off on a tangent, but he was soon brought back to the matter at hand. Nixon talked about having an economic summit meeting, but his newest Attorney General, William Saxbe, interrupted, saying, "Mr. President, I don't think we ought to have a summit conference. We ought to be sure you have the ability to govern."[1161]

George Bush was in attendance, as was his privilege according to the deal he worked out with Nixon when Bush became the Chairman of the RNC,[1162] but Bush was not supposed to participate in Cabinet discussions. He was officially just there as an observer, so it was quite a surprise to Nixon and Haig when Bush sought to speak. Bush was not recognized by the President or the Chief of Staff, but he spoke up anyway. Bush told Nixon that Watergate was dragging the whole country down, therefore the President should resign.[1163] According to Haig, "everyone present knew that whatever the President might say, he would have to resign."[1164] When the chairman of the party advocates resignation, what support does a President have left?

In his memoirs, Nixon mentioned that Bush wanted to be recognized, but Nixon glossed over it in his book, as if Bush never spoke up at all. Nixon did, however, record Kissinger saying that "We are not here to give the President excuses. We are here to do the nation's business." This was followed by an embarrassed silence in the room and then a resumption of talk about the economy.[1165] From just reading Nixon's account, one might think that the Cabinet was embarrassed for Saxbe and Bush. But Kissinger pointed out that Cabinet members in general are very deferential to the President because they are appointed by him, they get their power from him, and they can be fired at his pleasure. The Vice President and the Chairman of the RNC were not technically Cabinet members, but the Attorney General was. And no one in the Cabinet stood up for the President when the threesome attacked him. The embarrassment the Cabinet members felt was for Nixon, not his chastised officers. Kissinger intervened when he did, not because he supported the President on Watergate, but to preserve a little dignity for the man. Kissinger actually encouraged him to resign, but the Secretary of State did it later in the day, after the meeting was over.[1166] Kissinger thought Saxbe was "weak-livered" and Bush was insensitive,[1167] but Kissinger did not exactly think they were wrong.

Also on August 6, Bob Haldeman called Alexander Haig. Haldeman said he was opposed to Nixon resigning. However, Haldeman said, if

Nixon was determined to step down, the last thing he should do in office was pardon all of his men who were in trouble with the law. Haldeman furthered argued that Nixon could help sell his decision by pardoning all of the Vietnam draft dodgers at the same time. John Ehrlichman called Rose Mary Woods and one of the President's daughters with a similar plan. Interestingly, Nixon mentioned this idea in his memoirs, and the fact that he followed up on it by talking to Haldeman on the phone himself, but Nixon did not elaborate on the issue. He did not follow through on the pardons, and he does not explain his reasoning behind not following through.[1168] Alexander Haig recorded, "Nixon barely listened when I mentioned these suggestions to him; he had already made up his mind that there would be no blanket pardons for his former associates."[1169] But, like Nixon, Haig offered no rationale for the President's seeming indifference to the concerns of his two most loyal lieutenants. Perhaps Nixon was afraid that if he let all the others off, then the full fury of his adversaries would be directed solely at him. Maybe he was so numbed at the thought of being the first President in American history to resign that he had no mental energy left to care for anyone else at the time. But Nixon's thinking on the subject will remain a mystery.

Nixon told Woods that he needed her help telling his family that he had to resign because he had lost too much of his support in Congress. Translation: she had to tell Nixon's family for him and by herself. Like so many members of Nixon's staff, Woods had to handle an assignment that Nixon found too difficult to do personally.[1170] Nixon was fortunate that Woods was still around after so many other aides had left him for one reason or another. As Stanley I. Kutler observed, "At the end, Nixon seemed comfortable only with Rebozo, Rose Mary Woods, and possibly Press Secretary Ron Ziegler."[1171]

Nixon announced his resignation on TV on August 8, effective the next morning. There was no confession of wrongdoing or acceptance of blame. The President simply acknowledged that he did not have "a strong enough political base in the Congress" to continue his fight against the various investigators and the impeachment process.[1172]

After his speech Nixon was met in the hallway by Henry Kissinger. Kissinger's treatment of others had always seemed proportional to the power they wielded, and here was Nixon who was soon to be walking away from power altogether. Kissinger said, "Mr. President, after most of your major speeches in this office we have walked together back to your house. I would be honored to walk with you again tonight." It was a touching display of graciousness from a master diplomat. Kissinger told Nixon that history would judge his presidency kindly, but Nixon replied, "That depends, Henry, on who writes the history."[1173]

Back with his family afterwards, Nixon was so keyed up that he was sweating through his suit. Pat Nixon heard a commotion outside the White House, so she called her husband over to the window. It took them a moment to realize that the crowd was chanting "Jail to the Chief."[1174]

The next day, as Nixon was preparing to walk out of the White House and into civilian life, he said to Gerald Ford, "Good luck, Mr. President. As I told you when I named you, I know the country is going to be in good hands with you in the Oval Office." As usual, Nixon seemed to rise to the occasion in the face of immense adversity. The classiness that sometimes eluded Nixon when things were going smoothly had once again manifested itself. The new President thanked Nixon for his kind words. The new First Lady told him to "have a nice trip,"[1175] which seems kind of trite, given the circumstances, but knowing the right thing to say in such a uniquely awkward situation would be difficult for anyone.

Stephen Ambrose, a self described "Nixon-hater," wrote a three volume biography of the President. Ambrose's conclusion, despite his attitude going into the project, was, "When Nixon resigned, we lost more than we gained." It prompted the reviewer for the *Cleveland Plain Dealer* to write that the 2,155-page opus was "one sentence too long."[1176]

Regarding Nixon's demise, Special Prosecutor Leon Jaworski agreed with Pat Buchanan and many others. Jaworski believed that "what sank [Nixon] was his lying....People can tolerate a great deal in their public officials. If a person is big enough to say 'I did it,' he'll be forgiven."[1177] For the reminder of his life, though, "I did it" was not something Richard Nixon was willing to say. This was demonstrated when Bud Krogh went out to visit the ex-President in San Clemente. Krogh asked him, "Do you feel guilty, Mr. President?" Nixon replied, "No, I don't. I just don't."[1178] He was defeated but still defiant.

Gerald Ford soon decided to pardon Nixon, but the question of timing was an important one. As he said to one of his aides, Ford felt that if he had already decided to pardon Nixon, but was holding off for political reasons, and then something happened—like Nixon committed suicide or had a stress related heart attack—Ford would never have been able to forgive himself.[1179]

When Nixon was pardoned, it was controversial within the White House. Ford's Press Secretary Jerry terHorst had been a friend of Ford's for 25 years. TerHorst wrote to the President, "Try as I can, it is impossible to conclude that the former President is more deserving of mercy than persons of lesser station in life whose offenses have had far less effect on our national well-being." TerHorst resigned in protest.[1180]

When asked years later why he pardoned Nixon, Gerald Ford's rationale changed. "I had to get rid of him! I couldn't get the work done. Everybody was busy trying to crucify the guy. And I finally said to people, 'Enough already! Pardon him.' And [Counsel to President Ford] Phil Buchen said, 'On what basis?' And I said, 'I don't care. Get him out of here. I can't do this job until people stop. Enough.'"[1181]

There was a logistical concern at the time for Ford. On September fourth, Jaworski had sent a letter to Buchen, which said that it would be hard for Richard Nixon to get a fair trial in the United States.[1182] It was a point worth noting. One of Nixon's lawyers had already written a letter to that effect to Jaworski, pointing out that not only had the media coverage been overwhelming but the publicity was also compounded by the fact that so many politicians had weighed in with their views on the subject.[1183] The Watergate story was huge, and any prospective juror knew who the President of the United States from 1969 to August 1974 had been, so jurors would have definitive opinions on the defendant. Armed with that knowledge, Ford knew the issue could conceivably drag on for the remainder of his administration and beyond.

The pardon of Nixon on September 8th left the Watergate prisoners wondering if perhaps pardons might be coming for them, too. Chuck Colson was confident and Jeb Magruder was hopeful, but the public outcry against the pardon was such that Gerald Ford's hands were tied. The prisoners would have to wait it out.[1184] Colson tried to use his influence to help his cause. He contacted several men including Billy Graham, Colson's old boss Senator Leverett Saltonstall, and many others, asking them to intervene with Ford, but it was no use. Ford's hands were tied by public opinion on the matter.[1185]

Near the end of August, Magruder had been transferred to Fort Holabird. He was joined there by John Dean, who finally began serving his sentence on Labor Day. Magruder perceived Dean's treatment as much better than that of the rest of the Watergate prisoners and the prison population in general. Dean spent five days a week with the prosecutors during business hours, staying at the prison only at night and on weekends. While at the prison, Dean had a federal marshal stationed outside his cell door,[1186] though there was an explanation for this. As mentioned in the last chapter, Dean's enemies had circulated the rumor that he was afraid of being attacked in prison. It was felt that this would make Dean a target, so special protection might have been warranted. Dean's isolation was not such a disappointment for Magurder, who believed that "talking to [Dean] was a definite risk because he had a way of distorting the conversation at a later date so that he would come out on top, with everyone else on the bottom."[1187]

When John Ehrlichman first learned about the White House taping system from a reporter, Ehrlichman replied, "That's great. Now all the innuendos and questions will be answered with some hard evidence." Was this conviction or just bravado on the part of Ehrlichman? The former Domestic Policy Chief wrote in his autobiography, "When I was indicted in 1974, I was accused of a number of crimes, some of which I did not in fact commit." Ehrlichman complained that the quality of the tapes was so bad that transcribers attributed comments to him that were made by others. He also claimed that when he and Haldeman went to the CIA to try to get them to limit the scope of the FBI investigation of Watergate, Ehrlichman did not really know why he was there. So, what does Ehrlichman admit to? "During my last ninety days with Nixon my great crime was not forcing him to make a full disclosure." Also, Ehrlichman said he found out about the Fielding break-in after the fact, but he did not turn in the Plumbers.[1188]

The Watergate trial of Haldeman, Ehrlichman, Mitchell, and two other, lesser figures was rather unique. Though key Executive Branch figures had been in trouble with the law before, Mitchell was the first Attorney General of the United States to be put on trial.[1189] The proceedings were also somewhat unique in that the major codefendants had different strategies for surviving their ordeal. Haldeman's lawyer approached the Special Prosecutor with an intriguing offer. Haldeman was willing to plead guilty to one felony and testify against his good friend

Ehrlichman and the others if all the other charges were dropped against the former Chief of Staff. Haldeman's lawyer also said he believed that if Haldeman testified, then Mitchell would come clean also. The lawyers went to Judge Sirica to discuss the plea. Haldeman's lawyer wanted to know what kind of sentence his client would get, but Sirica said Haldeman would have to take his chances in court, which caused the deal to fall through.[1190] John Ehrlichman decided to base his defense on the idea that he was an innocent and honorable man who was used by a deceitful President.[1191] Ehrlichman's lawyers also attacked the quality of the White House tapes. Written transcripts were provided for the jurors because the sound quality of the tapes was so poor.[1192] This was not enough for Ehrlichman, who argued that the transcripts were riddled with errors. Judge Sirica, however, was unmoved.[1193] As Sirica described it, the lawyers did argue over the quality of the transcripts, but "much of the debate was meaningless and tedious." Sirica threatened to keep the lawyers in session long enough to miss a Washington Redskins game, which, he wrote, finally got them to reach an understanding. Ehrlichman also wanted former President Nixon to be brought in to testify. Ehrlichman sought to portray himself as a pawn of Nixon and Dean, but Nixon argued that he was too sick to travel. Sirica had some doctors confirm this, and he decided that the delay was not worth it. Furthermore, Sirica later wrote, "having [Nixon] in court was not really critical to Ehrlichman's defense."[1194] John Mitchell's lawyer tried to get a mistrial declared because each man's lawyer was trying to minimize his own client's guilt by incriminating the others. As Mitchell's lawyer put it, "The defenses here are so antagonistic that we are faced with the situation…where we have two prosecutors." But in Judge Sirica's opinion "the law is clear that defendants accused of committing the same crime can be tried together. It would have been an impossible burden to try to each one separately." One bit of strategy the defendants did agree on was blaming John Dean for the Watergate mess.[1195]

Nixon's pardon made things more complicated for the men on trial. If it was hard enough to get impartial justice before, it was even more so at this point. Some people thought that if Nixon was let off, his underlings should be shown the same mercy. But for those who felt Nixon got the easy way out, many wanted an extra pound of flesh from Nixon's men.[1196]

As the Big Three of Haldeman, Ehrlichman, and Mitchell were dealing with their trial, several of their associates saw things getting better. Bud Krogh was the first of the men focused on in this book to go in and out of prison.[1197] He served about four and a half months and had already gotten out on June 21, 1974. John Dean served for a slightly shorter period then was freed on January 8, 1975, the same day that Jeb Stuart Magruder was released.[1198] Judge Sirica, who had sentenced Magruder and Dean, decided these two men had been given rather stiff sentences in the first place, they had shown remorse, and they had been very helpful in the Watergate trial of Haldeman and the others. Sirica thus reduced their sentences to time served.[1199] But Sirica was not Colson's judge because Colson's lawyer had said that Colson would only plea bargain if he could do it with some other judge, such was the hostility towards Sirica.[1200] Since Colson had not been convicted in Sirica's court, when the decision was made to free the other two Colson was left behind. Magruder prayed that Colson would be freed soon[1201]—a remarkable development given the previous hostility of the two men.

The primary agent in the improvement of relations between the pair was that both had spiritual experiences in the midst of their Watergate agony. They, along with fellow Nixon staffer turned prisoner Herb Kalmbach, had become committed Christians as a result of their fall from power. They had even had their own private Christmas Eve worship service in John Dean's cell.[1202] As for Dean himself, he said, "My beliefs have remained unchanged before and after these events," and unlike the other three he chooses not to discuss those beliefs.[1203]

Shortly before Christmas, fellow prisoners Dean and Colson were talking about Watergate, trying to understand what happened. When Dean asked, "Chuck, why do you figure Liddy bugged the DNC instead of the Democratic candidates?" Colson did not have an answer. Dean suggested they invite Magruder in on their conversation. When Magruder joined them, and they asked a few questions about Watergate, Magruder said, "I don't think we ought to talk about that stuff" and walked out.[1204]

Dean and Colson could not understand why Magruder seemed so uncomfortable, but Colson had a theory. "I think he's still holding back what he knows," suggested the former hatchet man.[1205] Given that Magruder said decades later that Nixon pre-approved the Watergate break-in, Colson's theory might be correct. Also, Magruder might have been concerned about how Dean could twist their conversation.

John Ehrlichman, too, found himself turning to God for support in this difficult time. Ehrlichman spent a lot of time praying and thinking about Jesus in the Garden of Gethsemane, though Ehrlichman acknowledged that unlike Jesus, Ehrlichman was not without sin. Specifically, God was not the only one to whom Ehrlichman had turned for comfort. During his second trial, Ehrlichman had a brief affair, which he rationalized at the time because his marriage was an unhappy one, and his self-esteem was low.[1206]

Things got much worse for Colson, still stuck in prison, before they got better. His judge, Gerhard Gesell, did not want to look like he was being forced to be lenient because Sirica had been, so Gesell was not interested in shortening Colson's stay in prison. On January 20, the Virginia Supreme Court disbarred Colson from practicing law there. A short later, Chris Colson, son of Nixon's former hatchet man, was arrested for drug possession. The silver lining in this personal blow to Chuck Colson was that it prompted his judge to commute his sentence on compassionate grounds on January 30.[1207]

One prize unclaimed by the Special Prosecutor was Bebe Rebozo, but it was not just Leon Jaworski who was after him. Rebozo was also under investigation by the Government Accounting Office, the IRS, the Miami District Attorney, and the Senate Watergate Committee. Yet it was virtually ignored by the media when Leon Jaworski said on January 9, 1975 that his staff could not find any evidence of wrongdoing by Rebozo.[1208] The day after Magruder and Dean were freed, Bebe Rebozo was feeling free, too.

Bob Haldeman, John Ehrlichman, and John Mitchell were not sentenced until February 21, 1975, months after Nixon had already been pardoned. Haldeman was found guilty of all five of the charges against him. Ehrlichman was convicted of three of four counts related to Watergate,[1209] and he was convicted of one count of conspiracy and three counts of perjury for the Fielding break-in.[1210] Mitchell was found guilty of five of six counts.[1211] Judge Sirica noted that the three men even handled their final statements before sentencing differently from each other. Haldeman's lawyer noted that Nixon was free, and everything Haldeman had done was for Nixon. Ehrlichman's lawyer pleaded for alternative sentencing. Ehrlichman wanted to be placed in an institution in the southwestern United States, so he could give free legal advice to

Native Americans. Mitchell's lawyer said his client did not want to prolong the proceedings. Sirica sentenced all three men to two and a half to eight years.[1212]

On April 17, 1975 John Connally was found not guilty of two of the charges against him in the Milk Scandal. The Special Prosecutor moved to dismiss the remaining three charges the next day, and the judge agreed.[1213]

Almost two full years later, on April 12, 1977, President Jimmy Carter commuted Gordon Liddy's sentence from twenty years to eight, which made Liddy eligible for parole shortly thereafter. Liddy was finally released on September 7, 1977. Like his favorite President, a battler through and through, Liddy grew irritated as press cars followed him for miles after he left the prison. The uninsured Liddy took the wheel from his wife and lost the reporters after a high speed chase.[1214]

Henry Kissinger was moved by the plight of Mitchell to intervene on his behalf. Kissinger and Gerald Ford's Treasury Secretary, William Simon visited Judge Sirica in January 1977 to ask for mercy. Sirica did not want to discuss the matter with them, but by the fall of 1977 Sirica felt that justice had been served. He shortened the sentences of Mitchell, Haldeman, and Ehrlichman to one to four years, the same sentence, Sirica noted, that he had given to John Dean.[1215] Mercy seemed to be the order of the day with all of the Watergate figures.

Beaten down but not broken, Nixon the Battler continued to try to influence how he would be remembered. As he saw it, he would have a difficult job. Nixon said, "There is no such thing as history. There are historians and 85% of them are on the left."[1216] While Nixon genuinely believed this, it was also a convenient self-motivational tool for the man who strived on fighting.

Presidential historian Theodore H. White made a fascinating observation about Richard Nixon. White set the context for his remarks by observing that it has been said that "power is to liberals...what sex is to Puritans—liberals loathe it, yet lust for it." White noted, "The key belief of liberal intellectuals, shared with conservatives, is that power, in the hands of any but their own kind, conceals a hidden wickedness." White wrote that liberals were outraged by Nixon's big victory in 1972 because it showed that he understood the country better than they did.

But the unraveling of the Nixon administration by the Watergate scandal demonstrated that the liberals were right about Richard Nixon and his "hidden wickedness" all along.[1217]

Despite Nixon's personal weaknesses and public humiliation, his presidency was not wholly negative. There were some on both ends of the political spectrum who disliked Nixon's policies with the Soviets. Some liberals complained that Nixon ignored human rights abuses. Some conservatives felt the SALT talks did not benefit the United States as much as they did the Soviet Union.[1218] But as author John Robert Greene wrote, "Few scholars are left who attempt to argue that Richard Nixon's foreign policy was anything less than revolutionary." This was because of Nixon's successes in creating improved relations with both the Soviet Union and the People's Republic of China. And Nixon extricated his country from Vietnam.[1219] He did not do it as swiftly as his liberal critics would have liked, and the fragile treaty that was put it place did not last long, much to the consternation of Nixon's conservative critics. But Nixon got American troops out without accepting defeat. When Communist forces ultimately prevailed in Vietnam, it was not on Richard Nixon's watch.

On the other hand, and it seems that with Richard Nixon there is always another hand, maybe he does deserve responsibility for the fall of South Vietnam. As Nixon wrote, "Vietnam was lost, not because of a lack of power, but because of a failure of skill and determination at using power." Nixon also cited the changed status of the presidency as a factor, pointing out that "the presidency was weakened by the restrictions Congress placed on the President's war-making powers and by the debilitating effects of the Watergate crisis."[1220] Foreign policy concerns were used to justify efforts by the Executive Branch to break the law. When the lawbreaking was revealed, the President lost power and was unable to impose his will on the Vietnam situation. One is left to wonder if Nixon saw the irony of his situation.

Was there a double standard regarding Nixon and his men by the Democrats and liberal forces in the media? Yes, there was. The media had no moral problem with publishing the Pentagon Papers. These documents were obtained illegally, they even, rightly or wrongly, were classified as national security secrets, yet the media generally did not attack Daniel Ellsberg. Dirty tricks had been played not just by Republicans but by Dick Tuck and other Democrats. Human and electronic spying had been going on by both Democratic and Republican loyalists. Illegal propaganda had been distributed by Democrats and Republicans, too. But while that provides a context for the actions of Nixon and his men, it does not provide a sufficient excuse. Laws were broken—the system was broken—and the only way the country could hope that the system would be fixed and things might be a little better in the future was for someone, or a group of someones, to pay the price. The only one who really understood that a price might need to be paid was Gordon Liddy. The rest of them had to learn it the hard way.

Before Nixon's memoirs came out in 1978, Jeb Stuart Magruder wrote, "Someday Richard Nixon and his apologists will try to rewrite history, claiming that this tragic President was betrayed by his underlings and railroaded out of office by his enemies. When that time comes…it would help to have the record at hand."[1221] Magruder need not have worried. Between the dispassionate accounts of Watergate, and the writings of Nixon critics, history is in little danger of being unduly sympathetic to the 37th President. And right from the start there were Republicans who were not willing to give Nixon a pass. There were ten Republicans on the House Judiciary Committee who had voted against an impeachment resolution, but even they were under no illusions about the now ex-President. They wrote that though some would say Nixon was driven out of office by political and media enemies, it was Nixon's own actions that undermined him. And, the Republicans added, it was the Supreme Court, some of whose members Nixon had chosen, that ruled unanimously that Nixon had to turn over the evidence of his crimes.[1222]

Even Chuck Colson, who maintained a deep respect for Nixon through the Watergate scandal and Colson's own jail time, did not give the former President and his men a free pass. For Nixon and those who went to prison for him, Colson wrote, "We were guilty of hubris, callousness, moral indifference and ultimately, in the conspiracies that grew out of Watergate, crimes, that is, violations of the criminal code. Most of the things were not invented in the Nixon years, but we certainly advanced the state of the art, and none of us I suspect can look back on some of the excesses of that era with anything but a sense of regret and shame." Balancing out those comments, however, Colson added, "One must be fair and look at some very good things done during the Nixon presidency, particularly in the field of foreign affairs and arms reduction, a lot of which has been erased by Watergate and succeeding administrations."[1223] Perhaps it would be easier to see the "very good things" if it were not for the ethical lapses of Nixon and his men. Most of them found at least some form of redemption for their wrongdoings, but the actions taken during the Nixon years in the White House will leave his administration's legacy forever tainted.

Sources

Primary Sources

Bush, Barbara. *Barbara Bush: A Memoir.* New York: Charles Scribner's Sons, 1994.

Colson, Charles, W. *Born Again.* Grand Rapids: Spire Books, 1977.

Colson, Charles, W. "My Journey from Watergate," *Christianity Today.* (September 13, 1993): 96.

Dean, John. *Blind Ambition: The White House Years.* New York: Simon & Schuster, 1976.

Dean, John. *The Rehnquist Choice: The Untold Story of the Nixon Appointment that Redefined the Supreme Court.* New York, Touchstone, 2002.

Dean Maureen with Hays Gorey. *Mo: A Women's View of Watergate.* New York: Simon & Schuster, 1975.

Ehrlichman, John. *Witness to Power: The Nixon Years.* New York: Simon & Schuster, 1982.

Eisenhower, Dwight D. *The White House Years: Waging Peace 1956-1961.* Garden City, New York: Doubleday & Co., Inc., 1965.

Garment, Leonard. *In Search of Deep Throat: The Greatest Political Mystery of our Time.* New York: Basic Books, 2000.

Gold, Gerald, General Editor. *The White House Transcripts.* New York: Bantam Books, 1974.

Haig, Jr., Alexander M. with Charles McCarry. *Inner Circles, How America Changed the World: A Memoir.* New York: Warner Books, Inc., 1992.

Haldeman, H.R. *The Ends of Power.* New York: Dell Publishing, Co., 1978

Haldeman, H.R. *The Haldeman Diaries: Inside the Nixon White House.* New York: Berkley Books, 1995.

Jaworski, Leon. *The Right and the Power: The Prosecution of Watergate.* New York: Readers Digest Press, 1976.

Kissinger, Henry. *White House Years.* Boston: Little, Brown, and Company, 1979.

Kissinger, Henry. *Years of Upheaval.* Boston: Little, Brown, and Company, 1982.

Kutler, Stanley I. *Abuse of Power: The New Nixon Tapes.* New York: The Free Press, 1997.

Larson, Arthur. *Eisenhower: The President Nobody Knew.* New York: Charles Schribner's Sons, 1968.

Liddy, G. Gordon. *When I was a Kid, This was a free Country.* Washington DC: Regnery Publishing, 2002.

Liddy, G. Gordon. *Will.* New York: St. Martin's Press, 1980.

Magruder, Jeb Stuart. *American Life: One Man's Road to Watergate.* New York: Antheneum, 1974.

Magruder, Jeb Stuart. *From Power to Peace.* Waco, TX: Word Books, 1978.

McFarlane, Robert C. and Zofia Smardz. *Special Trust.* New York: Cadell & Davies, 1994.

Nixon, Richard. *The Memoirs of Richard Nixon*. New York: Grosset & Dunlap, 1978.

Nixon, Richard. *1999: Victory without War*. New York: Simon & Schuster, 1988.

Nixon, Richard. *The Real War*. New York: Warner Books, 1981.

Nixon, Richard. *Six Crises*. New York: Touchstone, 1990.

Nixon Eisenhower, Julie. *Pat Nixon: The Untold Story*. New York: Kensington Publishing Corporation, 1987.

Safire, William. *Before the Fall: An Inside View of the Pre-Watergate White House*. New York: Belmont Tower Books, 1975.

Schlesinger, Jr., Arthur M. *A Thousand Days: John F. Kennedy in the White House*. Boston: Houghton Mifflin Company, 1965.

Sirica, John J. *To Set the Record Straight: The Break-in, the Tapes, the Conspirators, the Pardon*. New York: W.W. Norton & Company, 1979.

Skinner, Kiron K., Annelise Anderson, and Martin Anderson. *Reagan in his own Hand: The Writings of Ronald Reagan that reveal his Revolutionary Vision for America*. New York: Touchstone, 2002.

Weinberger, Casper W. with Gretchen Roberts. *In the Arena: A Memoir of the 20th Century*. Washington DC: Regnery Publishing, Inc., 2001.

Interviews

Colson, Charles, interview with Prison Fellowship International official, date unknown.

Dean, John, interview with author, March 2006.

Krogh, Egil "Bud," interview with author, March 2006.

Magruder, Jeb Stuart, interview with author, April 2006.

Audio (Compact Discs)

The Nixon Tapes: Power Corrupts. DH Audio, 2000.

Watergate File provided by Prison Fellowship International

Colson, Charles. "Comments on Watergate," given to author March 2006.

Colson, Charles. "In the Image of Christ," original publication unknown, given to author March 2006.

Secondary Sources

Aitken, Jonathon. *Charles W. Colson: A Life Redeemed.* Colorado Springs: Waterbrook Press, 2005.

Aitken, Jonathon. *Nixon: A Life.* Washington, DC: Regnery Publishing, Inc. 1993.

Ambrose, Stephen. *To America: Personal Reflections of an Historian.* New York: Simon & Schuster, 2002.

Ambrose, Stephen. *Nixon: The Education of a Politician 1913-1962.* New York: Simon & Schuster, 1987.

Ashman, Charles. *Connally: The Adventures of Big Bad John.* New York: William Morrow & Company, Inc., 1974.

Berman, Larry. *No Peace, No Honor: Nixon, Kissinger, and Betrayal in Vietnam.* New York: The Free Press, 2001.

Brodie, Fawn M. *Richard Nixon: The Shaping of His Character.* Cambridge: Harvard University Press, 1983.

Cohen, Richard M., and Jules Witcover. *A Heartbeat Away: The Investigation & Resignation of Vice President Spiro T. Agnew.* New York: Viking Press, 1974.

Colodny, Len, and Robert Gettlin. *Silent Coup: The Removal of a President.* New York: St. Martin's Press, 1991.

Coulter, Ann. *High Crimes and Misdemeanors.* Washington D.C.: Regnery Publishing, Inc., 2002.

Crowley, Monica. *Nixon off the Record: His Candid Commentary on People and Politics.* New York: Random House, Inc., 1996.

Dallek, Robert. *Lone Star Rising: Lyndon Johnson and His Times, 1908-1960.* New York: Oxford University Press, 1991.

Dallek, Robert. *An Unfinished Life: John F. Kennedy 1917-1963.* Boston: Little, Brown, & Company, 2003.

Damore, Leo. *Senatorial Privilege: The Chappaquiddick Cover-Up.* New York: Dell Publishing, 1988.

DeGregorio, William A., *The Complete Book of U.S. Presidents.* Sixth Edition. New York: Gramercy Books, 2005.

Dogherty, James E. & Robert L. Pfaltzgraff, Jr. *American Foreign Policy: FDR to Reagan.* Harper & Row, 1986.

Dugger, Ronnie. "John Connally: Nixon's New Quarterback," *The Atlantic.* July 1971, pp. 82-90.

Ellis, Joseph J. *Founding Brothers: The Revolutionary Generation.* New York: Vintage Books, 2002.

Emery, Fred. *Watergate: The Corruption of American Politics and the fall of Richard Nixon.* New York: Time Books, 1994.

Evans, Jr., Rowland, and Robert D. Novak. *Nixon in the White House: The Frustration of Power.* New York: Random House, Inc., 1971.

Gelman, Irwin F. *Contender: Richard Nixon the Congress Years 1946-1952.* New York: Free Press, 1999.

Golan, Matti. *The Secret Negotiations of Henry Kissinger: Step by Step Diplomacy in the Middle East.* Trans. By Ruth Geyra Steran and Sol Stern. New York: Quadrangle, 1976.

Gormley, Ken. *Archibald Cox: Conscience of a Nation.* Reading, MA: Perseus Books, 1997.

Greene, John Robert. *The Presidency of Gerald R. Ford.* Lawrence, KS: University Press of Kansas, 1995.

Halberstam, David. *The Fifties.* New York: Villard Books, 1993.

Hay, Jeff, Editor. *Richard M. Nixon: Presidents and their Decisions.* San Diego: Greenhaven Press, Incorporated, 2001.

Hersh, Seymour M. *The Price of Power: Kissinger in the Nixon White House.* New York: Summit Books, 1983.

Higgins, George V. *The Friends of Richard Nixon.* Boston: Little, Brown and Company, 1975.

Hoff, Joan. *Nixon Reconsidered.* New York: Basic Books, 1994.

Holder, Timothy D., John A. Moretta, Carl J. Luna, and Jamie R. Olivares. *Public Pillars/Private Lives: The Strengths and Limitations of the Modern American Presidents.* Wheaton, IL: Abigail Press, Inc., 2005.

Isaacson, Walter. *Kissinger: A Biography.* New York: Simon & Schuster, 1992.

Kurz, Kenneth Franklin. *Nixon's Enemies.* Lincolnwood, IL: Lowell House, 1998.

Kutler, Stanley I. *The Wars of Watergate: The Last Crisis of Richard Nixon.* New York: WW Norton & Company, 1992.

Lasky, Victor. *It Didn't Start with Watergate.* New York: The Dial Press, 1977.

Manchester, William. *Glory and the Dream: A Narrative History of America 1932-1972.* New York: Bantam Books, 1990.

Mankiewicz, Frank. *Perfectly Clear: Nixon from Whittier to Watergate.* New York: Quadrangle, 1973.

Maraniss, David and Ellen Nakashima. *The Prince of Tennessee: The Rise of Al Gore.* New York: Simon & Schuster, 2000.

Mares, Bill. *Fishing with the Presidents.* Mechanicsburg, PA: Stackpole, 1999.

Marton, Kati. *Hidden Power: Presidential Marriages that shaped our History.* New York: Anchor Books, 2002.

McCullough, David. *Truman.* New York: Simon & Schuster, 1992.

Morris, Roger. *Richard Milhous Nixon: The Rise of an American Politician.* New York: Henry Holt and Company, 1990.

Olson, Keith W. *Watergate: The Presidential Scandal that Shook America.* Lawrence: University Press of Kansas, 2003.

Parmet, Herbert S. *Richard Nixon and his America.* New York: Konecky & Konecky, 1990.

Perry, John. *Chuck Colson: A Story of Power, Corruption, and Redemption.* Nashville: Broadman & Holman Publishers, 2003.

Pollock, John. *Billy Graham: Evangelist to the World.* San Francisco: Harper & Row, 1979.

Rather, Dan and Gary Paul Gates. *The Palace Guard.* New York: Harper and Row, Publishers, 1974.

Schmidt, Susan and Michael Weisskopf. *Truth at Any Cost: Ken Starr and the Unmaking of Bill Clinton.* New York: Harper Collins Publishers, 2000.

Schweizer, Peter. *Reagan's War: The epic story of his forty-year struggle and final triumph over Communism.* New York: Doubleday, 2002.

Starr, Kenneth W. *First among Equals.* New York: Warner Books, 2002.

Summers, Anthony. *The Arrogance of Power.* New York: Viking, 2000.

Thomas, Evan and Richard Wolffe. "Bush in the Bubble," *Newsweek.* (December 19, 2005): 31-39.

White, Theodore H. *Breach of Faith: The Fall of Richard Nixon.* New York: Atheneum Publishers, 1975.

White, Theodore H. *The Making of the President 1972.* New York: Bantam Books, 1973.

Wicker, Tom. *George Herbert Walker Bush.* New York: Viking, 2004.

Wicker, Tom. *One of Us: Richard Nixon and the American Dream.* New York: Random House, 1991.

Witcover, Jules. *The Resurrection of Richard Nixon.* New York: G.P. Putnam's Sons, 1970.

Woodward, Bob. *The Choice.* New York: Simon & Schuster, 1996.

Woodward, Bob. *Shadow: Five Presidents and the Legacy of Watergate.* New York: Touchstone, 2000.

Woodward, Bob, and Carl Bernstein. *All the Presidents' Men.* New York: Touchstone, 1994.

Woodward, Bob, and Carl Bernstein. *The Final Days.* New York: Simon & Schuster, 1976.

Television Documentary

PBS. *Watergate Plus 30: Shadow of History.* 2003.

Internet Sources

"Biography Resource Center." http://galenet.galegroup.com

"FindLaw." http://writ.corporate.findlaw.com/dean/

Kurtz, Howard. "Moving to the Right: Brit Hume's Path took him from Liberal Outsider to the Low-Key Voice of Conservatism on Fox News." ww.washingtonpost.com/wp-dyn/content/article/2006/04/18.

Index

Endnotes

Introduction

[1] Holder, Timothy D., John Anthony Moretta, Carl J. Luna, Jamie Ramon, Olivares, *Public Pillars/Private Lives* (Wheaton, IL: Abigail Press, 2005), p. 364.

[2] Safire, William, *Before the Fall* (New York: Belmont Tower Books, 1975), pp. 97-98.

[3] Haldeman H.R., *The Ends of Power* (New York: Dell Publishing, Company, 1978), pp. 96-97.

[4] Ibid., pp. 104-105.

[5] Walter Mitty was a fictional character who lived an exceedingly ordinary life but daydreamed of various sorts of greatness.

[6] Kissinger, Henry, *Years of Upheaval* (Boston: Little, Brown, and Company, 1982), pp. 73-74, 103.

[7] Safire, p. 180.

[8] Holder, et al, p. 345.

[9] Kissinger (1982), 74.

[10] Kissinger's true views were sometimes hard to pin down. At times these views varied based on his audience, as this book will demonstrate.

[11] Haldeman (1978), p. 75.

[12] Aitken, Jonathon, *Nixon* (Washington D.C.: Regnery Publishing, Inc., 1993), p. 345.

[13] Ambrose, Stephen, *To America: Personal Reflections of an Historian* (New York: Simon & Schuster, 2002), pp. 174-175, 183.

[14] Schmidt, Susan, and Michael Weisskopf, *Truth at Any Cost* (New York: Harper Collins Publishers, 2000), p. 5.

[15] Brodie, Fawn M., *Richard Nixon* (Cambridge, MA: Harvard University Press, 1983), p. 17.

[16] Greene, John Robert, *The Presidency of Gerald R. Ford* (Lawrence: University of Kansas, 1995), p. 17.

[17] Coulter, Ann, *High Crimes and Misdemeanors* (Washington D.C.: Regnery Publishing, Inc., 2002), p. 288.

[18] Magruder, Jeb Stuart, *An American Life* (New York: Atheneum, 1974), p. 252.

[19] Ibid., p. 118.

[20] Hoff, Joan, *Nixon Reconsidered* (New York: Basic Books, 1994.), p. 280.

[21] Haldeman (1978), p. 117.

[22] Ibid., pp. 225, 273-275.

Chapter One

[23] Haldeman (1978), p. 84.

[24] Ehrlichman, John, *Witness to Power* (New York: Simon & Schuster, 1982), p. 87.

[25] Nixon, Richard, *The Memoirs of Richard Nixon* (New York: Grosset & Dunlap, 1978), p. 185.

[26] Ehrlichman, p. 88.

[27] Kurz,Kenneth Franklin, *Nixon's Enemies* (Lincolnwood, IL: Lowell House, 1998), p. 289.

[28] Haldeman (1978), pp. 85-86.

[29] Magruder (1974), pp. 2, 7.

[30] Dean, John, *Blind Ambition* (New York: Simon & Schuster, 1976), p. 18.

[31] Kissinger (1982), pp. 108-109.

[32] Ibid., p. 112.

[33] Magruder (1974), p. 86.

[34] Haldeman (1978), p. 82.

[35] Ehrlichman, p. 83.

[36] Dean, John (1976), p. 25.

[37] Haldeman (1978), p. 111.

[38] Ibid., pp. 80-81.

[39] Ibid., pp. 75, 83.

[40] Ibid., pp. 76, 83.

[41] Haldeman (1978), p. 35.

[42] Dean, John (1976), pp. 46-47.

[43] Ehrlichman, p. 80.

[44] Kissinger, Henry, *White House Years* (Boston: Little, Brown, and Company, 1979), pp. 74-75.

[45] Safire, pp. 472, 474.

[46] Ehrlichman, p. 118.

[47] Evans, Jr., Rowland and Robert D. Novak, *Nixon in the White House* (New York: Random House, 1971), pp. 50-51.

[48] Weinberger, Casper W., with Gretchen Roberts, *In the Arena* (Washington DC: Regnery Publishing, Inc., 2001), pp. 195-196.

[49] Kissinger (1979), 76.

[50] Ehrlichman, pp. 80-81.

[51] Ibid., p. 77.

[52] Ibid., p. 75.

[53] Magruder (1974), p. 131.

[54] White, Theodore H., *The Making of the President 1972* (New York: Bantam Books, 1973), p. 365.

[55] See Chapter Nine.

[56] Haldeman (1978), p. 123.

[57] Evans, and Novak, p. 259.

[58] See Chapter Seven.

[59] Safire, pp. 157-158.

[60] McFarlane, Robert, *Special Trust* (New York: Cadell & Davies, 1994), pp. 153-154.

[61] Kissinger (1982), p. 4.

[62] Ehrlichman, p. 67.

[63] Haldeman (1978), p. 106.

[64] Ehrlichman, pp. 68-69.

[65] Safire, p. 614.

[66] White, Theodore H., *Breach of Faith* (New York: Atheneum Publishers, 1975), p. 119.

[67] Thomas Jefferson was politically active but very discreet. Ellis, Joseph J., *Founding Brothers* (New York: Vintage Books, 2002), p. 141, etc.

[68] Cohen, Richard M. and Jules Witcover, *A Heartbeat Away* (New York: Viking Press, 1974), pp. 138-140.

[69] Ehrlichman, p. 146.

[70] Ibid., pp. 65-66.

[71] Ibid., pp. 196-198.

[72] Haldeman (1995), p. 29.

[73] Pollock, John, *Billy Graham* (San Francisco: Harper & Row, 1979), p. 173.

[74] Magruder, Jeb Stuart, *From Power to Peace* (Waco, TX: Word Books, 1978), p. 29.

[75] Pollock, p. 174.

[76] Ibid., p. 173.

[77] Ashman, Charles, *Connally* (New York: William Morrow & Company, Inc., 1972), pp. 175-176.

[78] Safire, pp. 135-136.

[79] Schweizer, Peter, *Reagan's War* (New York: Doubleday, 2002), pp. 54-55.

[80] Haldeman (1978), pp. 139-140.

[81] Parmet, Herbert, *Richard Nixon and his America* (New York: Konecky & Konecky, 1990), pp. 567-568.

[82] Ehrlichman, p. 174.

[83] Nixon (1978), p. 387.

[84] Nixon (1978), p.378.

[85] Hoff, pp. 280-281.

[86] Nixon (1978), pp. 387-389.

[87] Schlesinger, Jr., Arthur M., *The Imperial Presidency* (Boston: Houghton Mifflin Company, 1973), p. 344.

[88] Garment, Leonard, *In Search of Deep Throat* (New York: Basic Books, 2000), pp. 55-56.

[89] Nixon (1978), p. 390.

[90] Garment, p. 57.

[91] Nixon (1978), p. 389.

[92] Ehrlichman, p. 170.

[93] Ibid., pp. 174-175.

[94] Dean, John (1976), p. 24.

[95] Magruder (1974), p. 72.

[96] Dean, John (1976), pp. 24-25.

[97] Safire, pp. 159-160.

[98] Kutler, Stanley I., *The Wars of Watergate* (New York: WW Norton & Company, 1992), p. 167.

[99] Magruder (1974), pp. 3, 56, 71.

[100] Ibid., p. 4.
[101] Haldeman (1978), p. 31.
[102] Ibid., pp. 32-33.
[103] Bush, Barbara, *Barbara Bush* (New York: Charles Scribner's Sons, 1994), p. 97.
[104] Ehrlichman, pp. 90-91.
[105] Ibid., pp. 94-97.
[106] Safire, pp. 171-178.
[107] Magruder (1974), pp. 56.-57.
[108] Ibid., p. 57.
[109] Ibid., pp. 57-58.
[110] Safire, pp. 342-343.
[111] Magruder (1974), p. 58.
[112] Ibid., pp. 58-59.
[113] Ibid., p. 68.
[114] Colson, Charles W., *Born Again* (Grand Rapids: Spire Books, 1977), p. 32.
[115] Magruder (1974), p. 69.
[116] Ibid., pp. 94-95.
[117] Parmet, pp. 563, 566.

Chapter Two

[118] Colson (1977), p. 34.
[119] Ibid., pp. 34-35.
[120] Magruder (1974), p. 69.
[121] Haldeman (1978), p. 93.
[122] Magruder (1974), p. 117.
[123] Haldeman (1978), pp. 91-92.
[124] Ibid., p. 92.
[125] Magruder (1974), p. 69.
[126] Ibid., pp. 132-133.
[127] Ibid., pp. 62, 66-67, 97.
[128] Mentioned below.
[129] Safire, pp. 470-472.
[130] Magruder (1974), pp. 118-119.

[131] Ehrlichman, p. 126.

[132] Magruder (1974), pp. 119-121.

[133] Ibid., p. 122.

[134] Parmet, pp. 4-6.

[135] Nixon (1978), pp. 380-381.

[136] Ibid., pp. 382, 498.

[137] Magruder (1974), p. 122.

[138] Nixon (1978), p. 457.

[139] Isaacson, Walter, *Kissinger: A Biography* (New York: Simon & Schuster, 1992), p. 269.

[140] Parmet, p. 7.

[141] Hay, Jeff, Editor, *Richard M. Nixon: Presidents and their Decisions* (San Diego: Green Haven Press, Incorporated, 2001), p. 106.

[142] Parmet, pp. 7-8.

[143] Parmet, p. 8.

[144] Isaacson, p. 270.

[145] Safire, p. 205.

[146] Parmet, pp. 8-9.

[147] Safire, p. 205.

[148] Evans and Novak, p. 274.

[149] Liddy, G. Gordon, *Will* (New York: St. Martin's Press, 1980), p. 135.

[150] Magruder (1974), p.73.

[151] Parmet, p. 3.

[152] Safire, p. 205.

[153] Parmet, p. 9.

[154] Safire, p. 205.

[155] Haldeman (1978), p. 101.

[156] Parmet, pp. 9-10.

[157] Safire, p. 206.

[158] Parmet, pp. 10-11.

[159] Ibid., pp. 11-12.

[160] Nixon (1978), p. 466.

[161] Isaacson, pp. 270-271.

[162] Pollock, pp. 107-109.

[163] Emery, Fred, *Watergate* (New York: Time Books, 1994), p. 28.

[164] Dean, John (1976), pp. 11-12.

[165] Magruder (1974), p. 183.

[166] Dean, John (1976), pp. 16-17.

[167] Magruder (1974), pp. 147-148.

[168] Haldeman (1995), p. 278.

[169] Dean, John (1976), pp. 17, 20, 25.

[170] Emery, pp. 28-29.

[171] Liddy (1980), p. 133.

[172] Magruder (1974), pp. 100, 183.

[173] Dean, John (1976), p. 39.

[174] Ibid., pp. 32-33.

[175] Ibid., pp. 33-34.

[176] Ibid., p. 34.

[177] Ibid., p. 35.

[178] Kutler (1992), pp. 96-98.

[179] Nixon (1978), pp. 474-475.

[180] Kurz, p. 286.

[181] Ibid.

[182] Mankiewicz, Frank, *Perfectly Clear* (New York: Quadrangle, 1973), p. 130.

[183] Dean, John (1976), pp. 36-38.

[184] Liddy (1980), pp. 141-142.

[185] See Chapters Seven and Eight.

[186] Nixon (1978), p. 491.

[187] Ehrlichman, p. 103.

[188] Nixon (1978), 492-493.

[189] Cohen and Witcover, p. 49.

[190] Mgruder (1974), p. 138.

[191] Maraniss, David and Ellen Nakashima, *The Prince of Tennessee* (New York: Simon & Schuster, 2000), pp. 123-125.

[192] Bush, p. 80.

[193] Evans and Novak, p. 321.

[194] Ibid., p. 322.

[195] Nixon (1978), p. 494.

[196] Magrduer (1974), p. 144.

[197] Mankiewicz, p. 9.

[198] Magruder (1974), pp. 145-146.

[199] Kissinger (1982), pp. 385-386.

[200] Erhlichman, 257.

[201] Ashman, pp. 36-38.

[202] Haldeman (1978), p. 344.

[203] Greene, p.

[204] Cohen and Witcover, p. 12.

[205] Kutler (1992), p. 102.

Chapter Three

[206] Haldeman (1978), p. 94.

[207] Perry, John *Chuck Colson* (Nashville: Broadman & Holman Publishers, 2003), p. 51.

[208] Summers, Anthony, *The Arrogance of Power* (New York: Viking, 2000), pp. 312-313.

[209] White (1975), pp. 190-193.

[210] Perry, p. 87.

[211] Kutler (1992), p. 166.

[212] White (1973), p. 367.

[213] Magruder (1974), pp. 153-154.

[214] Haldeman (1978), pp. 31-32.

[215] Magruder (1974), p. 155.

[216] Dean, Maureen, with Hays Gorey, *Mo: A Woman's View of Watergate* (New York: Simon & Schuster, 1975), p. 93.

[217] Magruder (1974), p. 155.

[218] Ibid., p. 174.

[219] Bush, p. 97.

[220] Magruder (1974), pp. 174-178.

[221] Haldeman (1978), pp. 32-33.

[222] Magruder (1974), p. 179.

[223] White (1975), p. 154.

[224] Higgins, George V., *The Friends of Richard Nixon* (Boston: Little, Brown, and Company), pp. 248-249.

[225] Magruder (1974), p. 158.

[226] Ibid., p. 144.

[227] Mankiewicz, p. 133.

[228] Perry, p. 81.

[229] Haldeman (1978), pp. 154-155.

[230] Isaacson, p. 330.

[231] Haldeman (1978), p. 155.

[232] Brodie, p. 504.

[233] Haldeman (1978), pp. 157-158

[234] Ibid., pp. 162-164.

[235] Liddy (1980), pp. 144-145.

[236] Hoff, p. 279.

[237] Olson, Keith W., *Watergate: The Presidential Scandal that Shook America* (Lawrence: University Press of Kansas, 2003), p. 19.

[238] Liddy (1980), pp. 146-148.

[239] Colodny, Len, and Robert Gettlin, *Silent Coup* (New York: St. Martin's Press, 1991), p. 10.

[240] Hay, pp. 125-126.

[241] Nixon, Richard, *1999: Victory without War* (New York: Simon & Schuster, 1988), pp. 243-244.

[242] Skinner, Kiron K., Annelise Anderson, and Martin Anderson, *Reagan in his own Hand* (New York: Touchstone, 2002), p. 43.

[243] Ehrlichman, p, 294.

[244] Ibid., pp. 294-295.

[245] Ibid.

[246] Weinberger, pp. 205-206.

[247] Nixon (1978), pp. 520-521.

[248] Rather, Dan and Gary Paul Gates, *The Palace Guard* (New York: Harper and Row Publishers, 1974), p. 281.

[249] Liddy (1980), p. 157.

[250] Ibid., pp. 158, 164.

[251] Sirica, John J., *To Set the Record Straight* (New York: W.W. Norton & Company, 1979), p. 44-45.

[252] Liddy (1980), pp. 165-167.

[253] Ibid., pp. 167-168.

[254] Mankiewicz, p. 137.

[255] Liddy (1980), pp. 168-169.

[256] Safire, p.15.

[257] Liddy (1980), p. 170.

[258] Ibid., pp. 171-172.

[259] Nixon Eisenhower, Julie, *Pat Nixon: The Untold Story* (New York: Kensington Publishing Corporation, 1987), p. 479.

[260] Liddy (1980), pp. 172, 180.

[261] Dean,John (1976), p. 76.
[262] Liddy (1980), p. 182.
[263] Ibid., p. 182.
[264] Ibid., p. 183.
[265] Dean, John (1976), p. 76.
[266] Ibid., pp. 48-49.
[267] Magruder (1974), p. 185.
[268] Liddy (1980), p. 185.
[269] Magruder (1974), p. 187.
[270] Dean, John (1976), p. 78.
[271] Liddy (1980), p. 182.
[272] Magruder (1974), p. 188.
[273] Liddy (1980), p. 188.
[274] Ibid.
[275] Ibid.
[276] Dean, John (1976), p. 77.
[277] Liddy (1980), pp. 195-196.
[278] Dean, John (1976), pp. 78-79.
[279] Ibid., p. 79.
[280] Rather and Gates, pp. 214-215.

Chapter Four

[281] Nixon Eisenhower, p. 488.
[282] Dean, John, *The Rehnquist Choice* (New York: Touchstone, 2002), p. 126.
[283] Like veteran newsmen John Osborne and James "Scotty" Reston.
[284] Ehrlichman, p. 275.
[285] White (1973), p. 96.
[286] Ibid., p. 148.
[287] Ibid., pp. 102-103.
[288] Ibid., pp. 316-317.
[289] Pollock, p. 174.
[290] Ibid., p. 175.
[291] Kutler (1992), pp. 82-83.

[292] Liddy (1980), p. 196.

[293] Magruder (1974), p. 193.

[294] Liddy (1980), p. 197.

[295] Magruder (1974), p. 194.

[296] Liddy (1980), pp. 197-199.

[297] Magruder interview with author, April 2006.

[298] Liddy (1980), p. 200.

[299] Magruder (1974), p. 195.

[300] Dean, John (1976), p. 83.

[301] Ibid., pp. 82-83, 85.

[302] Ibid., p. 85.

[303] Liddy (1980), p. 200.

[304] Ibid.

[305] Magruder (1974), p. 195.

[306] Liddy (1980), p. 200.

[307] Dean, John (1976), p. 85.

[308] Magruder (1974), p. 196.

[309] Dean, John (1976), p. 85.

[310] Ibid., pp. 86-87.

[311] Liddy (1980), p. 203; Magruder (1974) p. 197.

[312] Liddy (1980), pp. 203-204.

[313] Haldeman (1978), pp. 55-56.

[314] Magruder (1974), p. 197.

[315] Olson, p. 34.

[316] Liddy (1980), p. 212.

[317] This diplomacy included working through Pakistan and Romania. Nixon Eisenhower, p. 506.

[318] Kissinger (1979), p. 127.

[319] Summers, p. 393.

[320] Hay, p. 127.

[321] Kutler (1992), p. 80.

[322] Skinner, et al, p. 45.

[323] Liddy (1980), p. 212.

[324] Magruder (1974), pp. 208-209.

[325] Liddy (1980), p. 212.

[326] Magruder (1974), p. 209.

[327] Liddy (1980), pp. 212-213.

[328] Magruder (1974), p. 209.

[329] The entire conversation between Liddy and Magruder and the phone call from Dean to Magruder were found in Magruder (1974), pp. 209-210.

[330] Liddy (1980), pp. 214-215.

[331] Dean, John (1976), pp. 51-58.

[332] Ibid., p. 55.

[333] Kurtz, Howard, "Moving to the Right," www.washingtonpost.com/wp-dyn/content/article/2006/04/18.

[334] Summers, pp. 72-73.

[335] Liddy (1980), p. 211.

[336] John Dean interview with author, March 2006.

[337] Emery, p. 311.

[338] White (1975), pp. 157-158.

[339] Colodny and Gettlin, pp. 123-125.

[340] Magruder did not make this claim until 2003 in a documentary called *Watergate Plus 30: Shadow of History*.

[341] Magruder interview.

[342] Aitken, Jonathon, *Charles W. Colson*, (Colorado Springs: Waterbrook Press, 2005), p. 169.

[343] Nixon Eisenhower, p. 511.

[344] Haig, Jr., Alexander M. with Charles McCarry, *Inner* Circles (New York: Warner Books, Inc. 1992), pp. 282, 284.

[345] Liddy (1980), p. 219.

[346] Colodny and Gettlin, pp. 133-134.

[347] Magruder interview.

[348] Magruder (1974), p. 213.

[349] Dean interview.

[350] Berman, Larry, *No Peace, No Honor* (New York: The Free Press, 2001), pp. 129-130.

[351] Haig, pp. 275, 285.

[352] Rather and Gates, pp. 281-283.

[353] Ashman, p. 258.

[354] White (1973), p. 316.

[355] Summers, p. 406.

[356] Olson, p. 35.

[357] Liddy (1980), pp. 224-225.

[358] Olson, p. 35.

[359] Nixon Eisenhower, p. 533.

[360] Magruder (1974), pp. 228-229.

[361] Ibid., p. 230.

[362] Liddy, G. Gordon, *When I was a Kid* (Washington DC: Regnery Publishing, 2002), p. 167.

[363] Ibid., pp. 180-182.

[364] Olson, p. 39.

[365] Haig, p. 323. A large part of Haig's disdain for *Silent Coup* stems from the fact that the authors of that book spent an entire chapter creating a connection between Haig and reporter Bob Woodward, (Colodny and Gettlin, pp.69-90) who wrote many articles and two books with Peter Bernstein dealing with Watergate. Colodny and Gettlin try to make the case that Haig was Deep Throat, Woodward's famous informant. Haig debunks this in his memoirs, pp. 322-326, and in 2005 it was revealed that Deep Throat was actually Mark Felt, a high-ranking FBI official.

[366] Sirica, p. 47.

[367] Olson, pp. 38-39.

[368] Summers, pp. 412-413.

[369] Liddy (1980), pp. 231-233.

[370] Ibid., pp. 236-238

[371] Magruder (1974), pp. 229-230.

[372] Liddy (1980), p. 238.

[373] Haig, p. 292.

[374] Liddy (1980), pp. 242-244.

[375] Magruder (1974), p. 237.

[376] Haldeman (1978), pp. 197-198.

[377] Sirica, p. 44.

[378] Liddy (1980), pp. 244-245.

Chapter Five

[379] Aitken (1993), pp. 197-198.

[380] Nixon Eisenhower, p. 218.

[381] Aitken (1993), p. 198.

[382] Holder, et al., pp. 315-316.

[383] Nixon (1978), p. 117.

[384] Ashman, pp. 50-51.

[385] Isaacson, pp. 19-20.

[386] Rather and Gates, pp. 120, 134-136.

[387] Ehrlichman, p. 18.

[388] Aitken (1993), pp. 302-303, 374.

[389] Holder, et al., pp. 316-317.

[390] Liddy (2002), pp. 31-33.

[391] Liddy (1980), pp. 1-6, 10-14.

[392] Holder, et al., p. 317.

[393] Nixon (1978), pp. 16-17.

[394] Holder, et al., pp. 317-318.

[395] Parmet, p. 82.

[396] Magruder (1974), p. 13-18.

[397] Aitken (1993), pp. 63.-64.

[398] Ashman, p. 52.

[399] Holder, et al, p. 318.

[400] Ambrose, Stephen, *Nixon: the Education of a Politician* (New York: Simon & Schuster, 1987), p. 75.

[401] Nixon (1978), p. 20.

[402] Aitken (1993), pp. 66-67.

[403] Ambrose (1987), pp. 76-77.

[404] Ibid.

[405] Aitken (1993), p. 70.

[406] Ambrose (1987), p. 77.

[407] Nixon (1978), p. 21.

[408] Aitken (1993), p. 73.

[409] Ibid., p. 71.

[410] Summers, p. 21.

[411] Aitken (1993), p. 71.

[412] Kutler (1992), pp. 453-455.

[413] Aitken (1993), p. 73.

[414] Colson (1977), p. 84.

[415] Ambrose (1987), p. 76.

[416] Nixon (1978), pp. 20-21.

[417] Ambrose (1987), 76.

[418] Ibid., p. 98.

[419] Summers, p. 354.
[420] Ambrose (1987), p. 80.
[421] Ibid., p. 80.
[422] Morris, Roger, *Richard Milhous Nixon: The Rise of an American Politician* (New York: Henry Holt and Company, 1990), p. 177.
[423] Nixon (1978), p. 21.
[424] Ambrose (1987), p.80.
[425] Summers, p. 21.
[426] Nixon (1978), p. 629.
[427] Colson (1977), p. 22.
[428] Isaacson, pp. 28-31.
[429] Haberstam, David, *The Fifties* (New York: Villard Books, 1993), p. 318.
[430] Aitken (1993), pp. 80-81.
[431] Nixon (1978), p. 22
[432] Ambrose (1987), p. 88.
[433] Ibid., pp. 89-90.
[434] Parmet, p. 85.
[435] Aitken (1993), pp. 84-85.
[436] Ambrose (1987), pp. 89, 91.
[437] Biography Resource Center.
[438] Dallek, Robert, *Lone Star Rising* (New York: Oxford University Press, 1991), pp. 186-187.
[439] Ashman, p. 54.
[440] Ibid., pp. 55-60.
[441] Nixon (1978), p. 25.
[442] Liddy (1980), p. 24.
[443] Nixon (1978), p. 26.
[444] Ibid., p. 28.
[445] Ambrose (1987), p. 105.
[446] Dallek (1991), pp. 229-231.
[447] Rather and Gates, p. 213.
[448] Evans and Novak, p. 51.
[449] Biography Resource Center.
[450] Ambrose (1987), p. 113.
[451] Aitken (1993), pp. 108-109.
[452] Erhlichman, p. 18.
[453] Isaacson, pp. 38-39.

[454] Ibid., pp. 39-42.

[455] Ibid., p. 45.

[456] Parmet, p. 85.

[457] Nixon (1978), pp. 29-33.

[458] Ibid., p. 33.

[459] Liddy 1980), p. 30.

Chapter Six

[460] Gelman, Irwin F., *Contender: Richard Nixon the Congress Years 1946-1952* (New York: The Free Press, 1999), pp. 451-452.

[461] Halbertam, pp. 320-321.

[462] Gelman, p. 47.

[463] Morris, pp. 319-320.

[464] Gellman, p. 452.

[465] White (1973), p. 364.

[466] Haldeman (1978), p. 76.

[467] Rather and Gates, pp. 136-137, 154.

[468] Gelman, p. 160.

[469] Ibid., pp. 161-162.

[470] Ibid., pp. 162-163.

[471] Liddy (1980), pp. 34-35.

[472] Dallek (1991), pp. 296, 301, 303, 304, 336-346.

[473] McCullough, David, *Truman* (New York: Simon & Schuster, 1992), pp. 521-522.

[474] Gellman, p. 452.

[475] Aitken (1993), p. 303.

[476] Gelman, p. 236.

[477] McCullough, p. 759.

[478] Gellman, pp. 196-234.

[479] Summers, p. 77.

[480] Ibid.

[481] Gellman, p. 241.

[482] Nixon, Richard, *Six Crises* (New York: Touchstone, 1990), p. 37.

[483] Ibid.

[484] MucCullough, pp. 759-760.
[485] Colson (1977), p. 24.
[486] Perry, p. 16.
[487] Ibid., p. 17.
[488] Gellman, p. 272.
[489] Nixon Eisenhower, p. 155.
[490] Aitken (1993), p. 188.
[491] Morris, pp. 578, 581-583.
[492] Aitken (1993), p. 190.
[493] Nixon Eisenhower, pp. 155, 159.
[494] McCullough, p. 844.
[495] Rather and Gates, p. 28.
[496] White (1975), p. 73.
[497] Nixon Eisenhower, p. 159.
[498] Pollock, p. 171.
[499] Aitken (1993), p. 198.
[500] Nixon Eisenhower, pp. 217-218.
[501] Aitken (1993), p. 342.
[502] Nixon (1990), pp. 76-77.
[503] Rather and Gates, pp. 137-138.
[504] Isaacson, p. 70.
[505] Aitken (1993), pp. 205-206.
[506] Halberstam, p. 312.
[507] Ibid., pp. 314-315.
[508] Aitken (1993), p. 206.
[509] Gellman, p. 443.
[510] Aitken (1993), p. 207.
[511] Nixon (1978), p. 377.
[512] Aitken (1993), p. 207.
[513] Gellman, pp. 443-444.
[514] Aitken (1993), p. 207.
[515] Ibid. p. 206.
[516] Halberstam, p. 315.
[517] Mares, Bill, *Fishing with the Presidents* (Mechanicsburg, PA: Stackpole, 1999), p. 46.
[518] Halberstam, pp. 328-329.
[519] McCullough, pp. 909, 976.
[520] Liddy (1980), 36-39, 42.

[521] Nixon (1990), p. 73.

[522] Ibid., pp. 77, 81-82, 85.

[523] Manchester, William, *Glory and the Dream* (New York: Bantam Books, 1990), p. 629.

[524] Nixon (1990), p. 106.

[525] Manchester, pp. 630-631.

[526] Nixon (1990), p. 109.

[527] Ibid., p. 110.

[528] Ibid., p. 110.

[529] Ibid., p. 113.

[530] Ibid., p. 115.

[531] Morris, pp. 835-836.

[532] Nixon (1990), pp. 119-123.

[533] Aitken (1993), p. 221.

[534] Halberstam, pp. 326-327.

[535] Aitken (1993), p. 225.

[536] Dallek (1991), pp. 417-418.

[537] Ashman, p. 4.

[538] Magruder (1974), pp. 15, 18-22.

[539] Egil "Bud" Krogh interview with author, March 2006.

Chapter Seven

[540] Aitken (1993), p. 206.

[541] Nixon (1990), p. 131.

[542] Holder, et al, p. 324.

[543] White (1975), p. 65.

[544] Aitken (1993), p. 223.

[545] Summers, p. 140.

[546] Ibid.

[547] Nixon (1978), pp. 144-148.

[548] Nixon Eisenhower, p. 220.

[549] Manchester, p. 718.

[550] Summers, p. 140.

[551] Nixon (1978), p. 119.

[552] Ibid., p. 120.

553 Ibid., pp. 125-126.
554 Ibid., pp. 130-131.
555 Magruder (1974), pp. 22-23.
556 Ibid., pp. 24-25.
557 Hay, p. 26.
558 Colson (1977), pp. 26-27.
559 Liddy (1980), pp. 52-53.
560 Kurz, pp. 156-157.
561 Aitken (1993), p. 234.
562 Ibid., p. 235.
563 Mares, p. 46.
564 Aitken (1993), p. 235.
565 Summers, p. 148.
566 Aitken (1993), p. 236.
567 Ibid., p. 136.
568 Ibid., pp. 236-237.
569 Ibid., p. 237.
570 Summers, p. 148.
571 Nixon (1978), p. 173.
572 Aitken (1993), pp. 237-238.
573 Ibid., p. 238.
574 Ibid., p. 238.
575 Eisenhower, Dwight D, *The White House Years: Waging Peace 1956-1961* (Garden City, New York, Doubleday & Co., Inc., 1965), pp. 7-9.
576 Brodie, p. 352.
577 Parmet, p. 264.
578 Larson, Arthur, *Eisenhower* (New York: Charles Schribner's Sons, 1968), p. 8.
579 Summers, p. 149.
580 Aitken (1993), p. 239.
581 Parment, p. 265.
582 Ibid.
583 Brodie, p. 353.
584 Nixon (1978), p. 170.
585 Aitken (1993), p. 240.
586 Brodie, p. 353.
587 Aitken (1993), p. 239.

[588] Parmet, p. 274.
[589] Nixon (1978), p. 172.
[590] Eisenhower, p. 9.
[591] Parmet, p. 274.
[592] Eisenhower, p. 6.
[593] Ibid., p. 10.
[594] Larson, pp. 8-9.
[595] Eisenhower, p. 10.
[596] Aitken (1993), p. 242.
[597] Ibid.
[598] Nixon (1978), pp. 174-176.
[599] Aitken (1993), pp. 242-243.
[600] Eisenhower, p. 3.
[601] Kurz, p. 136.
[602] Aitken (1993), p. 243.
[603] Haldeman (1978), p. 75.
[604] Aitken (1993), p. 303.
[605] Haldeman (1978), p. 75.
[606] Ibid., pp. 79-80.
[607] White (1975), p. 93.
[608] Haldeman (1978), p. 78-79.
[609] Rather and Gates, pp. 122-123.
[610] Ashman, p. 4.
[611] Parmet, p. 292.
[612] Brodie, p. 358.
[613] Manchester, p. 720.
[614] Ibid.
[615] Summers, p. 143.

Chapter Eight

[616] Isaacson, pp. 94-100.
[617] Aitken (1993), p. 248.
[618] Ibid., pp. 248-249.
[619] Ibid., pp. 248-249.
[620] Ibid., p. 249.

[621] Liddy (1980), p. 74.

[622] Ibid.

[623] Ibid., pp. 76-77.

[624] Liddy (1980), p. 77.

[625] Ibid., p. 82.

[626] Ibid., p. 76.

[627] Isaacson, p. 99.

[628] Aitken (2005), pp. 67, 69-70.

[629] Nixon (1978), p. 186.

[630] Not to be confused with journalist and author Bob Woodward.

[631] Nixon (1978), p. 186.

[632] Ibid., pp. 187-188.

[633] Brodie, p. 362.

[634] Nixon (1978), pp. 187-188.

[635] Ibid., p. 188.

[636] Ibid., pp. 188-189.

[637] Summers, p. 170.

[638] Nixon (1978), p. 189.

[639] Marton, Kati, *Hidden Power* (New York: Anchor Books, 2002), p. 172.

[640] Kurz, pp. 172-173.

[641] Nixon (1978), p. 191.

[642] Summers, pp. 169-170.

[643] Ibid., p. 169.

[644] Nixon (1978), p. 191.

[645] Kurz, p. 173.

[646] Ibid., pp. 173-174.

[647] Ibid., p. 175.

[648] Summers, p. 168.

[649] Eisenhower, p. 382.

[650] Aitken (1993), p. 254.

[651] Ibid., p. 255.

[652] Ibid., p. 255.

[653] Ambrose (1987), pp. 515-516.

[654] Summers, p. 171.

[655] Hersh, Seymour, *The Price of Power* (New York: Summit Books, 1983), p. 12.

[656] Aitken (1993), p. 259.

[657] Nixon (1990), p. p. 235.

[658] Summers, p. 171.

[659] Nixon (1978), pp. 208-209.

[660] Aitken (1993), p. 259.

[661] Garment, pp. 32-33.

[662] Aitken (1993), pp. 261-262.

[663] Ibid., p. 264.

[664] Parmet, pp. 288-289.

[665] White (1975), p. 93.

[666] Ehrlichman, p. 18.

[667] Ibid., p. 20.

[668] Rather and Gates, p. 140.

[669] Summers, p. 209

[670] Magruder (1974), p. 34.

[671] Ibid., p. 35.

[672] Liddy (1980), pp. 88-89.

[673] Colson (1977), p. 31.

[674] Colson, Charles, "My Journey from Watergate," *Christianity Today*, September 13, 1993, p. 96.

[675] Colson (1977), p. 28.

[676] Ibid.

[677] Ibid., pp. 28-29.

[678] Ashman, pp. 69-71, 76-77.

[679] Witcover, Jules, *The Resurrection of Richard Nixon* (New York: G.P. Putnam's Sons, 1970), p. 209.

[680] Ambrose (1987), pp. 562.-563.

[681] Ibid., p. 463.

[682] Aitken (1993), pp. 274-275.

[683] Nixon (1978), pp. 218-219.

[684] Aitken (1993), p. 269.

[685] Summers, pp. 207-208.

[686] Nixon (1978), p. 221.

[687] Aitken (1993), p. 279.

[688] Ibid., p. 280.

[689] Ibid., p. 282.

[690] Parmet, p. 389.

[691] Aitken (1993), p. 282.

[692] Ibid., p. 281.
[693] Parmet, p. 389.
[694] Ambrose (1987), p. 553.
[695] Aitken (1993), pp. 282-283.
[696] Ibid.
[697] Brodie, p. 360.
[698] White (1975), p. 66.
[699] Nixon (1978), p. 222.
[700] Brodie, p. 360.
[701] Nixon (1978), p. 222.
[702] Brodie, p. 360.
[703] Nixon (1978), pp; 222-223.
[704] Ibid., p. 223.
[705] Ibid., p. 216.
[706] Aitken (1993), p. 288.
[707] Summers, p. 205.
[708] Haldeman (1978), pp. 111-112.
[709] Summers, p. 154.
[710] Aitken (1993), p. 286.
[711] Summers, p. 155.
[712] Aitken (1993), p. 286.
[713] Ehrlichman, p. 171.
[714] Ehrlichman, p. 171; Parmet, p. 406.
[715] Parmet, p. 409.
[716] Aitken (1993), p. 287.
[717] Nixon (1978), p. 225.
[718] Summers, p. 211.
[719] Ibid., p. 220.
[720] Nixon (1978), pp. 224-225.
[721] White (1975), p.71.
[722] Aitken (1993), p. 290; Nixon (1978), p. 224.
[723] Ibid.
[724] Nixon (1978), p. 224.
[725] Ibid., p. 226.
[726] White (1975), p.70.

Chapter Nine

[727] Ambrose (1987), pp. 626-627.

[728] Hersh, p. 13.

[729] Ashman, p. 77.

[730] Krogh interview.

[731] Mankiewicz, p. 126.

[732] Ambrose (1987), p. 633.

[733] Ambrose (1987), p. 632.

[734] Dallek, Robert, *An Unfinished Life* (Boston: Little, Brown, and Company), p. 370.

[735] Schlesinger (1965), p. 673.

[736] Weinberger, pp. 129-130.

[737] Witcover, pp. 28-29.

[738] Nixon (1978), p. 237.

[739] Dallek (2003), p. 502.

[740] Ambrose (1987), p. 652.

[741] Ehrlichman, p. 102.

[742] Magruder (1978), p. 51.

[743] Ambrose (1987), pp. 656-659.

[744] Ibid., p. 666.

[745] Nixon Eisenhower pp. 315, 317.

[746] Ambrose (1987), pp. 668-669.

[747] Nixon Eisenhower, p. 317.

[748] Ambrose (1987), pp. 669-671.

[749] Nixon Eisenhower, p. 318.

[750] Schlesinger (1965), p. 833.

[751] Ambrose (1987), p. 672.

[752] Weinberger, p. 131.

[753] Ashman, p. 101.

[754] Liddy (1980), pp. 98-99.

[755] Witcover, pp. 36-38.

[756] Nixon Eisenhower, p. 320.

[757] Witcover, p. 39.

[758] Lasky, Victor, *It Didn't Start with Watergate* (New York: The Dial Press, 1977), pp. 71-72.

[759] Ashman, p. 199.

[760] Wicker, Tom, *One of Us* (New York: Random House, 1991), p. 267.
[761] Nixon (1978), p. 252.
[762] Hersh, p. 13.
[763] Liddy (1980), pp. 99-100.
[764] White (1973), p. 365.
[765] Wicker (1991), p. 415.
[766] Rather and Gates, p. 207.
[767] Aitken (2005), pp. 103-104.
[768] Ibid., pp. 104-105.
[769] Kutler (1992), p. 198.
[770] Witcover, pp. 96-99.
[771] Wicker (1991), pp. 278-279.
[772] Nixon (1978), p. 268.
[773] FindLaw.
[774] Ehrlichman, pp. 84-85.
[775] FindLaw.
[776] Dean, John (1976), p. 145.
[777] Rather and Gates, pp. 220-223.
[778] Aitken (2005), pp. 92-98.
[779] Liddy (1980), pp. 101-102.
[780] Kutler (1992), p. 166.
[781] Witcover, p. 178.
[782] Pollock, p. 172.
[783] Aitken (1993), p. 338.
[784] Ibid., p. 339.
[785] Cohen and Witcover, p. 30.
[786] Nixon (1988), pp. 241, 244.
[787] Haldeman (1978), p. 131.
[788] Ashman, p. 126.
[789] Summers, p. 268.
[790] Pollock, p. 172.
[791] Magruder (1978), p. 70.
[792] Witcover, pp. 312-313.
[793] White (1975), p. 86.
[794] Rather and Gates, pp. 145-146.
[795] White (1975), p. 87.
[796] Rather and Gates, pp. 145-146.

[797] As covered in Chapter One.
[798] Ehrlichman, p. 38.
[799] Aitken (1993), pp. 344-345.
[800] Ehrlichman, pp. 63-64.
[801] Aitken (2005), pp. 112-113.
[802] Witcover, pp. 181-182.
[803] Ibid., pp. 371, 373-374, 442-443.
[804] Hersh, pp. 13-14.
[805] Nixon Eisenhower, p. 532.
[806] Hersh, p. 11.
[807] Wicker (1991), p. 362.
[808] Ibid., p. 363.
[809] Aitken (2005), p. 113.
[810] Safire, p. 70.
[811] Wicker (1991), pp. 357-360.
[812] Aitken (2005), p. 115.
[813] Wicker (1991), pp. 681-682.
[814] John Dean interview.
[815] Nixon (1978), pp. 317-318.
[816] Hersh, p. 21.
[817] Nixon Eisenhower, p. 367.
[818] Jaworski, Leon, *The Right and the Power* (New York: Readers Digest Press, 1976), p. 276.
[819] Witcover, p. 451.
[820] Nixon Eisenhower, pp. 368-369.
[821] Summers, p. 310.
[822] Magruder (1978), p. 70.
[823] Haldeman (1978), pp. 118-119.
[824] Wicker (1991), p. 282.
[825] White (1975), p. 206.
[826] Krogh interview.
[827] Ehrlichman, p. 84.
[828] Krogh interview.
[829] John Dean interview.
[830] Liddy (1980), pp. 125-128.

Chapter Ten

[831] Woodward, Bob, and Carl Bernstein, *All The President's Men* (New York: Touchstone, 1994), pp. 19, 129.

[832] Olson, p. 41.

[833] Ehrlichman, pp. 347-348.

[834] Magruder (1974), pp. 230-233.

[835] Liddy (1980), p. 251.

[836] Haldeman (1978), p. 34.

[837] Ibid.

[838] Haldeman (1978), p. 36.

[839] Ibid.

[840] Ibid., p. 37.

[841] Colson interview with Prison Fellowship International official, date unknown.

[842] Nixon (1978), 629; Aitken (2005), p. 167.

[843] Aitken (2005), p. 167.

[844] Woodward and Bernstein, (1994), p. 26.

[845] Ibid., p. 19.

[846] Colodny and Gettlin, pp. 281, 288.

[847] Aitken (2005), pp. 167-168.

[848] Dean, John (1976), p. 90.

[849] Ibid., pp. 91-92.

[850] Ibid., p. 92.

[851] Ibid., p. 93.

[852] Dean, John (1976), p. 94.

[853] Ibid.

[854] Ibid.

[855] Dean, John (1976), p. 97.

[856] Ibid.

[857] Liddy (1980), p. 217.

[858] Dean, John (1976), p. 98.

[859] Ibid., pp. 98-99.

[860] Colodny and Gettlin, p. 206.

[861] Dean, John (1976), pp. 101-103.

[862] Ehrlichman, p. 348.

[863] Aitken (2005), p. 169.

[864] Haldeman (1978), pp. 38-39.

[865] Dean, John (1976), p. 108.

[866] Ehrlichman, pp. 348-349.

[867] Dean, John (1976), pp. 109-110.

[868] John Dean interview.

[869] Ehrlichman, p. 349.

[870] Haldeman, H.R., *The Haldeman Diaries* (New York: Berkley Books, 1995), pp. 575-576.

[871] Summers, p. 412.

[872] Nixon (1978), pp. 634-635.

[873] Dean, John (1976), pp. 115-116.

[874] Aitken (1993), p. 474.

[875] As mentioned in Chapter Four.

[876] Aitken (1993), pp. 476-477.

[877] Haldeman, (1978), pp. 60-63.

[878] White (1973), p. 368.

[879] Hoff, pp. 306-311.

[880] Colodny and Gettlin, pp. 206-207.

[881] Olson, p. 55.

[882] Magruder (1978), pp. 37-38.

[883] Ashman, pp. 263, 266.

[884] Magruder (1974), pp. 290, 293.

[885] Kutler (1992), p. 205.

[886] Dean, John (1976), pp. 145-146.

[887] Perry, p. 98.

[888] Kissinger (1982), p. 77.

[889] Jaworski, p. 116.

[890] Magruder (1978), p. 37.

[891] Ibid.

[892] Nixon Eisenhower, pp. 523-524.

[893] Dean, John (1976), pp. 128-130.

[894] Olson, p. 57.

[895] Dean, John (1976), p. 132.

[896] Lasky, p. 30.

[897] Liddy (1980), p. 275.

[898] Olson, p. 175.

[899] Haldeman (1978), p. 226.

[900] Dean, John (1976), p. 142.

[901] Sirica, p. 50.

[902] Dean, John (1976), p. 142.

[903] Sirica, p. 51.

[904] White (1973), pp. 396-397.

[905] Ibid., p. 397.

[906] Dean, Maureen, pp. 62-64.

[907] Ibid., pp. 65, 69.

[908] Ibid., pp. 72-73.

[909] Hay, p. 120.

[910] Ibid., pp. 120-121.

[911] Damore, Leo, *Senatorial Privilege* (New York: Dell Publishing, 1988), pp. 415-416.

[912] The reference to "Connally oil" pertained to Connally's influence with the rich oil magnates in Texas.

[913] Pollock, p. 175.

[914] White (1973), p. 400.

[915] DeGregorio, William A., *The Complete Book of U.S. Presidents* (New York: Gramercy Books, 2005), p. 591.

[916] White (1973), p. 355.

[917] Brodie, p. 509.

[918] Ehrlichman, p. 342.

[919] Bush, p. 98.

[920] Nixon Eisenhower, p. 550.

[921] Colson (1977), p. 74.

[922] Haldeman (1978), p. 230.

[923] Ehrlichman, p. 142.

[924] White (1975), p. 179.

[925] Rather and Gates, p. 176

[926] White (1975), p.179.

[927] Weinberger, p. 151.

[928] Dean, John (1976), pp. 157.

[929] Wicker, Tom, *George Herbert Walker Bush* (New York: Viking, 2004), pp. 30-31.

[930] Weinberger, p. 151.

[931] See Chapter Thirteen.

[932] Colson (1977), pp. 73-74.

[933] Dean, John (1976), pp. 152-154.

[934] Kissinger (1979), p. 1456.

[935] Ibid.

[936] As covered in Chapter One.

[937] Liddy (1980), pp. 275-276.

[938] Ibid., p. 276.

[939] Higgins, pp. 165-166.

Chapter Eleven

[940] Crowley, Monica, *Nixon off the Record* (New York: Random House, Inc., 1996), p. 149.

[941] Kissinger (1982), pp. 5-6.

[942] Ibid., p. 77.

[943] Ibid., pp. 77-78.

[944] Berman, pp. 227-228, 233.

[945] Hay, p. 121.

[946] Jaworski, pp. 273-274, 276.

[947] Ibid., pp. 56, 182.

[948] Liddy (1980), pp. 277-278.

[949] Ibid., p. 278.

[950] Magruder (1974), pp. 307-308.

[951] Bush, p. 105.

[952] Magruder (1978), pp. 33-36.

[953] Colodny and Gettlin, p. 240.

[954] Magruder (1978), p. 39

[955] Colodny and Gettlin, pp. 240, 242.

[956] Discussed at length in chapter three.

[957] Jaworski, p. 72.

[958] Nixon (1978), p. 779.

[959] Colodny and Gettlin, p. 258.

[960] Dean, John (1976), p. 191.

[961] Ibid., pp. 191-192.

[962] White (1975), p. 199.

[963] Aitken (1993), p. 487.

[964] Ehrlichman, p. 369.

[965] Ibid.

[966] Haldeman (1995), p. 721.

[967] Gold, Gerald, General Editor, *The White House Transcripts* (New York: Bantam Books, 1974), p. 29.
[968] Dean, John (1976), p. 203.
[969] Gold, pp. 26, 31.
[970] Aitken (1993), pp. 487-488.
[971] Kutler, Stanley I., *Abuse of Power* (New York: The Free Press, 1997), pp. 256-257.
[972] Gold, p. 28.
[973] Kutler (1997), pp. xvi, 257.
[974] Nixon (1978), p. 799.
[975] Sirica, p. 98.
[976] Jaworski, pp. 179-180.
[977] Ibid., p. 133.
[978] Ehrlichman, p. 370.
[979] Colodny and Gettlin, pp. 268-269.
[980] Jaworski, p. 88.
[981] Sirica, p. 98, 145.
[982] Ehrlichman, p. 371.
[983] Aitken (1993), p. 489.
[984] White (1975), p. 204.
[985] Higgins, p. 69.
[986] Ibid., p. 254.
[987] Ibid., pp. 56-57.
[988] White (1975), p. 205; Sirica, p. 96.
[989] Ehrlichman, pp. 372-373.
[990] Sirica, pp. 109, 271.
[991] Ibid., pp. 109, 115.
[992] Magruder (1978), pp. 45-49.
[993] Liddy (1980), pp. 302, 304-305.
[994] Ibid., p. 305.
[995] Colson (1977), pp. 92-93.
[996] Emery, p. 422.
[997] Colson (1977), p. 94.
[998] Gold, p. 258.
[999] Liddy (1980), p. 307.
[1000] Ehrlichman, p. 376.
[1001] Nixon Eisenhower, p. 574.
[1002] Ehrlichman, pp. 576-378.

[1003] Kissinger (1982), pp. 79-80.

[1004] Nixon (1978), pp. 826-827 834.

[1005] Ehrlichman, p. 381.

[1006] Haldeman (1978), p. 330.

[1007] Nixon (1978), pp. 827, 834.

[1008] Magruder (1978), p. 55-56.

[1009] Kissinger (1982), pp. 89-90.

[1010] Ibid., p. 99.

[1011] Haldeman (1978), pp. 368-369.

[1012] Haldeman (1995), pp. 821-822.

[1013] Haldeman (1978), p. 108.

[1014] Ibid., p. 374, 376.

[1015] Woodward, Bob and Carl Bernstein, *The Final Days* (New York: Simon & Schuster, 1976), pp. 21-22.

[1016] Ehrlichman, p. 343.

[1017] Colson interview.

[1018] Woodward and Bernstein (1976), p. 244.

Chapter Twelve

[1019] Kissinger (1982), pp. 102-103.

[1020] Haldeman's wife.

[1021] Bush, p. 103.

[1022] Kissinger (1982), pp. 103-104.

[1023] Crowley, pp. 149-150.

[1024] Sirica, pp. 130-131.

[1025] Cohen and Witcover, pp. 97-98.

[1026] Kissinger (1982), p. 104.

[1027] Marton, p. 194.

[1028] Kissinger (1982), p. 104.

[1029] Haig, pp. 332-333.

[1030] Ehrlichman, pp. 407, 410.

[1031] Haig, p. 336.

[1032] Ehrlichman, p. 407.

[1033] Colson (1977), p.213.

[1034] Sirica, p. 136.

[1035] Olson, p. 151.

[1036] Dean, John (1976), p. 286.

[1037] Kissinger (1982), pp. 108-109.

[1038] McFarlane, pp. 154-155.

[1039] Kissinger (1982), pp. 109-110.

[1040] Liddy (1980), pp. 310-311.

[1041] Haldeman (1978), p. 218.

[1042] See last chapter.

[1043] Haldeman (1978), p. 219.

[1044] Colson (1977), p. 192.

[1045] Jaworski, pp. 34-35.

[1046] Emery, p. 421.

[1047] Haig, p. 338.

[1048] Gormley, Ken, *Archibald Cox* (Reading, MA: Perseus Books, 1997), p. 244.

[1049] Ibid., pp. 115, 204-205, 232.

[1050] Ibid., p. 280.

[1051] Starr, Kenneth, *First Among Equals* (New York: Warner Books, 2002), p. 251.

[1052] Haig, pp, 385, 387.

[1053] Aitken (2005), p. 227.

[1054] Gormley, p. 280.

[1055] Ibid., p. 233.

[1056] Ibid., p. 240.

[1057] Magruder (1978), pp. 56-58.

[1058] Rather and Gates, p. 282.

[1059] Woodward and Bernstein (1976), p. 198.

[1060] White (1975), pp. 244-245.

[1061] Haig, pp. 347-348.

[1062] Woodward and Bernstein (1976), p. 47.

[1063] Ibid., pp. 51-53.

[1064] Ibid., p. 54.

[1065] Summers, pp. 453-454.

[1066] Nixon Eisenhower, p. 579.

[1067] Ehrlichman, p. 344.

[1068] Haig, pp. 375-376.

[1069] Ibid., p. 377.

[1070] Ibid., p. 379.

[1071] Ibid., p. 380.

[1072] Haig, pp. 383-384.

[1073] Ibid., pp. 388-389, 391.

[1074] Olson, p. 112.

[1075] Ehrlichman, pp. 142-143.

[1076] Sirica, p. 163.

[1077] DeGregorio, p. 592.

[1078] Haig, pp. 390-392.

[1079] McFarlane, Robert, p. 159.

[1080] Aitken (1993), p. 514.

[1081] Ibid., pp. 514-515.

[1082] Jaworski, p. 58.

[1083] Golan, Matti, *The Secret Conversations of Henry Kissinger* (New York: Quadrangle, 1976), pp, 46, 50.

[1084] Ibid., pp. 214-215.

[1085] Haig, pp. 392-397.

[1086] Ibid., pp. 398-403.

[1087] Ibid., pp. 402, 406-407.

[1088] Schmidt and Weisskopf, p. 160.

[1089] Haig, p. 404.

[1090] Woodward and Bernstein (1976), p. 113.

[1091] Aitken (1993), p. 509.

[1092] Dean, John (1976), p. 341.

[1093] Haig, p. 399.

[1094] Dean, John (1976), pp. 339-340.

[1095] Haig, p. 437.

[1096] Ibid., p. 343.

[1097] Woodward and Bernstein (1976), pp. 79-81.

[1098] Ibid., pp. 84, 88.

[1099] Emery, pp. 421-422.

[1100] Jaworski, p. 35.

[1101] Colson (1977), pp. 192-193.

[1102] Magruder (1978), p. 81.

[1103] Olson, p. 128.

[1104] Krogh interview with author.

[1105] Ashman, p. 295.

[1106] Pollock, p. 177.

[1107] Nixon, Richard, *The Real War* (New York: Warner Books, 1981), p. 127.
[1108] Haig, p. 443.
[1109] Ehrlichman, p. 407.
[1110] Summers, p. 463.
[1111] Jaworski, pp. 45, 48.
[1112] Summers, p. 464.

Chapter Thirteen

[1113] Kutler (1997), pp. 638-639.
[1114] Woodward and Bernstein (1976), p. 103.
[1115] Dean, John (2002), p. 99.
[1116] Haig, p. 436.
[1117] Olson, pp. 130-131.
[1118] Aitken (1993), p. 513.
[1119] Haig, pp. 444-445.
[1120] Jaworski, pp. 85-86.
[1121] Ibid., pp. 36-37.
[1122] Ehrlichman, p. 405.
[1123] Jaworski, p. 38.
[1124] Nixon (1978), p. 987.
[1125] Summers, p. 467.
[1126] Woodward and Bernstein (1976), p. 200.
[1127] Thomas, Evan and Richard Wolffe, "Bush in the Bubble," *Newsweek*, (December 19, 2005), p. 33.
[1128] Haig, pp. 448, 452.
[1129] Ibid., p. 451.
[1130] Jaworski, p. 130.
[1131] Haig, p. 452.
[1132] Olson, p. 143.
[1133] Haig, pp. 451-453.
[1134] Olson, p. 144.
[1135] Pollock, p.181.
[1136] Magruder (1978), pp. 82-83.
[1137] Jaworski, pp. 131-132.

[1138] Haig, pp. 454-456.

[1139] Jaworski, p. 137.

[1140] Magruder (1978), pp. 87, 89, 94-95.

[1141] Ibid., pp. 98-103.

[1142] Magruder interview.

[1143] Woodward and Bernstein (1976), pp. 206-207.

[1144] Haig, pp. 457-458.

[1145] Kissinger (1982), pp. 118-119.

[1146] Nixon (1978), p. 1020.

[1147] Ibid., p. 1021.

[1148] Colson, Charles, "In the Image of Christ," (Original publication unknown, provided by Prison Fellowship International to author in March 2006), p. 47.

[1149] Colson (1977), pp. 230-231.

[1150] Woodward and Bernstein (1976), p. 221.

[1151] Jaworski, p. 158.

[1152] Colson, "In the Image of Christ," p. 48.

[1153] Aitken (2005), p. 250.

[1154] Colson, "In the Image of Christ," p. 49.

[1155] Woodward and Bernstein (1976), pp. 238-241.

[1156] Olson, p. 152.

[1157] Woodward, Bob, *Shadow* (New York: Touchstone, 2000), pp. 3-4.

[1158] Jaworski, p. 272.

[1159] Woodward, Bob, *The Choice* (New York: Simon & Schuster, 1996), p. 147.

[1160] Wicker (2004), p. 34.

[1161] Kissinger (1982), pp. 1203-1204.

[1162] See chapter Ten.

[1163] Wicker (2004), pp. 34-35.

[1164] Haig, p. 493.

[1165] Nixon (1978), p. 1066.

[1166] Kissinger (1982), pp. 1204-1205.

[1167] Woodward and Bernstein (1976), p. 389.

[1168] Nixon (1978), pp. 1067, 1071.

[1169] Haig, p. 494.

[1170] Nixon (1978), pp. 1067-1068.

[1171] Kutler (1997), p. xix.

[1172] Nixon (1978), pp. 1077, 1083.

[1173] Ibid., p. 1084.

[1174] Summers, p. 483.

[1175] Nixon (1978), p. 1089.

[1176] Ambrose (2002), pp. 183-184.

[1177] Coulter, p. 306.

[1178] Summers, p. 485.

[1179] Woodward, p. 22.

[1180] Ibid., p. 22-23.

[1181] Ibid., p. 30.

[1182] Higgins, p. 275.

[1183] Jaworski, pp. 230, 236.

[1184] Magruder (1978), pp. 176, 178.

[1185] Aitken (2005), p. 252-253.

[1186] Magruder (1978), pp. 157, 163-164.

[1187] Ibid., p. 164.

[1188] Ehrlichman, pp. 342-346.

[1189] Sirica, p. 256.

[1190] Jaworski, pp. 268-269.

[1191] Higgins, p. 170.

[1192] Readers can actually listen to the tapes themselves and hear how poor the quality was if they can track down a copy of *The Nixon Tapes*, DH Audio, 2000.

[1193] Ehrlichman, p. 345.

[1194] Sirica, pp. 246, 287-288.

[1195] Ibid., pp. 281-282.

[1196] Magruder (1978), pp. 177-178.

[1197] Jaworski, p. 283.

[1198] Ibid., p. 280.

[1199] Sirica, p. 293.

[1200] Ibid., p. 243.

[1201] Magruder (1978), p. 183.

[1202] Aitken (2005), pp. 263-264.

[1203] John Dean interview.

[1204] Dean, John (1976), pp. 388-390.

[1205] Ibid., p. 390.

[1206] Ehrlichman, pp. 411, 413.

[1207] Aitken (2005), pp. 266-268.

[1208] Nixon Eisenhower, pp. 663-664.

[1209] Jaworski, p. 281.

[1210] Ibid, p. 159.

[1211] Ibid, p. 281.

[1212] Sirica, pp. 293-294.

[1213] Jaworski, p. 286.

[1214] Liddy (1980), pp. 355, 359-360.

[1215] Sirica, pp. 294-295.

[1216] Parmet, p. 633.

[1217] White (1973), pp. 348-349.

[1218] Dougherty, James E. & Robert L. Pfaltzgraff, Jr., *American Foreign Policy* (New York: Harper & Row Publishers, 1986.), pp. 274-275.

[1219] Greene, 117.

[1220] Nixon (1981), p. 134.

[1221] Summers, p. 486.

[1222] Jaworski, pp. 220-221.

[1223] Colson, Charles, "Comments on Watergate," from unpublished file provided by Prison Fellowship, 2006, pg. 1.